Business Coaching & Mentoring

FOR

DUMMIES®

A Wiley Brand

Business Coaching & Mentoring

FOR DUMMIES®
A Wiley Brand

by Marie Taylor and Steve Crabb

Business Coaching & Mentoring For Dummies®

Published by: **John Wiley & Sons, Ltd., The Atrium, Southern Gate, Chichester,** www.wiley.com

This edition first published 2016

© 2016 by John Wiley & Sons, Ltd., Chichester, West Sussex

Registered Office

John Wiley & Sons, Ltd., The Atrium, Southern Gate, Chichester, West Sussex, PO19 8SQ, United Kingdom

For details of our global editorial offices, for customer services and for information about how to apply for permission to reuse the copyright material in this book, please see our website at www.wiley.com.

For general information on our other products and services, please contact our Customer Care Department within the U.S. at 877-762-2974, outside the U.S. at 317-572-3993, or fax 317-572-4002. For technical support, please visit www.wiley.com/techsupport.

Wiley publishes in a variety of print and electronic formats and by print-on-demand. Some material included with standard print versions of this book may not be included in e-books or in print-on-demand. If this book refers to media such as a CD or DVD that is not included in the version you purchased, you may download this material at http://booksupport.wiley.com. For more information about Wiley products, visit www.wiley.com.

A catalogue record for this book is available from the British Library.

Library of Congress Control Number: 2016930230

ISBN: 978-1-119-06740-5 (pbk); ISBN 978-1-119-07378-9 (ebk); ISBN 978-1-119-07377-2 (ebk)

Printed and Bound in Great Britain by TJ International, Padstow, Cornwall.

10 9 8 7 6 5 4 3 2 1

Contents at a Glance

Table of Contents

Introduction

*T*here was a time when business owners who told colleagues they had a coach or mentor were asked 'Why do you need a coach? What's wrong with you?' The thinking used to be that if you have a coach, you must have problems you can't sort out for yourself. Meanwhile, in sports and the arts, it has long been common practice for top-class athletes to have performance and psychological coaches and for stars of stage and screen to have voice and acting coaches.

Fortunately, in the past 15–20 years, the coaching conversation in business has shifted. Savvy business leaders are reaping the benefits of having a professional coach or mentor by their side. It's not uncommon for such leaders to ask each other, 'Do you know a really great business coach or mentor?' as they would for any other professional, such as an accountant. Business coaching and mentoring is becoming widely regarded as an essential professional service.

One of the reasons for the growing demand for professional business coaching and mentoring is that today's business landscape is changing quicker than ever. Who would have imagined 20 years ago the transformations brought about by technology, the emergence of the Chinese and Indian economies and the global effects of the credit crunch, recession and depression of the last decade. A lot has changed. Business coaching is all about change, dealing with change and assisting clients to deliver and adapt to political, economic, social and technological changes. Business coaching is about supporting business leaders to create businesses that flourish and thrive. A more exciting time to be in business and to be a business coach would be hard to find. The changes in thinking and in the ways business operates means even more demand for great coaches. You can find opportunities to do great work everywhere.

About This Book

With a combined coaching experience of three decades between us, we (co-authors Marie and Steve) have seen the positive differences that great coaching can have in any business. In *Business Coaching & Mentoring For Dummies*, we share some of that experience and introduce you to approaches, tools and techniques that enable you to be an amazing business coach or an amazing business person equipped to handle changing circumstances.

This book is about inspiring coaching excellence and about encouraging peak performance for the coach and business user alike.

If you're a coach, read the chapters and use the techniques with yourself first so you not only have a hands-on approach to coaching clients but can do so congruently, knowing that you have practised what you're coaching. In addition, you get the benefits of making positive changes to your own coaching practice.

We include mentors, and this book is for you too. We consider that mentors use the coaching skill set and can apply many of the models described in this book. The difference is that mentors are often sharing specific knowledge and skills from their professional area of expertise. For more detail on the distinctions between coaching, mentoring and other helping professionals, see the explanatory grid in Chapter 1.

If you're a business owner or entrepreneur, or are reading this book because you want to self-coach or are simply curious to know more about coaching, then read the chapters and practise the techniques as if you're being coached.

To help you navigate this book and use it as an easy, accessible reference, we have set up a few conventions.

- ✔ We have used sidebars to add extra gems of information. These contribute to the chapter subject and can be skipped if you want.

- ✔ Where we introduce a new term we *italicise* and then define it.

- ✔ We have numbered exercises and techniques so you can easily work your way through the steps.

- ✔ Throughout, we have used stories to coach concepts. These stories are in the forms of real-life examples from our own work and metaphors.

- ✔ Within this book, you may note that some web addresses break across two lines of text. If you're reading this book in print and want to visit one of these web pages, simply key in the web address exactly as written in the text, pretending that the line break doesn't exist. If you're reading this text as an e-book, you've got it easy – just click the web address to be taken directly to the web page.

Foolish Assumptions

We've written this book with two readers in mind: primarily the professional coach and secondly the business person. We've also made a few assumptions about you, whether you're a coach or a business person.

- ✔ You've heard about the benefits of coaching and are curious to know more. Previous experience of coaching isn't necessary for you to benefit from this book.

- ✔ If you have previous experience of coaching or are already a coaching professional, we assume that you're open to learning and trying new things. We have included much that you will not have seen or read before that's from our own personal experiences.

- ✔ You're willing to try something different that makes a difference.

- ✔ You're willing to learn by experience and application rather than simply from 'bookish knowledge'. We've included many exercises that you can learn from by doing them rather than just reading about them.

Icons Used in This Book

All *For Dummies* books use distinctive icons throughout to draw your attention to specific features within a chapter. The icons help you to quickly and easily find particular types of information that may be of use to you:

This icon highlights a practical tip to help you with a technique or your coaching practice.

When you see this, we are highlighting a valuable point that you'll want to remember. It saves you underlining or using a highlighter pen as you read, but feel free to highlight key points as you go through the book.

This icon highlights where you can try out an experiment or technique. As you read the steps, you get an idea about the technique, but the great coach always experiences the exercise by following the steps.

Nothing makes a point better than a real-life example, so we have included some of our own coaching experiences, not to impress you but to impress upon you the ideas made in the chapters.

Every once in a while, you may want to do one thing when it would actually be better to do the opposite (or not do anything at all). We call attention to these situations with the Warning icon.

This icon contains a more detailed discussion or explanation of a topic; you can skip this material without missing anything.

Beyond the Book

In addition to the material in the print or e-book you're reading right now, this product also comes with some access-anywhere goodies on the web. Check out the free Cheat Sheet at www.dummies.com/cheatsheet/businesscoachingmentoring for tips on keeping your business coaching practice running smoothly, a checklist of tasks to do before and after a coaching session and a list of questions to help you keep your work and personal life in balance.

We've also includes some additional information online at www.dummies.com/extras/businesscoachingmentoring. These Extras articles address

- Ways to help clients conduct better meetings
- How to help a client rethink her identity when she takes on a new role in business
- Why professionals take on mentoring roles and what they get out of them
- Actions to take to become the best coach around

Where to Go from Here

The Monty Python team has a wonderful sketch 'The 100 yards for people with no sense of direction'. The sketch is about an Olympic event, and when the starting pistol fires, the contestants run off in all directions.

This book can be read in just the same way; it's not meant to be linear with a start and a finish line for you to cross. Browse through the parts and chapter headings and see what you're attracted to. Feel free to explore the pages and dip into what seems most relevant to you in the moment. Think of the chapters and sections as tools that all serve a purpose in their own right. You don't need to read the book cover to cover, although you may find yourself compelled to do so as each tool adds up to a complete and comprehensive toolkit.

Part I

Getting Started with Business Coaching and Mentoring

getting started
with

business
coaching

web extras

Visit www.dummies.com for free access to great Dummies content online.

In this part . . .

- ✔ Discover the distinctions between different models of coaching and mentoring, and understand how a coach can train to meet the differing needs of a wide variety of clients.

- ✔ Find out how to demonstrate added value to clients and ensure that they understand that coaching is a worthy investment.

- ✔ Explore some of the best coaching methodologies and how to work with a wide range of differing business categories and business needs.

- ✔ Adapt coaching and mentoring for individuals, groups and organisations.

Chapter 1

Navigating the World of Coaching and Mentoring

*B*usiness is about people and organisations are complex systems and they're co-dependent. We need to move fast to deliver effectively and efficiently. Our digital world is connected in real time 24 hours a day. This reality takes its toll on the capacity of business leaders' ability to think and reflect. When human beings don't take the time to think things through, we make poor decisions, become less effective and can become lousy managers. We can lose perspective on what's important in our personal lives too. We start communicating with colleagues, family, friends and associates like we're speed dating, taking just long enough to get the bite-size essentials to filter for yes or no. Constantly matching our relationships to the speed at which we receive information and are expected to respond isn't sustainable. We're a social species who need to relate, to be motivated, to create and to have our contribution acknowledged by ourselves and others.

Coaching and mentoring are a late 20th-century pre-emptive gift from the gods, designed with 21st-century living in mind. The value of business coaching is well documented with studies on return on investment (ROI), engagement, motivation and innovation linked to coaching and mentoring. Businesses that have used coaching over a number of years see it as an integral part of their talent development strategy with both disciplines weathering the storm of recession. It's lonely at the top, and when people are lighting fires under your feet, you want someone you trust to help you gain clarity and perspective. This input is the value-add that a coach or mentor brings.

In this chapter, you discover some of the professional fundamentals of coaching. The roles at play in organizational coaching and mentoring are outlined, together with the distinctions between these and other helping professions.

Spotlighting the Business Benefits of Coaching and Mentoring

In her research looking at 106 studies on organisational mentoring, professor Christina Underhill (University of Memphis, 2005) found that organisational commitment, job satisfaction, self-esteem, work stress and perceptions of promotion or career advancement opportunities were statistically significant for those who had been supported in their careers through informal mentoring compared to those who had not. *Mentoring* in this context refers to ongoing career support from a more experienced colleague.

Similarly, a study conducted in 2011 by the Institute of Leadership and Management (creating a coaching culture) asked 200 organisations why they used coaching. Here's what they said:

- Support personal development (53 per cent)
- Improve a specific area of performance (26 per cent)
- As part of a wider leadership development programme (21 per cent)
- Provide development for senior management (19 per cent)
- Enable progression within the organisation (12 per cent)
- Support achievement of specific organisational objectives (12 per cent)
- Address a specific behaviour issue (8 per cent)
- Provide support after a change in position or responsibilities (6 per cent)
- Provide support to new employees (5 per cent)
- Support organisational change (4 per cent)
- Engage with individual employee concerns (2 per cent)

The strongest individual benefits were increased self-awareness, increased confidence and improving business knowledge and skills. The report highlights that the key organisational outcomes were improvements in leadership, conflict resolution, personal confidence, attitudinal change, motivation and communication and interpersonal skills.

In short, coaching and mentoring make a tangible difference to how leaders lead in business.

Defining Coaching and Mentoring

At their simplest level, coaching and mentoring are conversations where insight and learning take place; a space to slow down and make time to think; and time open up to possibility and maybe think differently.

A few nuances are apparent in the definitions of coaching and mentoring. In reality, a lot of overlap is evident, and the boundaries can get fuzzy in the business context. The following sections describe just a few definitions to help you understand the nuance.

Coaching is the art of co-creation

Coaching as we know it has been informed by a raft of disciplines including psychology, sports training, organisational development, behavioural science, sociology and therapy. Sports coaching had the biggest influence in developing leadership and business-related coaching with early coaching looking at the concepts of focus, developing excellence and high-level personal and team competence in the late 1970s and 80s.

There are myriad definitions of coaching. We define it as follows:

> Coaching takes place on a spectrum from short and medium shifts in performance to significant life transformation. This sometimes requires a metaphorical demolition truck to pull down old patterns of belief and behaviours before co-creating new thinking and building blocks for growth. Oftentimes consistent, regular, focused dialogue with a sprinkling of gentle challenge and a bag full of coaching tools is enough.

We see the role of a coach as

- ✔ A co-creator – a facilitator and thinking partner who helps clients develop, appraise and crystalise ideas
- ✔ An unconditional supporter who deals with a client's real-time life issues without judgment

✔ A sounding board when a client needs a listening ear

✔ The holder of the mirror when a client finds it difficult to see himself clearly

Coaches help clients

✔ See possibility

✔ Gain clarity

✔ Develop clear intentions

✔ Work on specific aspects of business to create great business

✔ Work on what they want to create in living a successful life "on purpose"

Key professional bodies maintain this holistic view of the whole person. They mostly embrace the personal and professional.

Executive coaching is

'A collaborative solution-focused, results-orientated and systematic process in which the coach facilitates the enhancement of work performance, life experience, self-directed learning and personal growth of the coachee . . . It is specifically focused at senior management level where there is an expectation for the coach to feel as comfortable exploring business-related topics as personal development topics with the client in order to improve their personal performance'.

–Association For Coaching

Mentoring is the art of imparting wise counsel

The work of a mentor is differentiated from coaching in that a mentor regularly shares his particular professional wisdom and experience with a mentee. It tends to be more specific and focused around a particular area of work or personal development. A mentor offers counsel on specific problems that a mentee brings and may share contacts, advocate on behalf of the mentee during her career and help her make useful connections.

The European Mentoring and Coaching Council (Switzerland) defines mentoring as

A developmental process in which a more experienced person shares their knowledge with a less experienced person in a specific context through a series of conversations. Occasionally mentoring can also be a learning partnership between peers.

Mentoring originated with a goddess

Odysseus, king of Ithaca, left his wife, Penelope, and infant son, Telemachus, to fight in the ten-year Trojan War. He left his son with a male guardian called Mentor to guide him. Odysseus was prevented from returning home for a further ten years. Young noblemen demanded that Penelope choose one of them to marry and deny Telemachus his birthright.

Mentor was rather useless as a trusted guide and adviser during the 21 years he was left as guardian. Telemachus was an emotional, indecisive wreck, apparently lacking confidence in his ability to undertake his royal duties and retain power. He needed help.

The goddess Athena wanted Odysseus back on the throne and appeared to Telemachus in a number of forms to give him wise counsel. One incarnation was a wise version of Mentor. With this guidance, Telemachus eventually slayed the would-be suitors, and his father returned. This intervention by Athena as trusted adviser in the form of mentor is the origin of the term we now use.

In other words, it wasn't a man called Mentor who was the wide counsel; it was in fact the female goddess of wisdom and heroic endeavour. We guess when the world of business mentoring adopted the term to describe a one-to-one relationship involving the nurturing of potential, it just couldn't cope with the idea of calling it 'goddessing'. Oh what fun we could have if they had!

Mentoring is used when a client needs

- ✔ To learn a specific skill
- ✔ To acquire particular knowledge
- ✔ Wise counsel from a more experienced critical friend

Note that the phrase is a 'critical friend', not a 'critic friend'. If you want to be a critic, maybe you need to look for a role in political or artistic journalism.

Distinguishing coaching and mentoring from therapy

Coaching isn't therapy or counselling, although some of the methods, models and techniques used in aspects of coaching are derived from these modalities. Anyone involved in a coaching or mentoring relationship needs to understand what coaching and mentoring are and are not.

Anthony Grant, a coaching psychologist at Macquarie University, highlights the difference between coaching and counselling simply:

> Coaching deals with clients who are functional. They want to improve their performance in a particular aspect of life. The emphasis in coaching is less on unravelling and understanding problems and difficulties, and more on focusing on finding solutions. It is very future oriented. Coaching does not deal with clinical issues, such as depression or high levels of anxiety; for those you need to see a doctor.

The same distinction applies equally in mentoring. You're dealing with the present and the future with your clients, rather than inviting them to recline on a chaise longue while you delve into their psyche in a parody of Freudian analysis.

In thinking about the distinctions, make sure you consider the professional roles that people commonly take in settings where people are being supported to learn. Table 1-1 describes the different roles in coaching and mentoring. It also highlights the distinction between facilitation and counselling.

Table 1-1	Dimensions of Coaching and Mentoring		
Role	**Relationship to Learner**	**Focus**	**The Narrative**
Organisational sponsor	Hierarchical/ parental Invested in and supporting long-term career direction	(3–10 years) Creating succession in an organisation or profession	'I will take a long-term interest in supporting, promoting and tracking your career'.
Mentor	Wise counsel/ senior yet collegiate Knowledge and experience gained over a number of years in specific professional area	(Months to years) Sharing exemplars of knowledge and experience to support an individual or group and to plan for and meet particular outcomes	'I will use my wisdom and long-term experience in a specific area to help you minimise mistakes in delivering in similar circumstances'.
External coach	Challenger/ facilitator of self-insight and business/ personal/career development	(3–12 months) Using a range of tools to resource an individual or group to achieve client-generated outcomes	'I will use my specialist skills to support you to gain clarity and confidence to maximise your contribution'.

Role	*Relationship to Learner*	*Focus*	*The Narrative*
Leader who coaches	Hierarchical with personal interest in outcomes	(Ongoing management) Uses a coaching style of leadership to support individuals and groups to deliver overall outcomes that the leader is responsible for delivering	'I will engage you in determining how you deliver against required organisational objectives and empower you to take right action'.
Facilitator of learning	Teacher/supporter	(Hours) Shares skills and knowledge to enable an individual or group to learn a specific skill or acquire knowledge using a range of learning methods	'I will help you deliver in your role more effectively by using my facilitation skills to teach you what I know or the skills I have'.
Counsellor/ therapist	Supportive listener	(6 sessions) Uses an identifiable approach to help an individual, couple or family make sense of their historical and current experience to learn new life management strategies	'I will support you to develop and sustain better relationship with yourself and others'.

Distinguishing Business Coaching from Other Types of Coaching

You can find many niche areas of coaching, and the profession is constantly developing. Niches even exist within niches. Whatever your bag, understand that a significant difference exists between personal coaching and business coaching.

Working with business requires a whole different level of relationship management, particularly if you're working in corporate organisations rather than with small, founder-led businesses. Managing triangulation becomes an art form as you navigate your way through dialogue with the client and *sponsor* (manager or person responsible for talent management) and sometimes a fourth player if the manager and talent manager are both involved in contracting and monitoring. The operations director or finance director (FD) may want to get involved in the contractual monitoring too if the budget is significant.

This situation is fine as long as everyone remembers what his role is and can maintain his boundary. As the coach, you not only have to manage the complexity of those relationships, you also need to act like a member of MI5 or the CIA in terms of confidentiality. Be prepared to be mentally water boarded by people who want to know the details of what's happening in the conversations with your client. Develop the art of answering a question without answering the question, of being really clear that you will report back into the organisation on the process of coaching and the delivery of the contract outcomes but not the content of coaching.

Empowering your client includes that you ensure that your client disclosures belong to your client, subject of course to the usual rules that apply if he's a danger to himself or others or has committed an illegal act or intends to. (See Chapter 4.)

Business coaching requires an understanding of business

If you don't know about how business operates and the language of business, get educated. This education doesn't have to be an MBA-level commitment; it may be reading business news in quality papers online, taking short seminars or joining a business club or a business institute. Learn as much as you can about how to run your own practice. Work on your own coaching business. Determine what you need to discover and find a way of learning that works for you. Get a mentor who can help you by sharing his experience and providing some challenge and stretch for you.

Defining expectations and determining fit

Clients want someone with knowledge of business – how it works, the language of business, the reality of running one. Specifying whether someone needs experience of a particular business process, discipline or business structure can be important. A sponsor looking for a coach or mentor to support a CEO or team in planning a merger likely wants that experience or knowledge to maximise impact.

Sometimes coaches need coaching too

Marie was mentoring a coach. He was a great guy and a successful coach with myriad coach trainings and seminars under his belt. He had never worked in the nuclear or gas industry and had never worked internationally. He had loads of experience in working with therapists, coaching charity workers from war-torn countries on their return to the US and in supporting leaders who were in organisations rescuing young people from human trafficking. His clients were often engaged in highly charged emotional and often dangerous work. They loved him. He was offered an opportunity by a consultancy to coach a group of ex-pat workers who had been injured or experienced trauma in Fukushima in 2011. He would have to go to Japan to do this work for around three months.

He saw this job as his big break – a place to make a name for himself. He had never worked in a disaster recovery zone or potentially dangerous conditions himself. He had never seen the devastation of a nuclear accident up close and personal. He wasn't a trauma therapist and had never undertaken any training in that area. The fact was that he had coached people who had distorted his view of his own ability to cope in that situation.

Marie worked with him carefully and helped him see how his lack of knowledge of the nuclear industry may have proved too much of a culture shock for him and even have compromised his own well-being; that he was being asked to help people return to work and fast, and he hadn't even contemplated what that could mean if he arrived in Japan and felt that those people weren't ready. In working together, they discovered some stretch goals for him that involved working with clients outside of the US, and he accomplished that quickly. The Fukushima offer catalysed an undiscovered desire in him, but he didn't need to compromise himself and those potential clients to get it.

A coach with years of experience in audit and accounting may be great in supporting a new FD on professional issues, but if he has inherited a staffing problem requiring team performance management due to poor customer service and attitude, a coach with experience in a people-oriented discipline may be best. Equally, someone who has 20 years' experience of coaching within the global corporate environment may not be the best choice for a small family business looking to retain its small family business identity.

Holding pre-contract conversations

Be prepared for exploratory conversations, not just sales conversations, in business. Accept that sometimes you aren't the right fit and that you may be able to refer someone else in who may do a better job of it than you. Sometimes it may be a partial fit but not right for now. Occasionally, you may not be able to see the problem because you're looking through the wrong lens.

If you don't know what you don't know, identify a coach or mentor you would like to emulate and ask him how he developed his business knowledge.

Coaching leaders to be difference-makers

Leaders in organisations are managing performance: business performance, key objectives, deliverables, key performance indicators (KPIs) – whatever terminology is used, it's about performance. Executives, leaders, managers, chief (fill in the blank) are resource managers driving results.

Senior people are expected to be self-directed, self-reflective and future focused. Often they seek the support of a coach or mentor (sometimes both) to help them meet those expectations. Organisations in effect provide one-to-one learning support for their senior staff and high performers to help them keep on track. From time to time, organisations also use coaches and mentors to help when a specific skill or knowledge gap needs honing or when an organisation anticipates that an executive may find work challenging due to organisational changes or because of a change in his personal circumstances outside of work. Organisations are effective when their leaders are emotionally intelligent, have self-mastery and are cognisant of their own well-being and the well-being of those around them.

If you're working in organisations managing major change or looking to shift culture, teach the leaders how to use the coaching skill set. It shifts accountability and delegation, increases creativity and innovation and keeps people focused to deliver the changing vision as that evolves.

Coaching the whole person to create business outcomes

Marie was asked to coach a partner in an international law firm at a particularly difficult period on her return to work after her husband's death. At the time, this client was expected to deliver a fairly challenging and complex case worth £3 million to the business – one that presented a substantial risk to a long-term client. The brief was to help keep the member of staff emotionally healthy and focused while paying attention to her overall well-being. The partner also had access to bereavement counselling paid for by the firm and a range of flexible arrangements to accommodate her needs.

The coaching focused on self-care, time planning and delegation to others. These issues were not particularly business issues on the face of it, and yet they were. Business operates effectively when people operate effectively in delivering what is required. In providing this kind of support, the business context is paramount. When organisations have key specialists, individual well-being can be the difference between pulling off a deal or not.

REAL WORLD EXAMPLE

Group coaching to increase accountability

Steve was coaching a director of an international nonprofit organisation when it became apparent that none of her team spread across four continents were pro-actively managing local income-generation staff well. Absence levels were high, and costs were rising against income targets. The team needed to place greater emphasis on accountability and to increase their understanding of the impact of lost working time on overall revenues. The situation was pretty urgent as they worked on annual income targets and were six months into their financial year.

Steve and the director agreed that he would develop an eight-session coaching programme for her top 15 managers and would coach them as a group with her over the eight sessions to help them deliver their income target. The coaching was focused on emergent performance issues in relation to people management and on delivering increased fortnightly targets. The overall goal was to help the managers become confident in managing ongoing performance and to increase the team's ability to discuss challenging local issues more openly with their manager and peers. They delivered their target.

Equipping Yourself to Help Other People in the Business Context

The global coach training industry is thriving. In any profession, this results in some great training programmes, some mediocre programmes and some downright awful programmes bordering on fraudulent. Some training schools promise that anyone can have a six-figure coaching practice in a month. Coaching flying pigs wearing grass skirts and playing the ukulele are not usually an option on the syllabus but wouldn't look out of place. Others suggest that professional coaching is a dark art requiring several rites of passage, years of inner soul searching and the ability to demonstrate 25 models of best practice before you can truly call yourself a coach or mentor. If you're looking to train or want to hone up your skills, do your research on the training available. Be clear and specific about what you want to learn and research the quality of the course and experience of the trainers.

REMEMBER

Choose training that encourages you to coach for a significant part of the training. Have clear outcomes, practise standard and supervision/mentoring to help you notice your own practice and get support when you hit issues that are beyond your experience.

To be a great coach or mentor in business you need

✔ To come from a place of

- Growth mind-set

- Respectful engagement with a client even when he's not at his best or respectful towards others (including you)

- Emotional resilience and a willingness to recognise when you're out of your depth

- Accountability for your own personal well-being

- Empathy and sympathetic understanding without joining in with the emotional roller coaster of your client's journey

- Self-reflective assessment and the desire to experiment, play and do more of what works

- Absolute focus on your clients and a desire to serve them

✔ To understand

- People learn and develop self-mastery in different ways, and you need to adapt to them

- Motivation theory is about belonging, not bucks

- How business works and the context of that industry

- Processes and functions involved in running a business and the language that business uses

- How personal change and transformation happen

- How organisations develop and change

✔ To be able to

- Give feedback in a constructive way to help your client rather than look clever and insightful

- Define clear outcomes and be flexible enough to move with your clients' needs as they change

- Manage your personal boundaries with a number of players

- Maintain confidentiality even when the person paying the fees really, really wants to know what's going on inside the coaching

- Think big picture and small chunks

- Challenge in order to help the client, not just for the sake of it

- Think purposefully and creatively

- Be comfortable with ambiguity and conceptual thinking
- Use the coaching skill set flexibly and be prepared to keep adding to the toolkit to resource a range of client needs
- Know when you're not the right person to support the individual or group at this time
- Refer someone to another helping service when he needs something beyond your experience, skills and boundaries
- Run your own business practice well and make a great living doing what you love

If you want to understand the specifics of the coaching skill set, take a look at Chapter 4.

Choosing a coach or mentor

In the real world of professional coaching and mentoring, you can find people with months of training but limited practice experience and some with lots of experience but little training. The research highlights two things in relation to coaching and mentoring outcomes. No positive correlation is shown between the length of time since a person qualified as a coach and coaching outcomes, and even less correlation between fees charged and coaching outcome. What's important is the relationship, and the onus is on the person commissioning the coaching or mentoring to establish what he's looking for from the relationship.

If a prospective client asks how you'll to manage the relationship, you can show him something like Figure 1-1, which shows a typical framework and the elements usually included. (This is the framework Marie uses.)

Becoming a business coach or mentor

If you're an experienced life coach or mentor with little experience of business, our suggestion is – get some experience of business. Work in one, run one or create your own start-up. No amount of reading books with titles such as *The 3-Minute MBA* equips you to work as a business coach. The learning for an experienced coach or mentor is to understand the functions of business, language, roles and duties, particularly in director-level coaching.

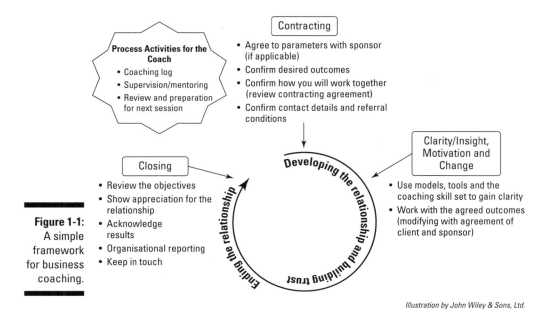

Process Activities for the Coach
- Coaching log
- Supervision/mentoring
- Review and preparation for next session

Contracting
- Agree to parameters with sponsor (if applicable)
- Confirm desired outcomes
- Confirm how you will work together (review contracting agreement)
- Confirm contact details and referral conditions

Clarity/Insight, Motivation and Change
- Use models, tools and the coaching skill set to gain clarity
- Work with the agreed outcomes (modifying with agreement of client and sponsor)

Closing
- Review the objectives
- Show appreciation for the relationship
- Acknowledge results
- Organisational reporting
- Keep in touch

Developing the relationship and building trust

Ending the relationship

Figure 1-1: A simple framework for business coaching.

Illustration by John Wiley & Sons, Ltd.

If you're an experienced business executive who wants to become a mentor, get some training in using the coaching skill set and in understanding how to develop mentoring relationships and contracting. (See Chapter 4 and Part II of the book.) The skills learning is often around how to avoid telling someone the answers that you can generate because of your experience. Get clear and specific on what you're offering in terms of expertise. If you're known for your stellar track record in winning large scale government contracts in the US, you could probably learn to mentor around that easily. Mentoring on cross-cultural contracting in the grain markets of Africa and Asia Pacific may be a stretch though.

If you're neither experienced in business nor an experienced coach, spend time in business deciding on the kind of environment you like and feel comfortable in. Discover how to develop the coaching skill set to facilitate people within that. It sounds simple, but we have seen many coaches who have been 'trained' to believe that all they need to do is six weekends of training and the world of coaching and mentoring is their oyster. It may be enough for securing a few clients for life coaching but is rarely sufficient in the world of business and executive coaching.

Being on the Other Side as Coachee or Mentee

Professional development and continuous learning is important in this business. You can't be in integrity and coach people to develop self-mastery if you aren't working on it yourself. If you think that you're 'cooked' and have nothing else to learn, there's a door plaque marked 'delusional' with your name on it, and you're the only one who reads it as 'desirable'. Please don't skip the information on the competency stairway if you're in this group, and pay particular attention to step one.

Most coaches are consummate learners who see continuous professional development as a feature of their business. This development is not an optional cost, but a core requirement. Coaches need to be able to identify learning needs in themselves and others, to notice the blind spots as they come into awareness and occasionally be prepared to have a colleague point them out gently (and sometimes not so gently, depending on how well you know them). Even writing this book has helped one of us see that we still have a propensity to correct like a track change pedant when asked to comment and the other one to recognise a rather unhealthy relationship with the apostrophe and the comma.

The Competency Stairway Model, shown in Figure 1-2, outlines the four stages of learning. Use it to consider your own learning or help others discover their learning needs.

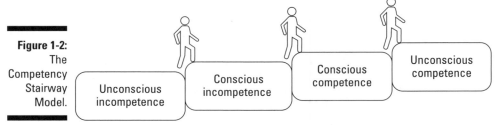

Figure 1-2:
The Competency Stairway Model.

Unconscious incompetence

Conscious incompetence

Conscious competence

Unconscious competence

Illustration by John Wiley & Sons, Ltd.

Here are the four stages of the competency stairway:

1. **Unconscious incompetence: The oblivious**

   You don't know what you don't know (blissful ignorance).

2. **Conscious incompetence: The Homer Simpson (Doh)**

   You become aware that you don't know (becoming self-aware).

3. **Conscious competence: The I'm sexy and I know it**

   Through experimentation, knowledge acquisition and/or practice, you're practising how to do it and improving (increasing in confidence).

4. **Unconscious competence: The accomplished performer**

   The doing of it comes so naturally to you that you don't even realise you're doing it. (Who me? What did I do? How do I do what? I don't know!)

Mentors help us see the blind spots.

 Think about the competency stairway as you consider the coaching skill set throughout this book. Notice where you're becoming aware of skills and knowledge you use that you're not consciously aware of. Notice where you feel your competence needs developing or honing for specific situations.

Understanding Professional Requirements

No legal requirements exist in relation to a standard of training or hours completed. However, you're likely to find it difficult to build a successful coaching practice without appropriate training and completion of practice hours to build your skill set. The required coaching standard for internationally recognised coach accreditation is between 35 and 100 hours coaching practice plus the training requirement. (See the accreditation guidelines in Table 1-2.) Most professional business coaches who coach at a senior level have more than 500 hours of coaching in the bag and coach regularly.

To keep it simple, we have produced two checklists that set out our view of the minimum requirements you need. Do your own homework and check out the professional institute websites for guidance.

Table 1-2	Accreditation Requirements for New Coaches		
	European Mentoring and Coaching Council	**Association for Coaching**	**International Coach Federation**
Membership requirements	Membership of a professional body	Hold appropriate level prior to submission of application	Completion of an entire ICF Accredited Coach Training Program or 60 hours of coach-specific training on an ICF-approved program plus 10 hours of coaching with an ICF accredited mentor
Client contact hours or coaching training	50 hours	35+ hours	Complete the Coach Knowledge Assessment
Coaching experience	1 year (from first practising as mentor/coach)	75+ hours	100 hours (75 hours paid)
Number of clients	At least 5 clients		At least 8 clients
Client feedback	5 within last 12 months (ending with submission date of application)	1 x Client reference	
CPD	16 hours per year	CPD record since initial coach training	40 hours every 3 years
Mentor/coach supervision	1 hour per quarter	Minimum 3 months' coaching supervision	
Website for more information	www.emccouncil.org	www.associationforcoaching.com	www.coachfederation.org

Checklist 1: Just do it:

- ✔ Contracting paperwork that sets out the financial agreement and the coaching agreement
- ✔ A clear disclaimer about any changes the client makes being his responsibility and choice
- ✔ Individual client next-of-kin details if you're meeting offsite or contracting with an individual rather than an organisation
- ✔ Clear terms and conditions regarding fees, payment, cancellation, travel and expenses
- ✔ Insurance to cover your professional liability and public liability if you have premises
- ✔ Confidential storage for your client records and ways of protecting and destroying confidential documents

Checklist 2: You don't have to, but please, just do it:

- ✔ A disclosure from the client regarding any therapy work he is engaged in or any medical conditions that may impact his work with you
- ✔ Your own system for session management, clearing the space, notes (coaching log) and review
- ✔ Sharing an open notes policy with the individual you're coaching
- ✔ Having a coach and/or mentor or supervisor
- ✔ Most important of all – loving your clients

Chapter 2

Presenting a Compelling Case for Coaching and Mentoring

In This Chapter

▶ Taking on the job of educating clients

▶ Showing the value of an outside perspective

▶ Establishing a strong return on investment (ROI)

▶ Making the most of the client's budget

▶ Considering the value of in-house coaching

*B*usiness coaching is above all about change and growth, whether for the individual or the organisation, a process that takes people on a journey from where they are now to where they want to go. The value in coaching lies in the degree of change that you, as a coach, help clients make. The more you can identify the difference before and after an intervention, the more a client sees the value and wants to work with you.

All the client really wants to know is 'What's in it for me?' In this chapter, we help you answer that question, forming such a compelling proposition that the client just has to say, 'Yes, I want your coaching programme'.

Taking the Role of Educator

Business coaching and mentoring is no longer regarded as just a new fashionable trend, nor as simply a feel-good substitute for good management. Business people increasingly see it as a valid methodology for assessing and re-evaluating goals and processes and for creating and delivering effective solutions to business needs.

Research on coaching

Unfortunately, few up-to-date studies exist that reinforce the credibility and value of implementing coaching programmes. What research there is, though, is encouraging, if not scientifically validated:

✔ The 2002 Chartered Management Institute and Campaign for Learning Coaching at Work study found that 80 per cent of managers disagreed with the statements

'Coaching is just another fad' and 'Coaching is too time-consuming', and believed that they would benefit from coaching (or more coaching) in their place of work.

✔ Studies show varying returns on investment, ranging from 5.7 to 7 times the initial investment, with some showing figures of 5,000 per cent!

Many companies are increasingly recognising that during and after coaching programmes, things are different. A company will, however, only make so much of an investment in coaching based solely on the idea that coaching will help. Successful companies won't throw endless amounts of money at programmes that don't have a positive impact on their bottom line – or, at least, they won't do so for long.

Coaches therefore need to educate potential clients in the benefits of coaching. Clients need to know how coaching translates into improved results, whether that be

✔ A better bottom-line profit

✔ Better communication

✔ Decreased levels of stress, illness and absenteeism

✔ Improved performance

✔ Increased loyalty and staff commitment

✔ Increased productivity

As coach, it's often left to you to substantiate the business case and plug the gaps in research data. To effectively educate clients in the potential change that can be achieved, we recommend that you

✔ Document your own experiences, analyse them and share them.

✔ Monitor your track record by collecting feedback from clients.

Valuing Third-Party Observation in Business

Here's a popular idiom: 'We're too close to the woods to see the trees'. What this saying means is that you can't see the whole situation clearly because you're looking too closely at small details or you're too closely involved to see what a third party might see.

A coach, however, can see each tree. She's unhindered by history, politics and habits, un-blinkered to all the possibilities. She can bring a fresh, new, *valuable* perspective to the business. That's what you need to get across when making the case for a coaching programme.

Showing that the coach's perspective matters

Most people already have an idea of the value of perspective. You hear people say 'I need to get some distance from this situation' or 'I have to rise above the problem'. Intuitively, they know that distance and perspective help them see solutions.

As coaches we don't claim to have a god-like, all-seeing, all-knowing perspective of the business. We're not the subject matter experts, nor do we claim to have all the answers. What we *do* claim is that we know the value of a third-party perspective and we purposefully bring that approach to work with us, cultivating and demonstrating an attitude of curiosity that challenges and provokes new ways of seeing the business.

A term often used in Neuro-Linguistic Programming (NLP) is 'looking for the elusive obvious' – finding subtle, small changes that can make big differences to results. Coaches do that. And beyond the subtle stuff, coaches also spot the self-evident or, as we like to call it, 'the bloody obvious'! Distance and objectivity enable us to see solutions, options and choices and then offer the appropriate interventions.

Being able to demonstrate this value of a third-party perspective to a client is worth more than being able to talk the theory. Wherever possible, a coach should be willing to roll up her sleeves and demonstrate a piece of coaching change work rather than explain it. If the opportunity presents itself to offer a new perspective for clients to consider, then we suggest you grab it with both hands.

Knowing how perspective feeds into change

An individual or business that needs coaching needs change – something isn't working or stands to be improved. The third-party perspective enables the coach to highlight where the change can take place. In an organisation, for example, areas identified for change may include

- Culture
- How the work is done
- Mission and values
- Organisational identity
- Processes used
- Relationships between members of staff
- Relationships between the organisation and its staff, customers, suppliers
- Roles
- The kind of work done

Understanding construal level theory

Construal level theory explores the psychology of 'can't see the woods for the trees'. In simple terms, the theory is based on the idea that people think in more abstract ways about problems they have some distance from or about problems relating to distant people. Thinking at a more abstract level means it's possible to be disconnected from the problem, to not be personally affected or associated to it. This detached perspective enables more creative solutions to be considered.

Two levels exist:

- **High-level construal thinking** is when people look at the bigger picture and don't focus on limitations or details. By their thinking, they change the framework or context in which the coach views the situation and sees other solutions. In other words, because of distance the coach is more solutions-focused compared to those in the situation, who tend to be problem-focused.

- **Low-level construal thinking** is when clients think in more concrete terms – like concrete, the terms are often fixed and rigid, with little or no flexibility. This fixed perspective usually comes about because someone has been involved with a problem for a long period of time. The fixation prevents her from seeing or even exploring other perspectives and new possibilities.

The following anecdote demonstrates high-level construal thinking and shows how co-author Steve's different perspective to the client's allowed him to take a step back from the situation and come to the task from a detached point of view, which greatly benefitted the client.

Scott was the marketing manager for a software provider. Steve was coaching him in the subject of persuasion and influence, with the view to examine the company's email marketing campaigns. The brief was to give the campaigns a persuasion and influence makeover to improve client enquiries and increase sales.

Scott's primary strategy had been to send emails to selected target audiences, and automated replies were triggered by the email recipients' actions. Scott called this strategy the 'drip campaign'. The recipients' actions determined which automated emails were triggered (or dripped out). The automated messages varied depending on whether the recipients opened the email, what landing pages they visited on the company's website, what they viewed and what links they followed.

Scott announced he didn't believe the drip campaign strategy was as effective as creating ad-hoc emails. He supported his assumption with statistics he had gathered that clearly showed that when he wrote and sent an independent one-off email, more people read it and took action. Scott was convinced that the drip campaign was a waste of time and ineffective.

Scott had also concluded that the drip campaign simply annoyed people, but he had no evidence to support this point of view. Steve challenged Scott's point of view by asking him, 'How do you know this to be true?' Scott was unable to answer this other than by saying he had a hunch.

Steve asked to see examples of the email messages. What Scott wasn't able to see because of his involvement over the course of a year was that his ability to write compelling and persuasive copy had improved over time. The earlier communications used in the drip campaigns were less compelling and persuasive than the ad-hoc emails sent out later. It was suspected that the quality of the copy – not the change in strategy – accounted for the improved results.

To test Steve's theory, new email copy was written using persuasion and influence language. The email was sent to the same database of prospective clients who had previously received emails in the drip campaign. The results were measured, and the new persuasive drip campaign clearly outperformed both the original drip campaign and the ad-hoc campaign, leading to a 130 per cent increase in company sales. An annual £30,000 ($45,000) email marketing campaign generated leads that converted to sales figures in excess of £2.3 million ($3.5 million) compared to £1million ($1.5 million) previously. (See Chapter 15 on how to engage, inform and influence.)

Wherever possible, measure and monetise to demonstrate to the client and to new prospective clients the value of coaching. (For more on this, see the later 'Measuring and monetising' section.)

Here are four simple ways to practise getting a new perspective and accessing high-level construal thinking for any situation or problem. (In Chapter 11, we explore additional creative thinking techniques for the coach and the client to practise high-level construal thinking.)

- **Temporal distance:** Change the perception and look through different timeframes (for example, looking ahead of time, or with hindsight, over the short, medium or longer term period). Getting temporal distance often reveals information that's not available to the client.

- **Spatial distance:** Seeing perspectives from a different physical space vantage point (see the Real World Example earlier in this section). Practise looking at a situation from multiple points of view by imagining the problem in front of you and literally standing up, walking around it, standing on a chair, lying on the ground. Ask yourself, 'From this perspective, what is another way of seeing this?'

- **Social distance:** The difference between the coaches and the groups they're coaching affects how any situation is perceived. It is said that 'a baker will want to bake and a surgeon will want to operate'. Our social identities have an impact on how we perceive the world. Value the difference between you and your clients and practise seeing a situation through the eyes of other people's perspectives. For example, ask how a child would see this situation? What would a Richard Branson, Donald Trump or other creative entrepreneur think and do here?

- **Hypothetical distance:** We all have beliefs about what we think is possible or not possible. As a coach, you bring blue-sky, out-of-the-box thinking to the client's situation. practise dreaming big and offering creative, totally unrealistic solutions.

Leading a client to the light-bulb moment

Many years ago, while being interviewed by a large multinational bank for some executive training programmes it wanted delivered, Steve was casually asked by the managing director, Alex, if and how coaching might help him to make an important and difficult decision. Did Steve have any techniques that would help? Although this exchange wasn't part of the interview, it was an opportunity to demonstrate the value of a third-party perspective. Manna from heaven for any coach!

Steve started by asking a few questions to get more specific information about what Alex meant by important and difficult. From the replies, Steve understood that Alex needed to get a bit of distance from the decision and a new perspective. He'd come up with two possible decisions and was in a dilemma over which to choose because the difference between each wasn't distinct.

Steve led Alex through a ten-minute coaching intervention where Alex visualised the choices and rose above the imagined future, looking off in time to see the futures unfolding to their inevitable outcomes. This intervention enabled him to see the choices over time and then review them with hindsight. Hindsight ahead of time is useful!

At no point did Steve need to know what the subject matter was. All he needed to do was guide Alex in exploring different perspectives.

This simple coaching exercise enabled Alex to experience high-level construal thinking in relation to time and space. As a result, Alex reached a point where the light bulb went on. From the new perspective, he had seen a new choice and another possible outcome. He then tested the choice in his mind, using the same visualisation technique, and was able to see that it was the best decision he could make at that moment in time with the information available to him.

Steve asked Alex the value to the business of this new choice. It turned out that the idea could save the bank £100 million ($150 million) over the next two years. 'Great', Steve said, 'that makes my fee seem very reasonable by comparison'.

The point of the story is as follows: to make a compelling business case for coaching, don't just tell clients the benefits; *show* them. Be willing to give someone the experience of discovering a number of alternative perspectives. The experience clients have of coaching with you will convince them of the value of coaching with you.

Not every new perspective you offer will work or resonate with clients, but many will, and a coach's responsibility is to help clients see the alternatives and then work through the choices.

Identifying the Client's Return on Investment

'So what's the cost?' or 'What do I have to invest?' are questions all clients ask, even if not quite so directly. In business speak, what they want to know is 'What's my return on investment?' and in plain speak, they're asking 'So what do I get in return for my money?'

Return on investment (ROI) isn't always easy to quantify and demonstrate, and existing quality data is often difficult to come by. A rigorous study needs to confirm to the rules of randomised double-blind controlled trials and requires

- ✔ Collecting critical performance data
- ✔ Analysing results and adjusting for causal influence and sustained impact
- ✔ Assigning a monetary value to business-outcome data
- ✔ Calculating the fully loaded cost of the solution design
- ✔ Calculating the ROI and its level of quality
- ✔ Predicting and quantifying performance improvement

Some coaching projects require this degree of commitment and professional enquiry, undertaken, usually, by analytics specialists. However, many clients aren't looking for a detailed report and want to hear from *you* how coaching equates to the bottom line. So in this section we offer a simple approach to demonstrating ROI to clients.

Selling the benefits

In business, everyone is a salesperson. All people have to sell something, whether selling a CV so they get a job, selling themselves for a promotion or selling a creative idea to a team. Whether you like it or not, business people are part of one of the oldest professions on earth. Professional coaches who embrace this idea and become experts in selling the idea of their coaching have full diaries and can choose whom they coach.

We've seen many a good coach fall by the wayside and return to a paid job because although they were good at coaching, they were poor at selling their coaching skills. They didn't have enough clients and ended going back to their day job. That doesn't have to be you!

Sales people commonly recognise that customers and clients buy the *benefits* and not the features of a product or service. Yet many ineffective sales people still talk about what their product or service looks or sounds like, and not what it's going to do for the customer, or give her or get her. Customers are only interested in what's in it for them. The case is the same for many coaches when it comes to explaining what they do and making a compelling business case for coaching.

Consider a networking event. Over the course of the event, people come over to meet you, and one of their first questions is, 'So what do you do?' If you answer 'I'm a business coach', you may well see people's eyes glaze over as they back away and head towards the nearest exit. You may as well say, 'I'm a lice infestation consultant' if you want to end the conversation quickly. If you're lucky enough to be given a second chance and the networker (who may be a prospective client) asks, 'So what exactly does that entail?', you now have an opportunity to redeem yourself.

You have two options:

- ✔ **List your job title or the features of your services.** For example:

    - 'I'm a stress management coach, and I run a stress management programme for overworked executives'.

    - 'I coach people in time management'.

    - 'I'm a business coach, and I coach and mentor executives in leadership and team building'.

- ✔ **Highlight the benefits for anyone choosing to coach with you.** For example:

    - 'It costs a lot to replace a burned-out executive, so I help businesses to better manage stress and create conditions for people to be happier with reduced levels of illness and absenteeism and raised productivity'.

    - 'I coach people to be more effective and efficient, which translates into greater output and increased profits'.

    - 'I coach executives to create and lead cohesive teams, which means that they reach project deadlines on time and on budget with minimal overruns and project slippage'.

The difference is clear. The first set of responses is uninspiring. The second set sells the benefits of coaching.

Doing a cost-benefits analysis

You can come at ROI from the angle of assessing:

- ✔ The costs of not having coaching
- ✔ The benefits of having coaching

 This exercise can be carried out with a client, or you can conduct a third-party assessment before holding a meeting. You can do it formally with pen and paper or just conversationally. We prefer to do the exercise formally with the client and with pen and paper because then the client gets to visibly see the business case for coaching unfold before her.

1. **Make a cost-benefits chart.**

    Take a piece of paper and draw a straight vertical line down the middle. Head up one side 'Costs of not coaching and staying the same' and the other, 'Benefits and value of coaching'.

2. Investigate the costs of staying the same (not coaching).

Ask good questions that root out hidden costs that may not be obvious to the client. For example:

- If coaching a sales team, what's the cost of not making appointments because they can't handle pricing objections?

- If coaching for stress management, what's the cost of sick leave due to stress?

- If coaching on customer service, what's the cost to replace a lost customer because they were dissatisfied?

- How do these costs add up over time – say a month, a year, three years?

- What are the other additional costs perhaps not fully considered, that is, staff morale, brand damage. How do these costs translate into downtime, project slippage, cost overruns and replacing staff? Given emerging market conditions, how does that picture of costs get even higher?

3. Examine the benefits of coaching.

Here are a few questions you can include:

- If coaching a sales team to handle pricing objections leads to on average 10 per cent more monthly sales, what's the value?

- If coaching stress management leads to on average a 10 per cent reduction in sick leave, what's the value?

- If coaching a customer service team to provide a better service leads to 20 per cent of customers renewing a service for a further two years, what's the value?

- How do these savings add up over time – say a month, a year, three years?

- What are the other additional benefits and values that may not have been fully considered or are difficult to monetise – that is, a happy work place, improved performance, better communication?

With your client, work to show the distinction between the cost of inaction and the potential benefits and values of coaching. When a client can see the comparative analysis between where she is now and where she can be after coaching, she's more likely to say, 'Yes, let's coach'. The bigger the gap between the two, the more value there is.

Measuring and monetising

In the cost-benefits analysis described in the preceding section, you can see an emphasis on measuring and monetising. Facts and figures are what matter most to clients.

In the earlier section 'Selling the benefits', we present two approaches to explaining what coaching is all about to a prospective client. But a third, even better approach exists: highlight the benefits *and give examples of measurables*. For example:

- ✔ 'It costs thousands to replace a burned-out, stressed executive. Did you know that work-related stress costs UK businesses more than £6.5 billion ($9.9 billion) a year, which equates to approximately 10.4 million productive days lost? So I coach businesses to better manage stress and create conditions for people to be happier, with reduced levels of illness and absenteeism and raised productivity. My clients report that, on average, illness and absenteeism is down by 30 per cent'.

- ✔ 'I coach people to be more effective and efficient, which translates into greater output and increased profits. Some of my clients have achieved savings of 15 per cent on average. That's thousands of pounds'.

- ✔ 'I coach executives to create and lead cohesive teams. It costs a company on average £20,000 ($30,000) in recruitment fees alone to replace a senior team member, let alone the cost of training to get new team members up to speed. So retaining talent is priceless. Plus experienced staff reach project deadlines on time and on budget with minimal overruns and project slippage. The savings made run into the thousands'.

 We recommend that wherever possible you offer clients measurable benefits – from your own experiences of coaching and from studies that show the change after coaching. And always look to monetise. So if a study shows percentages, translate the percentages into monetary terms, which are of more interest to the client.

Measuring the hidden benefits clients can't see

You can gain real value in being able to help a client see the often hidden benefits of coaching in these areas:

- ✔ Communication
- ✔ Culture and social change
- ✔ Happiness and well-being

While doing the costs-benefits analysis (see the earlier section 'Doing a costs-benefits analysis'), you notice the client start to talk about these areas. Monetisation isn't always possible or easy, and yet you can get real value in *measuring* to help the client see the value of coaching not just at the consultation stage but throughout the coaching process.

You need to define and agree with the client:

🖊 What she needs to see, hear or experience to know that a desired outcome has been achieved

🖊 What she needs to see, hear or experience to know that the programme is moving in a positive direction, which includes discussing:

 • How the programme is to be measured

 • How the programme is to be reported back

The following is a three-step process called the Hidden Value Process that enables you to measure and highlight the benefits resulting from coaching that can't be monetised:

1. **Calculate the *inputs*: the resources needed to implement a coaching programme.**

 They're measured as a cost. For example, the fees for running the programme include venue and equipment costs and staffing costs for the time spent. Assess the costs realistically because they give an accurate measure of investment.

2. **Estimate the *outputs*: the direct result of the programme's goal.**

 So, for example, if five members of staff are coached on improving customer service communication skills, how many customer service issues are you aiming to get resolved in one call compared to multiple calls? The outputs can be best estimates or a pilot study, or the results of the coaching programme can provide the feedback for future programmes and more accurate output assessments. If previous coaching programmes have been run with similar outputs, you can use the results to set the output goals.

3. **Measure the *outcomes*: the changes that have occurred over the longer term.**

 So, for example, the five members of staff resolved 10 per cent more issues in one call than before the coaching programme.

After you measure outcomes, you may often then find it easier to look for ways to monetise the results. In the example of customer service calls, this outcome may translate into improved customer satisfaction and improved customer retention. If so, what's the value to the business of the extended lifecycle of the customer? This information is the basis of a valuable case for further training or as a convincing argument for a new client.

What gets measured gets valued. When you show the value of benefits like happier staff and a more positive organisational culture, you validate ROI.

Investing now for a future return

Effective coaching brings about change. Sometimes the change isn't apparent or evident while the coaching is happening. For example, the process of learning a new skill and then practising it until it becomes behavioural takes time. Insights and creative ideas sometimes appear *after* coaching sessions in moments of quiet reflection. Many developments from coaching take time to settle and create results.

Amazing coaches remember to make clients aware of the value of change both in the coaching conversation and afterwards, in the near or distant future. A common mistake among coaches is to underestimate this value and fail to have future changes associated with the work they've done.

When change can't be easily measured or monetised, it's often useful to explain to a client that not all change work achieves immediate results. Explain that coaching has four component parts that have to be present for coaching to be effective:

- ✔ An awareness that something has to or can change
- ✔ A willingness to make the change
- ✔ The skills and ability to make the change
- ✔ The understanding that change takes time and can show up later or in other ways than those originally expected or anticipated

Giving a client this explanation is an effective way of influencing them to notice and associate future positive changes with the work they did with you.

Co-author Marie was coaching a seminar on designing a project for the future and testing the steps along the way when suddenly a member of the group stopped and shivered with delight. The businessman, Paul, explained:

> 'You probably won't remember, but we met at a seminar about six years ago and you did a self-confidence exercise with me. I felt amazing, and you told me to imagine what other amazing things would change in my life. You said that I may look back and remember that moment as being the catalyst. Well, I imagined my business being successful and being able to travel the world. And I just realised in the middle of this exercise that here I am! It's all come about because of working with you all those years ago'.

Marie's reply was as follows:

> 'That's amazing! I'm pleased you remembered that moment and experienced your success, which came about because of the actions you took. Now imagine what else can improve and change in your future. Perhaps one day you'll look back again and acknowledge the work we did here today'.

Don't employ false humility to disregard this phenomena and not associate with your coaching work. However, you need to strike a balance between bragging and making sure the client associates the positive changes with your work. This example shows how to make the association conversationally. Of course Paul did all the work; Marie had nothing to do with that. However, if a change happens for a client in a coaching conversation or afterwards, don't be shy about claiming it. Paul became a coaching client after the seminar – a deposit in the karmic bank paying dividends.

Stretching the Budget

Often the first thing a business cuts back on during any downturn is the budget for training – and that includes coaching and mentoring. Even without a downturn, savvy HR departments look for ways to stretch their training budgets to get more 'bang for their buck'.

Your job, then, as a coach convincing a client to hire you, is to demonstrate value for money by offering a blended mix of coaching that suits the budget of the client and still delivers results.

A benefit of coaching is its flexibility – you can effectively coach in many different ways:

- ✔ Email coaching
- ✔ Group coaching, off site and on site
- ✔ One-to-one, face-to-face sessions
- ✔ Peer-to-peer coaching
- ✔ Skype or similar online communications
- ✔ Telephone coaching

All methods of coaching can be delivered in isolation or in combinations. They can be used for one-off sessions or over spaced intervals, depending on which best suit the coach and the client. Each method of delivery has pros and cons that affect the ROI, especially the costs involved in delivery.

When presenting the business case to a client, the coach must evaluate all inputs from the client's perspective. Using the Hidden Value Process (see the earlier section 'Measuring the hidden benefits clients can't see) to calculate and demonstrate the costs and potential returns from the coaching programme helps budget-conscious clients make an informed decision to coach. When it comes to the bottom line price of a programme, great savings can be made for the client by careful consideration and delivering a blended mix of the ways to deliver coaching outlined in this section.

Adding Value by Training Leaders in Coaching and Mentoring Skills

As more companies recognise the value of coaching, they're looking for ways to get the best value for money from coaching. As a result, coaches are finding increasing demand for them to work alongside existing teams of coaches or to work with the company to develop its own in-house coaching talent and in-house coaching programmes. The company's logic is that the in-house team knows the business better than people brought in from the outside, and that in-house coaching is more cost-effective than bringing in an external coach. This logic is often based upon a hunch, because as yet little research has been done into the return on investment for in-house coaching.

When making the business case for working with in-house coaches or to assist in developing in-house talent, the coach must work with the client to create a programme that's fit for purpose. First, you conduct a needs analysis to help the client see which option best suits her specific needs. Highlighting the values we discuss in this chapter, such as the third-party perspective, enables the client to make an informed decision.

You can also talk through the upsides and downsides of training in-house staff to be coaches, in case the client decides an external coach would be better. On the positive side:

- ✔ The in-house coach brings to the coaching conversation one big advantage over the coach from the outside: she understands the culture because she's part of it.
- ✔ Line managers can coach on the job and are often experts at process tasks.
- ✔ Leaders who've been trained to coach and mentor generally have more access and time to coach compared to external coaches. Coaching can often be on demand or as needed.

The following potential drawbacks are worth exploring with the client:

- ✔ Being in the business can lead to low-level construal thinking – not being able to see the woods for the trees (see the earlier section 'Understanding construal level theory').

- ✔ Although line managers are experts in processes, the multi-billion-dollar question is: are they experts in coaching talent transfer? Being able to impart skills to another person is a different skill set from knowing how to do a process well.

- ✔ The in-house coach isn't immune to the politics of the workplace, and if dealing with personal information, coachees may be disinclined to open up and truly regard the coaching conversation as a safe place to be honest, open and vulnerable.

- ✔ A challenge for many managers who become coaches is ensuring that they adopt an empowering, supportive role rather than a dictatorial management approach to their coaching. That's not to say that managers are dictators; we're just emphasising that the skill set of a coach is different to the traditional one of a manager.

You can make a valid business case for the experienced coach working alongside the organisation to train coaches or to support in-house coaches. No fixed formula exists that has been tested or proven to be best practice – see it as fertile ground for coach and client to explore in search of which options provide the best value. In Chapter 3, we explore how to coach and support the in-house coaches and mentors.

Chapter 3

Assessing Clients' Needs before Coaching

. . . .

In This Chapter

▶ Focusing on organisations

▶ Guiding entrepreneurs

▶ Working with family-owned businesses

▶ Nurturing intrapreneurs

▶ Making a difference with socially oriented businesses

. . . .

*E*very organisation you get to coach is unique compared to any other organisation you work with, no matter how similar many may seem to be on the surface. Even organisations in the same industry sector have different people, processes, clients, values, suppliers and so on. In this chapter, we explore how to help different folks navigate through the complex array of decisions they must make, and ultimately guide them to say 'yes' to having a coach or mentor. We look at types of organisations that although unique, share common specific needs. Then we address how to tailor your coaching and mentoring to meet those needs.

The actual content of the coaching and mentoring sessions varies depending on the subject matter. We cover interventions, tools and techniques that can be used in Parts II and III.

Getting your attitude right

To tailor a coaching programme specifically to the client's needs, at the initial interview stages of consultation, when both you and your client are finding out if what you have to offer is suitable for his requirements, you need to be

✔ **Honest:** Honesty is the foundation of any good relationship, whether personal or professional. So from the outset you need to be willing to ask tough questions and point out what the client may not want to hear. Your honest advice helps clients navigate the decision-making process and manage the behind-the scenes stuff that influences how they think, behave and decide. Turn to

Part II for guidance on delivering an honest perspective that will highlight the value of coaching with you.

✔ **Non-needy:** We've heard it said that a *needy* coach is a *creepy* coach. Have you ever met a salesman or a friend or partner who was needy? The neediness is a big turnoff: the person is thinking only of himself. If you're needy, you compromise your coaching work. Through neediness, coaches can end up offering or accepting inadequate programmes or taking on client-led suggestions knowing that they'll both regret it later.

Creating Programs to Deliver Coaching and Mentoring in Organisations

In this section, we focus on evaluating the needs and wants of an organisation and how to devise a coaching plan that is a suitable fit. Remember, an organisation is made up of teams and the teams consist of individuals. You can adapt the approaches in this section and use them with both individuals and teams.

Figuring out what the organisation wants and what the organisation needs

When the phone rings or the email arrives that invites you to an initial consultation meeting, you're heading off to see someone who either

✔ Thinks he knows what coaching he wants

✔ Suspects he needs coaching but isn't yet sure what he wants

In both cases, you need to start with an honest enquiry to find out what the client *thinks* he wants and needs, and what he really wants and needs.

A *needs assessment*, whether for an individual, department or organisation, is a systematic process that identifies gaps between where they are now and where they would like to be. This process is the start of any planning process. Needs assessments identify problems, appropriate interventions and solutions.

Making the case for a needs assessment

A robust needs assessment is beneficial to the organisation and coach as follows:

✔ Ensures that the coaching programme maps to the needs of the organisation and not just what the coach has to offer.

✔ Provides a business case and validates the organisation's ideas that coaching will be beneficial.

✔ Identifies the hidden, often unconscious objections to coaching, which can then be addressed before coaching begins, preventing the objections from becoming obstacles to successful coaching.

✔ Identifies the obvious and potential obstacles that the coach and organisation are aware of that may affect the success of any coaching plan. Highlighting these early on enables a contingency plan to be put in place to minimise the effect they have or a coaching plan developed to ensure obstacles don't occur in the first place.

✔ Establishes an end game for post-coaching evaluation.

In short, a thorough needs assessment sets the foundations for the success of the coaching programme.

> *If you don't know where you are going, any road will get you there.*
>
> –Lewis Carroll

Where to start when conducting an assessment

Because of the unique nature of every organisation, no one assessment formula fits all businesses. Most organisations will already have ideas about what they think they want, so you can use this as a starting point for any assessment. This approach maintains rapport with the organisation from the beginning.

To identify where to start the assessment, consider the organisation's vertical needs and horizontal needs:

✔ A **vertical needs assessment** addresses three categories of need:

- **Organisational:** Evaluates the organisational performance, taking into account people and processes, demographics, technology, economy and political trends.

- **Occupational:** Evaluates the skills, abilities and knowledge to operate effectively and efficiently.

- **Individual:** Evaluates how an individual is performing.

✔ A **horizontal needs analysis** addresses the organisation's goals, possible solutions and what may affect the outcomes. Horizontal needs fall into four categories:

- **Performance:** Identifies where a level of performance in skills or behaviour is needed to change in order to function in a satisfactory way.

- **Instrumental:** Identifies where a new system, technology task or process intervention is needed to change in order to function in a satisfactory way.

- **Conscious:** Identifies needs that are known to those who want to function in a satisfactory way.

- **Unconscious:** Identifies needs that are unknown to those who want to function in a satisfactory way.

Stocking up your toolbox

Roger Kaufmman, regarded by many as the father of needs assessment, identified many tools that are useful for information gathering.

✔ **Observation:** Firsthand knowledge is invaluable. Ensure that your observing has minimal effect on performance so you don't bias the data. People often act differently when being observed.

✔ **Interviews:** Asking great questions reveals information that may not be available to the organisation. Create a safe, confidential space so people are willing to tell you the truth and not just say what they think the bosses or you want to hear.

✔ **Questionnaires:** Questionnaires enable feedback from large groups. Confidentiality enables individuals to express themselves and reveal valuable information that may not be otherwise forthcoming. Consider carefully how the person preparing the questionnaire pre-frames and presents the questions asked; this can influence the answers received. For example, if you head a questionnaire, 'What are the problems with customer service?', you presuppose there is a problem with customer service, and the questionnaire doesn't invite any solutions. A better heading may be, 'An enquiry into the strengths and weaknesses of customer service and how we can improve it'.

✔ **Job description analysis:** A study of all responsibilities and an evaluation of the skill sets and behaviours required to function satisfactorily reveals gaps. These gaps are due to attitude, skills deficits or simply having the wrong person doing the wrong job.

✔ **Difficulty analysis:** Where are the biggest challenges? This question reveals where small coaching interventions can have huge impacts.

- ✔ **Problem-solving conference:** Here, you can invite staff to create a solution-based programme to meet their needs. They know the business better than you do, so this approach has value. However, an important consideration is that although the staff are experts in what they do, they're not coaching experts.

- ✔ **Appraisal reviews:** Conducted within a performance review, these reviews carry out all the above enquiries.

Use these tools in combination because no one tool gives a full overview of what the client needs.

Using the Well-Formed Goals and Outcomes process

This the Well-Formed Goals and Outcomes process is a Neuro-Linguistic Programming (NLP) process that was originally used for therapeutic interventions. The process is a simple yet powerful needs analysis enquiry that is focused on solutions, asks great, revealing questions and works for all the categories of vertical assessment (see the earlier section 'Where to start when conducting an assessment').

The process highlights not only where the coaching must happen but also possible pinch points that may hinder success. The following is a series of questions that you ask your client. If his answers meet the definitions given by five criteria, they are said to have passed the tests for well-formed goals and outcomes. When his answers pass the tests, the client is more likely to achieve his goals and outcomes than when the tests are not met.

Here are the criteria and tests for well-formed goals and outcomes:

- ✔ **All goals and outcomes must be stated in the positive:** For example, if you ask people to not think of blue elephants, they have to first think of blue elephants in order to not then think about them. This result is akin to focusing on the problem and not the solution. You want the solutions, so you always want answers stated in the positive. 'Don't tell me what you don't want; tell me what you do want'.

- ✔ **All actions to be initiated and maintained by the person who desires the goal:** We can only control ourselves, so the desired actions must come from the individual. If it involves others to take action, these actions are potential 'pinch points'.

- ✔ **Goals and outcomes can be defined and evaluated according to sensory-based evidence:** This criterion ensures that the goals or outcomes are in a language that the brain understands, expressed as what we see, hear, feel and – if relevant – smell and taste.

- ✔ **By achieving the goals and outcomes, the positive intentions of the present situation are preserved.** If we accept that every behaviour or situation has come about through a positive intention, this positive intention must be preserved with any new solution. If the positive intention of the present situation isn't preserved, then goals and outcomes often fail to happen through unconscious self-sabotage.

✔ **Any changes must serve the ecology of the person or organisation.** Any changes have an effect on other parts of a system, so the ecology or well-being of the system must be preserved. If the changes sought adversely affect the ecology, the attempts to achieve goals and outcomes are often sabotaged.

Start the enquiry by asking questions to elicit the present situation:

✔ What is the problem/situation specifically?

✔ How do you know it's a problem?

✔ How do you know how to have it/do it?

✔ How do you know when to have it/do it?

✔ How do you know with whom to have it/do it?

✔ How do you know where to have it/do it?

✔ What stops you from changing the problem/situation?

Then ask questions to elicit the desired situation/outcomes:

✔ **All answers must be stated in the positive.**

- What do you want specifically?
- When, where, with whom do you want it?

✔ **All actions are to be initiated and maintained by the person who desires the goal.**

- What resources do you have to accomplish this?
- What resources are in your control?
- What resources are missing or could be better?
- What resources do you need that are out of your control?

✔ **Goals and outcomes must be defined and evaluated according to sensory-based evidence.**

- How will you know when you have it?
- What will you see, hear, feel, smell, taste?
- What will you look like, sound like? And so on.

✔ **Test to see whether achieving the goals and outcomes will preserve the positive intentions of the present situation.**

- What will happen if you get this result?
- What won't happen if you get it?

- What will happen if you don't get it?

- What won't happen if you don't get it?

- What do you get to have or keep by maintaining the current situation? (This question will reveal any unconscious secondary gain from staying with the situation as it currently is. This secondary gain can often show up as sabotage or resistance to change.)

- How do you know it's worth getting?

- When, where, with whom does not having the change or desired outcome work for you?

✔ **Any changes must serve the ecology of the person or organisation.**

How will these changes affect your life? Family? Friends? Colleagues?

- What will be different as a result of these changes?

Reviewing the answers reveals where coaching is needed. Then you can design and deliver coaching and mentoring programmes that meet the idiosyncratic needs of the organisation.

Working with talent management and succession planning

Key talent in an organisation are the people who are already experts in their work, have shown star potential to become experts or are critical to the company in their job, enabling the organisation to work effectively.

Traditionally, organisations tried to retain key talent by allowing employees to move in a progressive manner 'up the ladder'. Today, career development is more varied, so organisations need strategies to evolve continuous knowledge and skill development for their employees, to prepare them for the future growth of the organisation.

In order to release the talent potential already in the organisation, more organisations are identifying the need for

✔ **Talent management:** This involves creating and delivering coaching and training programmes to nurture existing talent within the organisation.

✔ **Succession planning:** This involves creating and delivering coaching and training programmes to disseminate existing knowledge and skills throughout the organisation and hands-on experience to the next generations of staff.

Organisations are increasingly asking coaches to construct and execute plans for talent and succession, and to develop and support the people who become the talent managers.

Here's a six-step process you can follow to design a talent management and succession strategy:

1. **Evaluate the readiness and willingness of the organisation to commit to the strategy.**

2. **Identify the talent management and succession planning goals and philosophies of the organisation.**

3. **Identify the metrics used to measure progress and outcomes.**

4. **Communicate and collaborate with executive stakeholders to ensure agreement and support.**

5. **Create the tools, systems and programmes to deliver the strategy.**

6. **Communicate the strategy to the stakeholders and begin the process.**

Supporting coaches and mentors

As companies recognise the benefits of coaching, they often look first within the organisation management to see who has skill, knowledge and experience that can be passed on to others. The role of management can be blended into the role of coach, and on some occasions this works. However, the skill sets of a great manager and a great coach are very different. Being able to support in-house coaches and mentors, especially those transitioning from management roles, is a worthwhile and profitable niche for any business coach to explore.

The benefits of supporting a coaching culture within an organisation are well recognised in the corporate world. The paradigm has shifted from the traditional top-down, control-and-command style of management to building a responsible, empowered workforce in which all employees act in a collaborative way and are committed to achieving objectives and sustained growth. Coaching the coaches is an integral part of this new way of running a business.

Supervising coaches and mentors is a collaborative learning process where the supervision coach engages in reflective dialogue with the coach for the ongoing development and benefit of the coach and the people he coaches.

Here are the key areas to focus on when you're supporting coaches and mentors in organisations:

- ✔ **Building trusting and collaborative relationships and being clear on the supervisory role.** Set out the pre-frames first and ensure the client is willing to listen to learn. The coach is there to support, not to do the in-house coach's work.

- ✔ **Agreeing on processes to review the supervision sessions and the coach's results.** Treat each coaching session with an in-house coach as you would any client. Hold regular reviews and ask what's working and what's not working. This keeps both parties focused on where improvements can be made.

- ✔ **Enabling coaches to become aware of their own weaknesses and blind spots and areas for growth and development.** Be willing to offer constructive criticism and encourage the in-house coach to be vulnerable, honest and open to feedback.

- ✔ **Distinguishing between managerial or direct control approaches; coaching by encouraging freedom, choice, personal responsibility and empowerment.** Keep reminding the in-house coach to be the coach and not the manager. Test this by observation; sit in on a coaching session or listen to a recorded coaching session.

- ✔ **Generating new coaching conversations that may not have occurred to the coach because he's too close to the business.** Be willing to introduce new techniques and coaching concepts to the in-house coach. Work with him to build a large and flexible toolbox of coaching techniques and approaches. The more choices he has, the better the coach he will become.

Coaching Wannabe Business Owners and Start-ups

In the UK at the start of 2014, the Federation of Small Businesses reported that small and medium-sized businesses employed 15.2 million people, with a combined turnover of £1.6 billion. ($2.4 billion). Each year in the UK alone, approximately 500,000 new companies are registered. Despite these encouraging statistics, 20 per cent fail within a year of start-up and half won't be around to see the second year of trading. Start-ups often fail for common reasons that can be avoided with proper prior planning and coaching – which is where you come in.

Helping start-ups see the value of coaching

Peak performance coaching in sports has a value that's widely recognised. It can mean the difference between promotion or relegation, between coming in fourth or winning an Olympic medal. The difference translates into prize money and won or lost sponsorship deals worth thousands or even millions. The distinction between a professional and an amateur isn't always about skills. It's about attitude. And a 'winning attitude' in sports translates equally well to the business arena.

Working hard and putting in long hours isn't what makes a business thrive – you need to work smart. To work smart, a start-up needs a winning attitude and must look for ways to be efficient, effective and successful.

Few start-ups will stop and ask smart questions – unless of course they are working with a smart coach. You and the new business owner can consider such questions as:

- ✔ Who is already doing what I'm doing? What can I learn from their successes and failures? What can I do better, quicker, easier, more profitably, have more fun doing?
- ✔ Who is successful in a different area of business to mine that I can model and learn from and integrate into my own business?

Coaching a business start-up to cultivate a winning attitude is best done at the start, before the new business owner acquires bad habits of mediocrity. You start by looking at all aspects of the business and ensuring that you coach where it counts most.

At the end of the 2012 London Olympics, the French cycle team complained that the British team were using specially designed tyres that allegedly gave them an advantage over the competition. The British team coach replied by saying that after the Beijing Olympics the British team decided to look at every aspect of the coaching programme and to look for any and every advantage. They investigated metabolism, diet and the design of every single component part of the bike and looked for marginal improvements. This professional approach paid dividends: The team target was for 10 medals, and they won 12, with the men's sprint team setting a new world record in the finals against France. The tyres used came from a French manufacturer.

Every winning sportsman or woman has a professional coach. Your job is to show clients how taking the same approach will reap rewards for them. Show, not just tell, clients how start-ups that hire a coach to ensure they take a professional approach in everything they do perform at the top of their game. Like the sportsperson, those who work smart achieve magnificent results.

Looking at areas for focus

Here are six areas in which start-up wonders frequently need support:

✔ **Business plan:** The strategy for the business – it contains all reviews of information and shows if a 'duty of care' has been undertaken. It also shows that the best assessments have been made with the information to hand. Some businesses fail to write a plan, or if they do, they file it away, never to be seen again. Even working with the coach to create a simple SWOT analysis, identifying the strengths, weaknesses, opportunities and threats to the business can reveal valuable insights about the business and show the coach what's needed (for more on SWOT, turn to Chapter 9).

A careful review of the business plan will point the coach in the direction of where coaching is needed. The maxim 'failing to plan is planning to fail' should always be remembered; if no plan exists, then begin by coaching the business to create one.

✔ **Marketing action plan (MAP):** Without this plan, many people get lost. Some start-up owners fail to test the market because they don't want to hear any news that may contradict their enthusiastic ideas. The market determines the success of the business after the market knows about the services and products and what they can do for them, give them or get them. Only then does the start-up have a chance to be successful. The start-up benefits from professional coaching for many areas of marketing, including branding, sales, customer service and advertising.

✔ **Financials:** As a coach, you must know when to coach and when not to. If offering any financial-related coaching, always check that you're qualified to do so. Underfunding is one of the main causes of businesses failing to make it to year three. Many start-ups overestimate sales and underestimate costs and the time it takes to achieve targets. Many free financial services are available for new business start-ups, and it's often best to refer a start-up client to a reliable financial expert rather than give financial advice yourself.

✔ **Fact-finding:** Some clients need coaching to set up processes and procedures that track the facts: new customer acquisitions, client loss rate and every cost incurred along the way. Without consistent metric tracking, clients never really know whether the start-up is thriving or striving.

✔ **Success:** Success can be a problem. Start by defining what success means to the client. As a business gets established and grows, scaling the business up from a start-up to meet increased demands can be tricky because it requires new staff or premises, and new systems and processes. There are times when coaching can support the growth plan to expand. Coaching from the start of a venture means that a business is more likely to have the right people in the right roles with the right processes in place at the right time.

✔ **Balance:** Clients may need help striking a balance between working on the business and actually doing the business. A coach can guide a client who may be drawn, in the early stages, to spending more time working on the business – designing letterheads, marketing plans and so on – rather than doing the business he set up to do. The following section has more on this theme.

Guiding the jack-of-all-trades and master of one

With so many aspects to running a business, many start-up owners fall into the trap of trying to do everything themselves. A common mistake is that they invest valuable time and expend energy in doing everything, including the things they're lousy at, rather than focusing on what they do best — their *area of genius*.

This exercise is called the Flow Matrix. You can use it to help clients identify work they're doing that they'd be better outsourcing to others.

1. **List the business tasks you engage in and grade yourself as follows:**

   • **Flow:** It's natural, it's easy and time flies. It's what I'm born to do.

   • **Excellent:** If someone gave me the task, I'd do an excellent job.

   • **Okay:** If someone gave me the task, I'd do an okay job.

   • **Lousy:** If someone gave me the task, he'd probably wish he hadn't.

Overcoming avoidance to excel in your area of flow

In a mentoring session with a coach, Steve asked him where his area of flow was. *Flow* is when your work is easy and effortless and is what you'd do even if you had to pay to do it. The coach's answer was quick and sincere: 'It's when I'm either training a group or coaching around creativity. It's not really work, and time flies when I'm doing it. And I'm brilliant at it!'

Then Steve asked another question: 'If that's where you're in flow, what part of the business are you lousy at?'

His answer was just as quick: 'Selling. I'm okay when I'm talking with a prospective client, but getting to that point – doing the networking, phoning people up, making appointments – I avoid doing'.

The coach spent longer avoiding doing something he was lousy at than just doing it or investing in someone who was in flow when doing the selling side of business, which would enable the coach to be in his 'space of flow'.

2. **Estimate what percentage of your time you spend doing these tasks on average per week.**

   Put the percentage in each of the four quadrants in Figure 3-1, with time spent totalling 100 per cent.

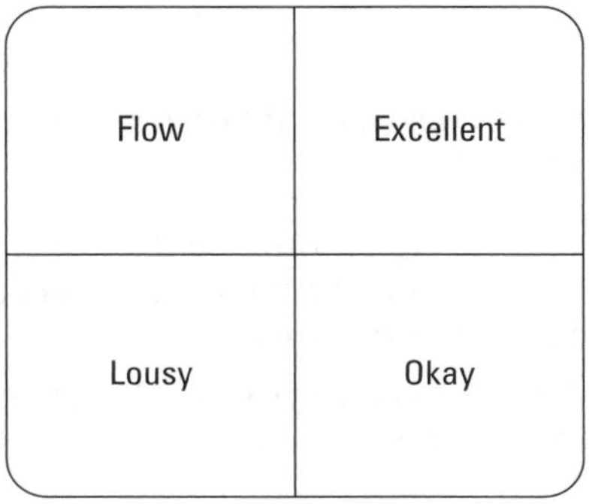

Flow	Excellent
Lousy	Okay

Figure 3-1: The Flow Matrix.

Illustration by John Wiley & Sons, Ltd.

Most people have an inclination to carry on doing tasks even if they're lousy or okay at them. They do them to save money or in the hope that with practise and study they'll get better and eventually get above the midline. These approaches are false economies and prevent someone from spending his valuable time doing what he does best. What works best is to realise the cost of doing tasks below the midline and then outsource the tasks to suppliers or colleagues for whom the tasks are in the grids of 'Excellent' or 'Flow'.

If you conduct this exercise with successful entrepreneurs, you find that most spend little, if any, time doing tasks below the midline. The pattern for success is to focus on tasks that you do in a state of flow and build a team of excellence and flow experts around you for the other tasks.

Helping the Family-Owned Business Survive and Thrive

In the US, family-run businesses account for 30 per cent of companies, with sales over $1 billion. In the UK, they account for 66 per cent of all small to medium-sized enterprises. The economic footprint left behind by family-run businesses is a large size 12. In the UK, they employ two out of every five people in the private sector.

This unique and active sector has specific traits and characteristics that can be both strengths and weaknesses. A needs analysis (see the earlier 'Looking at areas for focus' section) highlights these strengths and weaknesses and points to where coaching would best benefit the business.

Knowing where your support is most helpful

Here are a few areas in which you can make a big difference with coaching when working with family-run businesses:

- ✔ **Bringing in talent:** To keep up with competitors and to grow, businesses need to bring in new talent from outside the family. They need to know where to find that talent and how to integrate it.

- ✔ **Scaling up the business:** Old, traditional ways of working may need to evolve or be redesigned. What worked in infancy may not work as the business matures.

- ✔ **Making funding decisions:** The family-run business is concerned with how to separate family money from the business and how to raise and use funds.

- ✔ **Changing aspirations of the family members:** As needs change, personal aspirations may be in conflict with traditional family and business values.

- ✔ **Implementing new technological changes:** Organisations that embrace change and adopt new ways of working can be more successful, gaining a competitive advantage over those that aren't willing to move forward.

- ✔ **Organisational structure:** The unique and often volatile mix of personal family dynamics, business strategy, business values and ownership structure can create an emotionally charged environment that makes decision making and future planning (not to mention the day-to-day management) of a business challenging.

Also important are succession planning and prioritising professionalism over emotion. We explore these areas in the following sections.

Evolving the legacy

The LEGO Group is a globally recognised brand that began making wooden toys in the 1930s. Today, it employs more than 10,000 people and sells its modern plastic bricks in 130 countries. It remains firmly in the hands of the founding Kirk Kristiansen family, with Kjeld Kirk Kristiansen and his son Thomas sitting on the company's board. In the early 2000s, the family brought in professional management, a move that paid off handsomely with sales almost doubling annually since 2008, reaching £1.86 million ($2.79 million) in 2011. This evolution hasn't come at a cost for the founding family's values, particularly when it comes to quality, the community and the environment. 'Only the best is good enough' is the LEGO Group's motto.

Bringing in professional management, and looking at people and processes and new routes to market transformed LEGO in a few years. Such transformation requires flexibility and a willingness to evolve. This statement is never truer than with a family-run business, many of which are steeped in traditional ways of doing things often handed down through generations. For family-run businesses to evolve, thrive and grow in a global competitive arena, they have to adopt even more professional approaches (see the next section).

Sometimes someone outgrows the business, and sometimes the business outgrows the person. The modern nature of business with today's high-tech needs and the lifecycle issues for products and services may no longer suit older generations, just as traditional ways of operating may no longer suit the attitudes and aspirations of the younger generation. Either way, evolution rests on carefully managed succession, ensuring leadership and management continuity throughout an organisation.

 We advise using the six-step model in the earlier section 'Working with talent management and succession planning'. A robust succession plan ensures that replacements have been prepared to fill key vacancies and that individuals have the ability to assume greater and expanded management responsibilities in the business. It also helps to identify when home-grown talent isn't there and when and how to recruit the right people for the right roles.

Transition coaching can be valuable when an organisation is working to evolve. Moving on can seem traumatic, but with support, an individual can see that staying in a role where he's not happy or flourishing is of disservice to him and to the business.

Keeping business professional

Conflicts are part of a normal experience for any business. *Constructive conflict* is healthy because it demonstrates a willingness for individuals to speak their mind and for all to be willing to listen to constructive feedback, even if it doesn't agree with their views. A business requires a healthy organisational culture to encourage constructive conflict and deal with it professionally. Many a business meeting has ended with people nodding their heads in agreement to the proposals made and then walking off knowing that nothing will change simply because people weren't willing to speak up for fear of conflict. But create the right culture to encourage people to resolve any concerns, issues or disagreements, and you get people on board.

On the other hand, *destructive conflict*, when people make conflict personal or take it personally, can have a negative effect on the well-being of staff and the organisation as a whole. A business requires a formal management structure that encompasses policies and procedures to deal with destructive conflict. Many family-run businesses begin with informal management styles that don't have the structure to deal with destructive conflict.

Enter the coach or mentor. With your support, the organisation can come to encourage constructive conflict and deal with destructive conflict before it becomes a problem.

When you coach family-run businesses, always coach them to

- ✔ **Award roles on merit, not blood lines.** The ethos is, 'It's not personal, its professional'. Put family members on the payroll only if they're making a real contribution. This rule also goes for suppliers. Establish positions, roles, remuneration and reviews as with a nonfamily member.

- ✔ **Be equitable.** Be careful not to show family members preferential treatment. Doing so creates the culture of family versus nonfamily, which is a recipe for conflict. Treat family and nonfamily the same when it comes to rewards and discipline.

- ✔ **Be honest.** Secret meetings with family members to discuss key issues over dinner creates a divide and doubt for nonfamily members who ought to be privy to such discussions. Aim for open, honest communication.

- ✔ **Separate family decisions from business decisions.** Asking the question, 'What would you do if this person was not a family member?' helps keep the decision-making process professional.

- ✔ **Have a healthy work–life balance that separates personal from professional.** Create working rules where shop talk is off limits helps family members distinguish between the two.

Developing Intrapreneurs within Organisations

Successful companies such as Facebook, Google and 3M have embraced the concept of encouraging employees to take new initiatives without it being part of the job description. These so-called *intrapreneurs* have in some cases transformed ideas into innovative, creative and profitable ventures within an existing organisational environment.

The 3M intrapreneurship came about by accident when Dr Spencer Silver, a scientist at 3M, was working on a project to develop a strong adhesive to be used in the aerospace industry. Instead of a strong adhesive, he created a light adhesive that stuck objects to surfaces well and didn't leave behind any marks or residue adhesive when removed. Instead of seeing this result as a failure, Dr Silver persisted with looking for applications for the adhesive. He teamed up with colleague Art Fry, and together they developed the Post-it note, now found in virtually every office.

Intrapreneurs need the organisational culture and space to create ideas, and organisations need the strategies to turn their intrapreneurs' ideas into reality. This mix can create a number of challenges that lead to an SOS call to a coach or mentor. Intrapreneurship is an exciting, growing area where coaching and mentoring can support the birth and growth of innovation.

Creating the space to innovate

An *intrapreneur* is an employee working for an organisation, rather than striking out alone. But other than that difference, intrapreneurs act just like entrepreneurs. They take calculated risks. They see opportunities rather than obstacles. They pioneer innovation. They forge ahead with an idea without having to seek someone else's permission. They anticipate trends. They create solutions to needs and spot business opportunities that often create unexpected value.

To do all these things, intrapreneurs need creative space. That means the organisation must cultivate an entrepreneurial culture that allows the 'loyal rebels', as intrapreneurs are often called, to step forward and grow, while working within the organisational systems, job descriptions and traditional culture.

For an intrapreneur to step up and deliver an idea requires courage and commitment. So goes the saying: 'You can't be a prophet in your own land'. If the culture of the organisation isn't mature enough to respect this courage, then great ideas stay stuck in the minds of the intrapreneurs and never get to market. Alternatively, and worse for the organisation, the intrapreneurs will transform into entrepreneurs and take their great ideas elsewhere.

When an intrapreneur raises his head above the parapet with a new innovation, he's making himself vulnerable to being shot down. He may be putting a lot at risk, or at the least on hold, such as letting go current job responsibilities, perhaps benefits and promotion. The organisation has to create a politics-free zone for this type of initiative to thrive. The intrapreneur has earned his bulletproof jacket and should be given independence to develop his idea to the best of his ability with the support of the organisation.

Here are some areas where coaching and mentoring programmes can support the organisation in fostering a culture of intrapreneurship:

- 🖊 Establishing frameworks to empower people to make decisions and be willing to speak up. An organisation's existing culture may discourage this type of independent thinking, and that's where coaching the individual and organisation adds value.

✔ Developing strategies for creative thinking, enabling the intrapreneurs to be revolutionary and visionary.

✔ Understanding the strategies and attitudes of entrepreneurs and being able to apply them.

✔ Creating incentives to encourage ideas, including celebrating and rewarding contributions.

Turning the catalyst of an idea into reality

Launching intraprenurial ventures is similar to taking a start-up idea and having it become a large, multinational business in the space of a year. Each development phase for scaling-up requires different management skills and different coaching programmes to support it. In Chapter 9, we explore in detail how you can help clients transform a vision into a workable plan.

One of the key decisions a business has to make, after it has the idea and has done due diligence to ensure that the idea is workable, is who's best suited to take the project to market. The person who developed the idea may not be the right person to deliver the project.

You may coach the intrapreneurs to build their ability and capacity to take an idea to scale. Alternatively, you may coach the organisation to find or develop a different model in which different leaders manage different phases of an initiative or the whole project.

 Treat each innovative venture as you would a new start-up. This idea means you can use the same diagnostics as you would with a new business. Then you design the best-fit coaching programme, giving the venture the best possible chance of becoming a reality.

Working with the Socially Oriented Business

In recent years, there has been a growth in the number of books and articles published and talks given on the subject of socially oriented businesses. Philanthropy in business isn't a new concept; philanthropy has been around since the Quakers began in the 1600s and perhaps earlier. If we define a *socially oriented business* as an organisation that applies commercial strategies to maximise improvements in human and environmental well-being, rather than maximising profits for external shareholders, then we can find many modern-day examples of such organisations.

Behind each organisation, you find individuals who want to make a difference. Author J. K. Rowling's Volant Charitable Trust helps fight poverty and social discrimination, especially where it affects women and children. It has an annual budget of £5.1 million ($7.6 million). Oprah Winfrey's Angel Network funds scholarships, youth centres and women's shelters. Her contributions exceed £303 million ($454 million). In 1991, John Bird and Gordon Roddick established *The Big Issue*, which enables homeless people in the UK to earn money by selling copies of *The Big Issue* publication on the streets, and in doing so regain self-respect and confidence and the chance to support themselves.

Knowing types and makeups

Socially oriented enterprises take many forms. Professor Muhammed Yunus won the Nobel Peace Prize in 2006 for setting up the Grameen Bank. The bank helps poor people escape from poverty by providing loans on terms suitable to them and by passing on a few sound financial principles so they can help themselves. Professor Yunus describes socially oriented business as being in two forms:

- ✔ **Type One:** Focuses on businesses dealing with social objectives only.

- ✔ **Type Two:** Owned by the poor and the disadvantaged, who can gain through receiving direct dividends or by some indirect benefits. Through this type of enterprise, the investors can use the dividends to enter into other profitable businesses.

The two types can be mixed together within the same social business, as has happened in the case of Grameen Bank. A Type Three is evolving as more businesses become socially conscious: an organisation set up for profit that's transitioning into a socially oriented enterprise.

Identifying the challenges for the business

Socially oriented businesses have the following challenges in common, all of which benefit from coaching and mentoring:

- ✔ **Being diligent with others' money:** Grants have many conditions and outcomes attached to them, so businesses need to be careful not to go off purpose.

- ✔ **Communicating:** Finding the right people, getting them on board and keeping them interested and actively engaged are areas where excellent communication skills are essential.

✔ **Getting grant funding:** Grant funding is a competitive market, as it is for any other business. Knowing how best to pitch ideas, develop budgets, options and appraisals and comply with the terms of the funding are areas in which socially oriented businesses can need support.

✔ **Meeting responsibilities:** The structure of the social enterprise comes with responsibilities. For example, if the business is non-profit-making, transparency of financial operations is of vital importance.

✔ **Presenting and pitching the business case:** One of the biggest killers is running out of cash to run the core business or create new ventures and projects. Specialist venture capitalists support socially oriented business and really understand it. They can provide support as a private equity or venture capitalist partner would do in a purely profit-based business.

✔ **Pushing for profit:** Even a non-profit-making business must make a profit! They have overheads and bills to pay, so ventures must be profitable. In addition, the business needs a savvy commercial approach that enables it to attract and maintain financial support.

✔ **Staying on track:** The trick is to remember that socially oriented businesses are building an enterprise, and the goal is to become profit generating and to increase self-sufficiency as soon as feasibly possible. To do that, the business must have upside potential because people are only going to fund a nice philanthropic idea for so long. The client may love his business, his client group, the social good he's creating, but if his numbers don't add up, he's running a charity looking for a grant. In other words, your job as the coach is to help him move from being dependent on funding to creating funding.

Any coach or mentor offering professional advice in relation to finances must be sure to work within the regulations and framework of that country. The coaching and mentoring skill sets around finances and public accountability can be quite specialist and are best outsourced or passed over if not a specialisation of the coach.

Working with a socially oriented businesses is a valuable contribution to serving the greater good. The sector comes with its own challenges, but you can use many of the standard coaching principles, tools and techniques. Above all, your perspective can help the business step back and see beyond its vision and purpose to create plans that will transform philanthropic ideals into real-world businesses that make a difference.

Chapter 4

Developing the Skills and Knowledge Base of a Coach and Mentor

In This Chapter

▶ Creating great coaching conversations

▶ Knowing your client's business

▶ Managing client sessions

▶ Working with frameworks

▶ Supporting clients in particular circumstances

*S*kills and knowledge are often underestimated in the world of coaching.

Whether it's face-to-face webinars, online courses, reading, practice groups, supervision, coach mentoring or personal coaching, do whatever it takes to develop your practice for you and for your clients. 'Whatever it takes' doesn't mean you have to follow the latest fad sold to you by someone who swears that her practice has improved twentyfold since she went into the forest with a sensory awareness group and danced around a fire pit calling in the spirit of the goddess of coaching. No matter how much people try to convince you, these kinds of activities aren't a requirement in the world of business coaching and mentoring.

In this chapter, we set out some of the things we know work in developing your skills and experience to support business clients. Our aim is to give you a flavour of what you need to know and what you need to be able to do well.

Coaching and Mentoring Are Not One and the Same

Although we cover both coaching and mentoring in this chapter, they are not the same thing. A coach supports clients to achieve their articulated outcomes or wants and helps them gain clarity around their measures of success and the impact of achieving what they want. A coach helps her clients to focus on 'the how' of delivering those wants in ways that align with the clients' values and current or future operating context.

Mentoring is more appropriately used when a client needs to learn a specific set of skills, acquire particular knowledge or needs wise counsel from a more experienced person over a period of time. Table 4-1 highlights the differences between the two roles.

Table 4-1   Mentoring and Coaching: The Difference in Emphasis

Mentoring	*Coaching*
On-going relationship usually over a long period	Relationship of set duration and regularly recontracting
More informal – when mentee needs advice/support or for a specific duration and purpose	Structured, planned; regular interventions
Mentor chosen for experience or knowledge in a particular area	Coach chosen largely for facilitative skill, coaching experience and understanding of how to help individuals and groups self-maximise contribution in a particular context
Agenda set by mentee whose learning requirement drives the mentoring goals; outcome framework may be set by a sponsor	Agenda focused on meeting specific imminent goals and can be set by the coachee or sponsor responsible for the intervention
Focus more on professional development	Focus more on support to determine specific development or solutions

The differences between coaching and mentoring can be subtle. Clarity at the outset and at the contracting stage ensures that clients know what they can expect.

The coaching skill set

The key skills used within coaching are skills that you have used all your life, such as listening, questioning, state management and speaking. The differences between coaching and everyday conversations are in the intensity and quality of your listening, the structure of the conversation, the quality of the questions and the focus of attention on clarity, insight and outcome. The skills of coaching are evident throughout this book. Doing some kind of coaching skills health check can really help coaches, mentors and leaders who coach. The self-assessment questionnaire in Chapter 1 is useful for even the most experienced coaches and mentors to help you reflect from time to time.

If you haven't done the skills assessment yet, it may be helpful for you to complete that and keep your answers in mind when you read through the next sections of this chapter.

Some practical things can help in any coaching intervention, whether it's a face-to-face session, a telephone session, video, Skype or email. Make sure you review notes, remind yourself of coaching objectives and think about the session. Getting prepared in terms of your physical and mental state are important too.

The mentoring mind-set

The mentoring relationship is slightly different from the coaching relationship. Yes, you need to be present and listen actively, but the balance of conversation is different in mentoring. Mentors elicit less and illustrate, support and advise more than coaches do. So while mentors need a growth mind-set that is focused on the ability of the mentee to learn, you need to be on alert with your particular knowledge and experience at the ready. The mentee is looking to you for guidance, so the eliciting and listening needs to be focused around the issues you are mentoring on, particularly if you're mentoring around a specialist area.

When we're mentoring, the mentoring is usually around some kind of thinking activity such as helping someone devise a situational response or helping her understand and apply a proven methodology for handling something. The balance is more towards actively signposting and advising the mentee rather than resourcing her to find the answer herself.

In mentoring, the mentor is sharing experience, knowledge, networks and ideas generation with the mentee. Mentors need to contract with a client, work within a model/framework and help clients get clear on any actions they may take as a result of the session.

Coaching and Mentoring Skills

Coaches and mentors need to have a strong set of skills to manage session time well and to help their clients get the most from their time and make shifts in their thinking and approach. We walk you through each of these in this section. All these skills need to be honed and utilised to support clients effectively.

Being present for a session

In coaching, turning up for a session isn't being present. A lamp post can be present. Looking or sounding interested isn't enough either. A devoted dog can do that if you dangle the smell of a treat in its path. Presence is about being fully engaged with a client, and it demands everything of the coach. It's about full-on attention in body, heart and mind. Yes, we used the heart word. If a coach is physically there and has all her intellectual and thinking faculties on alert but has no emotional connection with her client's experience, the situation is like going to a doctor and getting a prescription drug without any acknowledgement that you have a pain that impacts you. Don't leave your compassion at home when you work in business – you're trying to help people create businesses that people love to do business with!

Business leaders are busy. Their coaching session can be one of the rare opportunities they get to stop and think in a focused way with another person. Part of the job is to help clients remove distractions and slow down the pace for a while so they can focus and get something from their session.

Coaches need to be present to mirror effective presence and encourage clients to be with them in the moment. Inviting a client to stop and breathe lower in the belly, to close her eyes for a second and allow the thoughts and distractions of the day to leave her for the next hour or so while you help her focus on whatever she came here for is all about cultivating presence.

Being present in mentoring is obviously as important as in coaching. You need to come to the conversation well prepared, but the emotional distance is greater in mentoring.

Active listening

Listening in coaching isn't listening for the sake of just hearing or listening to respond, which is what we do in most conversations. You're actively listening. When you actively listen, you focus only on the client and on listening fully. You're listening in order to understand the client's story, her dilemma and the issues she wants to address. You're listening for language, assumptions, generalisations, beliefs, facts and emotions. Listen for passion, panic, perception and pause. You also need to listen intently and be able to summarise what the client has told you. The client needs to know she has been heard for you to serve her well.

The client deserves your absolute attention in order to:

- ✔ Elicit the issue the client wants help with.
- ✔ Check understanding of the assumptions, generalisations, opinion and facts in the story you hear.
- ✔ Listen for language that tells you how the person has experienced the problem or situation. The way someone recalls a situation or describes an issue can be as important as the issue itself.
- ✔ Understand what you can pull out of your coaching toolkit to assist her.
- ✔ Ensure that the person feels heard and you can gain and sustain rapport.

Active listening is full-on listening with the power and volume turned up – full-on attention, not 'Oh could you repeat that? I got distracted by the lovely artwork on your wall' kind of attention. Sit up, be fully there and notice everything.

Part of your job is helping clients see themselves and their behaviour. You can't be a mirror of sparkling clarity unless your focus is entirely directed at your client. When your client says 'I think the suit was all wrong; they were dressed quite casually. I think they might take me for someone who is a bit too formal', you need to be in a position to say, 'It sounds like the presentation went well, and the investors loved the product. You have worked so hard to get here over the last four years. Your team are so excited to hear if you have secured funds to expand. They're all behind you on this. Sounds like you've done a great job. So when they're so supportive and behind you, why are you preoccupied about whether they're judging your suit?'

Why coaching is rarely about the first issue in the conversation

Contracting can be complex. Clients sometimes contract for a period of coaching, start the process and then overtly change their mind about what they want help with. Alternatively, a new and deeper, often more impactful issue emerges in the conversation. Clients may have been aware of the secondary issue (which is probably the primary issue) at the point of contracting, or the issue was something they were not consciously aware of. So why does it emerge? There may be several reasons. Trust and space stand out. It takes time for a coach to gain rapport with clients and for clients to trust enough to state the real issues they want to coach around. This situation is quite normal, and coaches need to be ready for it.

When any of us slow down and focus on things impacting us in business life, the mere fact that we create the space to think invites the possibility that other issues may show up.

Flexibility in coaching and on the part of the coach is imperative. Enabling a coachee to trust in the process and consider sessions as a continuum rather than one-off events can really help people look in the places they never considered initially.

Doing your homework and developing relevant business knowledge

If you want to support people in business, particularly at executive levels where decisions get taken about direction, strategy, resources, risk and rewards, you need to understand business and the language of business.

The depth of that knowledge really depends on the type and level of engagement you are looking for with clients. Ask yourself: What kind of clients do I want to work with? Do I want to specialise in a particular sector, an area of business, a subject area or defined niche? Do I want to work in territory or globally? Understanding your own ideal customer is key. If you think about your customers and the level at which they operate and want support, what does this indicate for you?

The following would be useful knowledge to have:

- An overview of business, how it operates, key features and key language used
- Detailed knowledge of a particular geographical market (national or global)
- In-depth knowledge of a professional area
- Knowledge of a profession across a range of markets
- Investor responsibilities and governance
- An understanding of board-level structures and director's duties

Getting really clear on this beneficial knowledge can help you develop your coaching practice, target sessions with specific emphasis and identify your own learning. It would be hard to work in parts of China if you don't speak Mandarin, and you'll find it equally hard to coach in business if you don't understand business.

An experienced coach doesn't necessarily need exposure in a particular type of business niche to coach people in that business; clients know that themselves. However, knowing how a business operates, the language of business, how to read an annual report, understanding organisational reporting requirements in overview and the generic features of domestic and global business is useful and gives credibility.

Know when you are comfortable and when you are out of your depth. Chapter 16 gives some indications of generic resources to help you develop your knowledge base. More generally, the best place to understand what you need to know starts with using your common sense.

If you are supporting around a specific professional area, keep your professional membership requirements up to date. If you are coaching global teams, make sure you read, ask and stay open to the different cultural norms inherent in a mixed group. Work with individual preferences as much as practically possible, bearing in mind the cultural context and operating environment of the parent company. If you normally coach in the pharmaceutical industry and get a contract to coach in a hospital setting, research the roles, structures and operating environment.

Structuring a Client Session

Planning sessions before sitting in front of a client is important, particularly at the outset of contracting and when ending a coaching relationship. In between, the structuring needs to be more of a review of notes, some consideration of what works with the client and a reminder of what her contracted needs were at the outset of coaching. The rest of the session time needs to be client led.

Getting into the right frame of mind

Managing your coaching mind-set means ensuring that you are relaxed yet alert before a coaching session starts. Coming from a mind-set of openness, learning and growth for the duration of the session really helps it along. Remember that your role is to be in service to the client. Stopping before a session to prepare before you start the face-to-face or pick up the telephone is the first step; simply stop for five to ten minutes to clear your mind of distractions and commit to focus only on the client in front of you. Grounding your state irrespective of what has been going on for you just before the session is an essential part of being in service to your client.

Contracting creates relationship clarity

Whether coaching individually or in groups, the agreement about why, what, where, when, who and how much needs to be absolutely clear. Getting this clarity up front saves any confusion or surprises at a later date. Your agreement needs to be in writing and in plain language. Table 4-2 shows, at minimum, what the agreement should include and who is responsible for following through with each issue.

Table 4-2	Issues to Address in a Coaching Contract	
Issue	*Coach Responsibility*	*Client Responsibilty*
Confidentiality	✓	✓
Ethics and standards regarding conduct and retention of information	✓	
Well-being and boundaries of responsibility	✓	✓
Limits of liability and notification of indemnity insurance	✓	
Who the agreement is with, fees and payment terms	✓	
Length of coaching period, frequency of sessions and session arrangements	✓	✓
Outline of coaching requirement	✓	✓
Outline of services and length of programme	✓	✓
Cancellation and penalties	✓	✓
Commitment to the work outside of sessions		✓

Disclaimer: This list isn't exhaustive and does not represent advice on the part of the authors or publisher.

If you already have a structure for managing sessions, you may want to check that the elements listed in Table 4-2 are covered.

In addition, the agreement should reflect a flavour of your brand and of how you like to work. We say more about developing your brand in Chapter 13.

Where third-party sponsors are involved in an organisation and they are responsible for fee payment, you need to engage them at the outset of contracting to gain agreement to the coaching outcomes and content of the contract terms. If the contract then needs to change during the period of coaching, the client or the coach must discuss that with the sponsor. You may want to create two levels of agreement. Your agreement needs to be in writing and in plain language. One would be a contract for services document; the other, an agreement about the coaching relationship between the coach and coachee. It should set out clearly who is responsible for what.

The contracting session

The first session with your client can reasonably be split into three parts: domestics, respecting the relationship and difference making.

- ✔ **The domestics:** Where and how you will work together; the details of the agreement and how these will operate in practice; what the agreement is with the employer (if applicable); where notes are stored and the like.

- ✔ **Respecting the relationship:** How you will behave towards each other, implications of cancellation, confidentiality, acting honestly, role boundaries and what happens if you need to suggest referral outside of coaching.

- ✔ **Difference making**: Expected outcomes, expectations of individual work outside of session time, assessing how the client and others will experience success and how the on-going coaching relationship will be evaluated.

Creating the right environment

It seems too simple to say that you need to pay attention to the coaching environment and to make it conducive to effective coaching, but we have heard tell of people coaching in unsuitable environments so often that it's worthy of a mention here.

In simple terms, this relationship is professional and, even though many a business deal is made on a golf course, we recommend that unless you are coaching or mentoring clients on their swing, it isn't a conducive environment. At its simplest level, the client is distracted by the game, and you can't possibly be fully present in the coaching if you are worrying about winning and upsetting your high-achieving competitive client.

Some simple dos for managing an environment:

- ✔ Hold the session in a quiet, professional space. No beds or therapy couches.

- ✔ Have natural light if possible.

- ✔ Make water available (hydration is an essential brain lubricant).

- ✔ Have a room that comfortably fits two to four people if you are coaching an individual.

- ✔ Have a table, preferably round, and sit at an angle rather than interview style.

- ✔ Use a circle of chairs if coaching a group.

- ✔ Keep the air conditioning and heat down and have some fresh air in the room if you can.

- ✔ Have as few distractions as possible.

- ✔ Turn all phones and electronic equipment off – it's a coaching conversation, not a 'fit you into a window while I do something else' appointment.

- ✔ Have blank paper and pens ready or a notebook for your client to write in if she chooses.

- ✔ If possible, track time using a clock on the wall behind your client's head and away from her gaze.

- ✔ Arrive early and set the room up as best you can when coaching away from your known environment.

- ✔ If coaching remotely, try to re-create these conditions in your space and encourage the client to do the same. In particular, suggest that any papers are cleared, computer alerts switched off and rooms have a sign outside asking not to be disturbed.

- ✔ Wear comfortable, appropriate clothing and your most welcoming smile.

Create the kind of welcoming environment that you would like to be coached in. No Skype calls from your bedroom in your PJs, even if you are working across time zones! We've even had coaches report holding sessions in the gym on a treadmill and in a sauna – please don't. Coaching is a professional relationship and needs to be treated as such. You wouldn't expect a lawyer or a doctor or an accountant to meet clients on a treadmill to discuss a contract, their health plan or their tax return would you?

Knowing your limitations

All coaches are not equal. There. We've said it. In the world of personal and professional development where we like to find the best in everyone and want people to be resourceful and successful, we shy away from saying such things. Truth is, we're like wine. A spectrum exists from supermarket plonk to fine reserve produced by Trappist monks on a secluded mountaintop accessible by swing bridge where only five bottles are released every 20 years. We may think that we're the reserve, we may promote ourselves as the reserve, we may charge fees closer to the reserve price, and . . . we don't always know if those nearer the plonk provider end of the spectrum are providing a reserve experience at a plonk price. What we do know is that some people think they're getting the reserve experience because the price is nearer to the price of the bottle with the Trappist monk picture on it. However, some clients are getting reserve standard wine at the plonk price because some great coaches don't know how to run a business or because, quite simply, they undervalue the difference they make.

The client must understand what they're paying for. It serves coaches well to get comfortable explaining their credentials, and it serves clients well to get comfortable asking about them. Experience, qualifications, training and professional background are important. Of all these, experience is the most important. By that we don't just mean coaching hours (which are important); we mean the experience of the clients the coach has worked with and the impact the coach has had. Recognising the boundaries of experience and knowing when a coach is punching above her weight is important. Taking a client that you're not yet a 'skills and experience fit' to coach can be a disaster. Knowing when to say 'No, this isn't my area of expertise, of comfort, of confidence, of competence' is important.

Why refusing work gets you the right work!

Co-author Marie was once asked to go to coach a team on an oil rig after the death of a colleague following an accident. This request was from a longstanding executive coaching client in the oil industry who had worked with Marie both one to one and in his team. He knew her work and trusted her judgement. He thought she could really help the people impacted by the loss of a colleague. He thought he had the emergency coaching rescue solution.

Marie had never been on an oil rig, had never dealt with post event trauma and wasn't particularly fond of helicopter rides at night. She wasn't too happy at the prospect of being surrounded by a deep expanse of open water either.

Her former client didn't know that. All he knew was that he felt she could help in a dire emergency during a rig investigation and that he had seven staff members relying on him to help and support them.

In terms of working with grieving colleagues on an isolated rig, Marie would be out of her depth.

She told him quickly that she wasn't the right person to do this particular work and helped him find an experienced coach and grief counsellor who was.

In truth, some coaches would have accepted that challenge based on flattery, and it may have worked out. The question that professional coaches need to ask is 'Am I best placed to fulfil this obligation right now, and will the clients get a great service from me based on my knowledge and expertise?' If the answer is no or even maybe no, think on and be confident enough in your own personal credibility and integrity to say, 'Thank you so much for thinking of me. I'm just not the right person to deliver this'. Don't even tell a little porky pie lie of being too busy. Be honest. Otherwise they may come back with the same issue later, and you wouldn't want to say 'No I'm too busy' again, would you? If you do, they will simply stop calling because they're busy too, and you have been filed under 'too busy to help'. Avoid the temptation to structure a contract you are not skilled, confident and able to deliver. Clients respect you for that.

Find out how to say no clearly and nicely when the work just isn't for you or you know you can't serve the client well. Keep your coaching network fresh, and recognise that sometimes your service to clients is in referring them to another great coach. As a business client, recognise that someone who is clear about the boundaries of her expertise is a great coach. You want to find out more about what she does and hang onto her contact details.

Using Models in Coaching and Mentoring

A *coaching model* is simply a process framework that coaches use to give some structure to coach within. Models can be useful to help keep sessions on track. Think of coaching as a way of enabling clients to be even more resourceful and models being the method you use to help clients navigate their way around an issue. The more you can use simple models, the easier it is for clients to learn a process or two to help them resolve issues when you're not around.

You can find literally thousands of coaching models. (A US search engine found 94 million references to the term 'coaching model'.) You need a couple of good tools to help you stay on track and manage session time effectively. In business, you're working with busy people who want results fast.

You'll find it useful to have more than one model in your toolkit to support clients in different situations or handling different types of issue. Sometimes clients with a particular learning style relate to a particular model of coaching more easily. In our experience, IT specialists, scientists and doctors seem to relate well to solution-focused techniques, whereas those with a more active learning style tend to prefer a more narrative approach such as the CLEAR model. This is just an observation, however, not a rule. We outline two models below that can be used in individual or group coaching.

Keep using what works for your client and mix the models up a little rather than sticking rigidly to a model that you think works based on your assumptions about a person's preference. One size definitely does not fit all in the use of coaching models. The issue for coaches is to discover and develop a range of models in order to develop and maintain behavioural flexibility. As a coach, you need to use models to serve the client, not yourself.

The CLEAR model

Peter Hawkins at Bath Consultancy Group developed the CLEAR model in the early 1980s. Like many coaching models, this model is defined using acronyms. It has five stages or elements (see Figure 4-1):

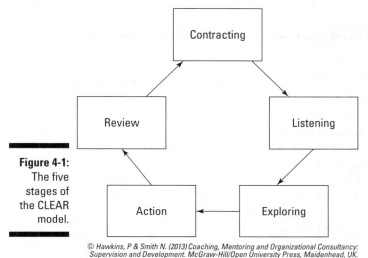

Figure 4-1:
The five
stages of
the CLEAR
model.

© Hawkins, P & Smith N. (2013) Coaching, Mentoring and Organizational Consultancy:
Supervision and Development. McGraw-Hill/Open University Press, Maidenhead, UK.

1. **Contracting:** Opening the discussion, setting the scope, establishing the desired outcomes and agreeing to ground rules.

2. **Listening:** Using active listening and interventions, and helping clients develop their understanding of the situation and generate personal insight.

3. **Exploring:** Helping clients understand the personal impact the situation is having on them and challenging them to think through possibilities for future action in resolving the situation.

4. **Action:** Supporting the clients in choosing a way ahead and deciding the next step.

5. **Review:** Closing the intervention, and reinforcing ground covered, decisions made and value added. Wherever possible, the client summarises her actions, insights and self-reflections at this stage. The coach also encourages feedback from the client on what was helpful about the coaching process, what was difficult and what she would like more or less of in future coaching conversations.

This model is effective for supporting a person in situ in an operational situation. It can easily be used to identify a way forward to an emergent issue/problem, which is current and immediate. The model is useful for generating ideas, helping a client see a situation differently or identifying and assessing possible alternatives.

The important thing about the CLEAR model is to keep it conversational. The conversation has a structure and a direction with the overall aim of giving the client what she wants from the session and leaving her in a better place than when she sat down to talk to you.

Using the CLEAR model

Here are some example questions to illustrate the different stages of the CLEAR model.

Contracting

We have around an hour, so let's check what would be useful to you today. Last time we met, you suggested you may like to focus on your lead responsibility for improving diversity in the workplace. Is that still the case?

Yes, I'd like to look at the board presentation I have next week.

Great. Where would you like to get to by the end of the hour?

The paper has gone in, and I am fairly confident but would like to walk through it and think about the emphasis and the questions I may be asked. I'd like to feel confident that I have covered all the issues.

What would you like from me in the session?

I'd like you to act as sounding board and help me identify the difficult questions.

Okay. I'll keep track of time and maybe make a few notes and give you a time check ten minutes before the hour is up so we can summarise and see if we need to discuss anything else. Okay?

Listening

So, walk me through the paper . . .

(The coach acts as a sounding board to test the paper, asking appropriate questions such as those following:)

✔ Can you explain what you mean by . . .

✔ Where did that figure come from on page 34?

✔ How do you know that you compare badly against your competitors in relation to women returners?

Exploring

The coach helps the client look around the issue using open questions, reflections, challenge and summary.

✔ So what I am hearing you say is that when you get to this midpoint in the presentation, you are worried that X will become challenging around the figures as he always picks up in the stats. Yes?

✔ I wonder if you notice how well you present information and how you are really good at presenting it using both the paper and the PowerPoint? You come across as being really confident about your data.

✔ So what is the worst thing that X could ask you? Where are you least confident about the paper?

✔ What happens when you get anxious about what X may say?

✔ What happens when you are not concerned about what he may ask? How can you do more of that on the day?

✔ You said he likes an injection of humour – you have some of that – how can you use that more if challenged by X?

✔ So let me summarise what you have said about what you are confident about and what you might do differently . . .

Action

So given what we have discussed, what can you do between now and next week?

Who needs to action that? You or someone on your team?

How are you feeling about delivering this presentation right now?

How can you get to that positive state before you go into the board meeting?

What other actions have you highlighted today?

Review

In summary, what will you do as a result of this session?

What has been helpful? What has been less helpful to you today?

Is there anything else you want to mention before we close?

Solution-focused coaching model

Solution-focused coaching helps people see the range of possible solutions open to them and how they can take action to achieve that solution. It can be particularly useful when a client is finding it difficult to discuss the content of a situation or perceives the problem as overwhelming and can't break it down into its component parts.

The question for the coach in solution-focused work isn't 'Where is the client coming from, and what is the issue she is facing?'; it's more like, 'Where is the client aiming to get to, and what steps can she take to get there?'

The coach supports the client by working through these four steps:

1. **Positive forward-focused pictures.** What will the client be doing (rather than not doing) that will indicate that the problem is getting resolved?

2. **Identifiable and specific actions.** If the client is to know that she is being successful, she needs to know specifically what she will be doing that will make her know that the situation is improving.

3. **Small, incremental changes.** She needs to identify the small indicators that she or others will notice, indicators that demonstrate that she is on the right path.

4. **A preferred future.** This future is one that the client defines and thinks she is capable of achieving. You aren't looking for the preferred future or the perfect future that the client thinks the coach wants for her.

This model is simple and can be used quickly if a client has limited time. It also works well as a self-coaching tool. We often teach clients how to use the model themselves and with their teams. It can be used in group coaching where a group is focused on the delivery of a change outcome or introducing a new product for example.

A solution-focused team intervention

Co-author Marie was working with a leadership team in the home care and housing sector who were responsible for identifying whether a potential partnership with a 1:1 care provider in a new geographical area would be a positive move for them.

They were in the process of building and renovating 60 properties for older people and adults requiring temporary supported housing solutions for 6–36 months while they were rehabilitated following serious and permanent physical disability.

The team of seven were struggling to identify whether they ought to create a joint venture with care provider 'Independent You' (not their real name) as an alternative to providing the care service alongside the housing themselves. They hadn't yet identified what that solution may require.

Marie walked them through a solution-focused process using the following questions:

1. What will you be doing if this situation is resolved and you have determined an agreed course of action?

Summary answers: By the end of June, we will have a partnership agreement with Independent You. It will be a joint venture where we provide the housing and Independent You delivers the care service for the Newcastle region.

2. What specifically will you be doing/leading between now and the end of June if you have a partnership agreement in place? What are you doing well at the moment and know will be required to make this joint venture successful?

Summary: Identifying broad client needs

Determining what equipment needs we have

Developing 10–60 specifications for service

Undertaking due diligence on Independent You

Getting to know the Independent You management team and their capabilities in more detail

Working with lawyers in legal agreements

Working with local politicians on the build, the PR and the service plans

(We elicited four pages of specific detail.)

3. How will you know that all these elements are being successfully managed and you are on track?

The risk matrix will show that legal and operational risk is managed.

Residents will feel involved, and the January survey will indicate that.

The individual specifications will be agreed and plans to deliver them set out month by month.

The lawyers will be able to develop a single agreement with a break clause after two years of operation and that will be accepted.

(We elicited seven pages of detail here with rough dates and milestones.)

4. If this is the preferred future, what does that look like? Describe the full picture to me that you have now. (Marie asked them to draw it as a team and to imagine some of the things that their customers and key stakeholders would be saying.)

As they did this activity, they realised why they were reticent about this option. They anticipated strong objections and blocking from two stakeholder groups. They realised that their vision needed to be shared earlier than anticipated to get these groups on board, as that could be a deciding factor in the organisation's ability to deliver this option. As they went through the work, three of the leadership team were articulating real reservations about the option and wanted to work up the alternative option which we did using the same method. In defining two alternative potentially successful futures, the team fleshed out the requirements of each for them to be successfully executed. As a result they were able to decide on a preferred option, work up detailed plans, justify their rationale and manage stakeholder objections.

They developed a joint venture on budget and on target.

A model for mentoring

As a fan of the mnemonic, co-author Marie has used the following model in training mentors to think about their role. It acts as a useful aide memoire and is similar in structure to the CLEAR model, described earlier in this chapter. The model is simple, and we like simple.

In the following mentoring model, the mentor leads and manages the session around six stages (coaches and mentors do love a series of stages and steps).

The mentee typically brings an issue. The mentoring session opens up with ideas and sharing, and moves through examination of likely scenarios. The difference in mentoring as opposed to coaching is in the amount of personal experience the mentor shares from her own professional life. The mentor uses her experience to highlight the issues the mentee needs to consider and helps the mentee think through his options and proposed actions. The mentee produces a clear plan of action.

1. **M**otivate by generating ideas and options and sharing own experience.
2. **E**xplore ideas, solutions, roles and scenarios.
3. **N**otice the mentee's response and degree of movement towards a solution.
4. **T**heorise as to possible impacts of the ideas and options generated.
5. **O**utline a plan of proposed action.
6. **R**eview the session and usefulness of the intervention.

Developing flexibility in utilising models and tools

The beauty of coaching models is that when you have a few under your belt, you can mix them up and identify what works with your client. We have mentioned several models throughout this book. We invite you to mix them up and notice what works for your client. Even with the two models outlined in this chapter, you can insert a bit of solution focus into the CLEAR model. You can mix models readily when looking at exploring what may be required or at the action stage when defining the how of getting things moving forward.

The invitation is to use coaching models like a knickerbocker glory ice cream rather than four flavours in single cones. This mixture is how business operates. It doesn't play out in a vanilla fashion. Business is more like chocolate chip and raspberry ripple mixed in with a few bits of rocky road biscuit and a few nuts!

 Don't be greedy and possessive with your toolkit. If you want to resource clients, let them know what you are doing when you use models. Share your models so they can learn to use them too. Some coaches behave like they are holding onto state secrets with their toolkit. Models are just information. What you do with them in service to a client is what creates magic results.

Working in Particular Circumstances

Coaching business leaders can be difficult to manage, given their operating circumstances and work patterns. This difficulty is even more evident if they are operating across time zones in a multi-site or global environment. Equally, if you are working with leaders from a different culture or operating across cultures, you need to actively consider this. Whatever the method, remember to keep it professional and give your client time. You are engaged in a conversation, not a transaction.

Sometimes you need to use different methods of coaching to meet the client's needs. The following sections outline a few practical things you can do.

Coaching and mentoring via telephone, web and email

When your client isn't sitting in front of you, create the conditions to act as if she is. If you're running a session on the phone or email, aim for the following if you can:

> ✔ **Clear away anything that distracts you.** Turn off you mobile phone and computer alerts; move papers off of your desk. Have only those things that relate to the client in front of you. If you have a photo of your client, take a quick look and remember whom you're talking to before you start. Imagining her sitting in front of you sounds a bit far-fetched, yet it works.

✔ **Be prepared to hear the silences like a deafening gap.** Silence always seems to last longer on the telephone or webcam. Keep in mind that the client needs time to explore her thinking. She can't do that if you keep interrupting her.

✔ **Be prepared to walk the client through the process you are following to give her signals of what you are about to do.** Doing so is good practice anyway but becomes even more important when a client can't see you. For example, if you were using the CLEAR model (see the earlier section 'The CLEAR model') when you had identified the broad issue she wanted to focus on, you may say something like, 'I'm just going to listen for the next few minutes and take a few notes while you think about the issue. When you're ready, tell me what I need to know to help you today'.

In short, acknowledge what you are doing to facilitate the client's thinking.

Using the telephone

Your active listening skills need to be on high alert when you use the phone for coaching. You are not simply listening for the words but for any pauses that may indicate confusion, discontent or some other emotion. When you sense something is interrupting the client's thoughts, it's useful to check. You could ask, 'Is your hesitation because you need a minute to pause and think, or for another reason?'

When people are face to face, you can coach them through a range of scenarios and steps easily. When Marie is coaching on the telephone, she often suggests that a client pops the phone down for ten minutes to write out quick ideas in a mind map or bullet points. This activity can be useful if clients want to generate a communication piece or would like to walk through a conversation they intend to have with a third party. It can be more effective to use a teleconference service so you can stay on the line and have the client dial back in when she is ready.

Using Skype or videoconferencing services

While videoconference is preferable to email and telephone coaching, it only works for the client if you can guarantee a reliable connection. Marie once tried to get a signal using the Bluetooth connection via her phone to power a connection to Skype on a laptop in the middle of the Arizona desert. Not her finest coaching hour.

Dial in and test the connection in advance. Sending the client a reminder of your soft rules of engagement also makes for a better session. Maybe you can schedule a message the morning of the call just reminding her of any sign-in details (Skype name or any passcodes), time of call (in both time zones if relevant), and suggest that the client will have a better experience if she can be at a clutter-free desk or private room with no phone or other distractions. Make sure she has a mobile or landline number in case something goes wrong. We mentioned working in your PJs earlier – don't do it. Dress as if you were seeing a client face to face.

Emailing

While email coaching isn't ideal because so much can be misinterpreted without the rapport-building that happens face to face or through the voice, some coaches and clients prefer it.

If you're coaching on email, you can't clarify things with each other quickly. You must make sure that the communication is clear and short. Remember that you are in dialogue, not writing an essay. Check in frequently with the client on where you are in the coaching process. Also, as with telephone coaching, the process needs to be made more explicit. So you can write, 'It seems like you have explored all angles of this issue. So if you were to move to action now, what steps can you take to execute your idea?'

To coach on email well, you need to be good at using language and spotting deletions, distortions, assumptions and generalisations (see Chapter 5). Getting good at reframing written sentences quickly helps too. Resisting the temptation to shorten sentences in our increasingly sound bite, fast-focused world needs to be considered.

You probably notice a world of difference between

> *I think you're saying that Mary is causing a real problem in your team.*

And

> *So I can understand that Mary's work isn't at the level you would like, and she isn't delivering to target at the moment.*

And even greater difference if you talk in tweetage such as

> *I hr u say M's wk is prob @ mo n u need 2 do somat*

Doesn't look professional and thought out, does it?

The format of email coaching is important. Emailing in two different colours (one each) can really help. Be wary of using too much emphasis like bold, capitals, exclamation marks and the like. These can signal a feeling that the client may misinterpret.

Cross-cultural and multicultural work

Cross-cultural work can be a complex subject because so many permutations exist. If you work in a business wholly owned and led from the US and you are in Europe but manage staff in Singapore, Russia, Australia and India, this situation is significantly different to managing a UK subsidiary of a US-owned company where you have a small office in Geneva and one in Germany. If you are coaching clients with complex responsibilities, you need to understand those to serve the client well.

If clients are managing people from a different culture to their own but situated in their country of origin, this situation is wholly different to coaching a client from a different culture operating outside of her country of origin.

People commonly group areas together using convenient umbrella terminology such as 'Asia' or 'Europe' when you can find myriad nuances of culture inside those labels. If you think about the tiny island that is the UK, you have Welsh, Scottish, Irish, English, northern and southern cultures and regional subcultures. No wonder thinking about the notion of cross-cultural working is complex!

Some of the questions you're looking to understand to help the client include:

- What country is the company led from in terms of governance?
- Overall, what factors are dominant in that country in terms of values, issues of gender, equality, religion, appetite for risk, governmental system (democratic or autocratic) and power relationships?
- What is the culture within the company? What five descriptive words or sentences would your client use to describe it?
- What is valued in the company – what gets rewarded and what doesn't?
- How does culture differ in the country of the person/people you are coaching? (Walk through questions 2–4.)
- Where are the customers that the client's staff are serving, and what are the features of their culture? (See question 2.)

When coaching businesses that work across different cultural contexts, with staff from a variety of cultural backgrounds, you need to work harder at understanding their context in order to coach them through the additional challenges and rewards that this variety may bring.

Most large-scale business is in a state of constantly learning how to get results in different ways, usually in different markets. Often, coaching leaders who work cross-culturally is about helping them develop flexibility and get clear on what factors are important in delivering results for the company in different territories. You need to help them focus on outputs while paying attention to the dominant country culture, the culture in the organisation itself and the various norms that operate in the organisations that the client is responsible for.

Part II
Coaching and Mentoring to Get a Business on the Right Track

Logical Levels model

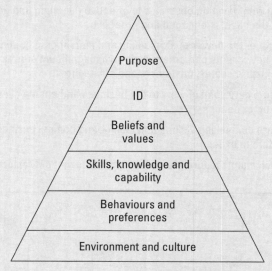

Illustration by John Wiley & Sons, Ltd.

Meetings are a must in business. Find out how to coach clients to conduct better meetings with the free online article at www.dummies.com/extras/businesscoachingmentoring.

In this part . . .

- ✔ Deal with common obstacles to effective coaching and ensure that the client is engaged and proactive.

- ✔ Discover the power of storytelling and metaphor in coaching and how clients can create their own magnificent stories that will inspire clients, customers and colleagues.

- ✔ Bring a new point of view to the business and enable clients to see other options.

- ✔ Create compelling visions that inspire and compel business leaders to excel.

- ✔ Coach clients to turn great ideas into plans that get results.

Chapter 5

Coaching Clients through Their Blind Spots

. . . .

In This Chapter

▶ Preparing to coach with the pre-frame

▶ Breaking down barriers to learning

▶ Exploring the ego, eccentricity and empathy

▶ Moving beyond drama to see clearly

▶ Considering incongruency

. . . .

Someone once asked Dr Richard Bandler, co-creator of Neuro-Linguistic Programming (NLP), 'Do you work with the deaf, dumb and blind?' His exasperated reply: 'Every single day'.

There are none so blinkered as those who don't *want* to see. Have you ever had an insight into a problem and later realised that the solution had been staring you in the face for ages? Or been given advice that you didn't listen to, only to later find that it was correct? We're sure you have – we've all been there.

Blindness to the obvious or to new ideas is one of the biggest blocks to effective coaching, and you're best dealing with it at the start of any coaching relationship. Socrates said, 'I cannot teach anybody anything. I can only make them think'. A coach can't make someone change; he can only guide a client through reflective conversations, metaphors, enquiry and inquiry, and insights gained through tools, techniques and processes. The coach can be teasing, chiding, provocative, caring and supportive – whatever the client needs to help him see clearly.

This chapter explores how to create the environment and the attitudes for clients that enable coaching to be effective. We cover what stops people from learning and seeing the obvious, and we look at what a coach can do to shine a light in the darkness of ignorance and misunderstanding.

As a coach, you must be aware of your own blind spots, so throughout this chapter consider how the information applies to you as well as your client.

Being aware of your own blind spots and working on them helps you to become a better coach.

Pre-framing the Coaching Conversation

Before you can start any coaching conversation with a client, you need to *pre-frame* it. To do so means you lay down the guidelines, rules, agreements and conditions for coaching that enable positive change to happen. In Chapter 4, we outline the practicalities of rules for the pre-frame (switch off your mobile, for example, and be punctual).

Here, we offer general principles that we recommend you lay down with your client in the pre-frame to help create the right conditions for tackling those blind spots. Guide your client to be

- ✔ Totally present in the room and focused on the coaching

- ✔ Fully engaged in the coaching process, not just dabbling

- ✔ Open-minded and willing to listen and learn

- ✔ Ready to learn by experience – to do assignments

- ✔ Willing to make mistakes and learn from them

- ✔ Honest about limitations and obstacles – if he's stuck or unsure, he needs to say so

- ✔ Selfish – this is special time for the client; he must make the most of it

- ✔ Respectful

- ✔ Fun-seeking

The preceding guidelines are for your client and are flexible, which is very different to rules, which are fixed. Switching off mobile devices when coaching is a rule. But a pre-frame guideline to 'have fun' is optional – after all, some subjects are serious and emotionally charged and don't naturally lend themselves to having fun.

Talk through the pre-frame with the client and seek his agreement, out loud, for each point. If he disagrees with anything, you can now discuss it and agree what works for both parties.

Set the pre-frames up with your clients *before* you begin any coaching. You'll find it much more difficult to *reframe*: add in rules and conditions after you have started – clients are resistant to re-framing. Imagine having a potential client who stares out the window during your initial meeting instead of engaging in meaningful conversation with you; the time to address this problem is before it takes hold. 'A pinch of pre-frame is worth a pound of reframe' is the mantra to use!

Breaking Down Common Barriers

With experience, a coach will begin to see common patterns of behaviour. By being aware of the patterns that may hinder coaching, you can deal with the behaviours before they happen. In the following sections, we explore some of the common patterns that are barriers to clients being able to fully engage in the coaching experience, and we look at how best to deal with them before they arise.

Making clients aware of how they're preventing themselves from learning and changing is an essential coaching pre-frame. So the crux of the work in this section is building self-awareness in clients. *Self-awareness* – also known as *emotional intelligence* or *EQ* – is the state of being aware of emotions and thoughts and the behaviours that result from them. Research has shown that EQ has a significantly positive effect on managerial awareness and performance.

Valuing EQ more than IQ

Daniel Goleman, an internationally renowned psychologist and science journalist who studies and lectures on behavioural and brain sciences, has pioneered the concept that emotional intelligence or EQ matters more than IQ in terms of social and emotional learning. EQ is highly relevant to learning through coaching. Most blocks that prevent effective coaching are a result of clients being in stressed or fear-related states that adversely affect their EQ.

Two examples of how low EQ levels can have a negative impact on how the mind operates are when taking exams and when presenting. Most people have experienced studying for an exam or preparing a presentation; they have done the work, practised and know their subject matter well, yet as soon they entered the exam room or stood in front of an audience, their mind went blank. The low EQ stress-related state releases neuro-chemicals called *neuro-inhibitors* that effectively shut down large parts of the brain's operating system. They inhibit neuro-activity, taking valuable information offline and making it unavailable.

As soon as the student leaves the exam room or the presenter steps off stage, he breathes a sigh of relief, relaxes and changes his state. No longer in the stressed state, the neuro-inhibitors are replaced by different chemicals called *neuro-transmitters*, and these effectively switch the brain back on so all the information comes back online. This switching happens in fractions of a second. The student now knows the answers, and the presenter remembers all his lines.

Low EQ stress-related states block recall (output of data), and they also block learning (input of data), creating blind spots. In Chapter 10, we look at techniques that enable clients to change their states and raise their EQ so they can access optimal learning conditions.

Working on willingness to learn

A coach can open a door, but the client must enter by himself. For this action to happen, he has to be willing. If he isn't willing, what does the coach do next? Your ability as a coach to deal with unwillingness has a profound effect on your effectiveness as a coach.

First, explain to the client the importance of being willing to listen to learn and the positive impact this will have on his coaching experience. Then, after you directly cover the pre-frame conditions for willingness to learn, indirectly reinforce them with metaphors.

Addressing willingness to learn before teaching

In 2011, Steve was invited to present a one-day 'Introduction to NLP' workshop in New York. The audience: 250 of the East Coast's finest cognitive behavioural therapists. (This situation is the equivalent of a South London comedian walking into a working man's club in Glasgow; it had the potential to be a lively event!) Steve started the day off with an analogy that was a little shot of pre-frame to begin the day. Steve began as follows:

'Imagine a large fan spinning. The fan represents your thinking. On the other side of the fan is your mind and body. In my hand imagine that I have cards. Written on them are metaphors, questions, tools and techniques that can transform your practice; they represent all that you can learn if you have an open mind. My role is to get the cards and the information on them past the fan and into your mind so they are embodied in your thinking and your behaviours. How do I do that?'

After a few suggestions – throw the cards faster or quicker, wrap them in an elastic band, time the throws so the cards go between the blades – eventually someone shouted, 'Switch the fan off'. Steve said:

'Excellent answer. Now I have a question: Are you willing to switch the fan of over-thinking off? Are you willing to be smart enough to be stupid and set aside all that you know in order to let new information in? If you're not willing, then the exit is over there, and you may as well go home'.

No one left, to the relief of the event organiser. Next, Steve told the story of a novice monk who went to see a master in order to become his protégé and attain enlightenment. The master listened to the novice explain how intelligent he was. He talked about his ideas, his theories, what he had done, what he knew and how keen he was to learn from the master. While the novice was talking, the master poured him a cup of tea. When the cup was full, he kept on pouring. The novice was shocked as the tea spilled over the rim across the table. The master explained that the novice's cup of knowledge was already full, and while he believed he was smart, he was in fact stupid because he was blocking himself from new ideas. Only by being willing to learn would he attain enlightenment.

Because the room was full of professionals who had been trained in a discipline that had different approaches to the subject being taught, Steve knew that people may not agree with what he presented. Their knowledge and experience may have created blind spots that prevented them from learning, So he pre-framed to address the issue of willingness to learn.

Metaphors are a powerful coaching device. Messages in the metaphors bypass conscious examination and critical evaluation and enable you to elegantly convey valuable information that gets accepted and goes unquestioned by the listener.

Sometimes you'll need to use multiple metaphors and analogies embedded within each other. Stacking metaphors within each other is called *nesting* and is a powerful way to convey ideas.

Time invested in getting clients to be willing from the start is well worth every second spent.

When you're working to overcome a client's unwillingness, aim to create a safe space where you have no smart questions and no smart answers, no dumb questions and no dumb answers, and it's fine to make mistakes.

Pushing beyond the comfort zone

Coaching is all about change, and change often means giving up what you know and entering into the unfamiliar: stepping out of the comfort zone. You need to make your clients understand that while they love what's familiar and comfortable, they learn by what's different and new. And as they practise what's different and new, it eventually becomes familiar and comfortable.

Here's a simple physical exercise you can use to demonstrate how people learn through focused repetition and how they can unconsciously be resistant to new learning. We call this 'The Thumbs of Wisdom'. The bold steps are the instructions you give directly to the clients.

1. **Hold your hands out straight in front of you and interlock your thumbs and fingers so they alternate.**

2. **Identify which thumb is on top and then notice how it feels in your body and describe it.**

   Most people, regardless of whether the left or right thumb is on top, describe their body as feeling 'okay', 'normal', 'natural' or 'comfortable'.

3. **Now pull your hands apart (still outstretched) and bring them back together, fingers alternating, but this time with the *other* thumb on top.**

   After a few moments of confusion, most people can do this seemingly simple task. Check to see whether they actually followed the instruction. Some have switched the thumbs but not the fingers; some have switched thumbs and some of the fingers but not all of them; some may say to you, 'I can't do it'.

4. **What does this feel like in comparison to the first way?**

   Most people say things such as 'weird', 'unnatural' and 'uncomfortable'. We've have even had people say 'evil'!

5. **Revert your hands to the first position (Step 1).**

   As they do this, you hear the sighs of relief. The first position is natural and comfortable – even when it comes to clasping hands, people have a pattern they unconsciously prefer.

6. **Slowly alternate between the two ways of interlocking fingers.**

   Keep going for a few minutes, and as you notice people finding the job easier, direct them to speed up.

7. **Stop; now for a final time, try the two positions. Notice how each feels.**

   By now, with a little bit of practice, most people notice that the second position feels just as comfortable and easy as the first.

Identifying the enemies of learning

When discovering new things, many experience what we call *enemies of learning*. These unconscious behaviours block people from trying new things for the sake of comfort and familiarity. As a coach, you need to have an awareness of your own enemies of learning and see them in others.

Here are the most common enemies of learning to look for:

- ✔ **Is this the same as that?** Humans are pattern-matching machines. They look for the sequences and familiarity in everything as a means to learn about the world. Is this like that? Is that like this? If someone operates by assuming what's being coached is the same as what he already knows, he's closing his mind to new ideas. If you identify that a client is pattern matching, first make him aware that he's doing it. Then explain the negative impact it can have and invite him to stop doing it.

- ✔ **I've heard this before.** If the client assumes he's heard this before, the open mind closes. Steve recalls sitting in an NLP trainers' training session, listening to Dr Richard Bandler tell a story. 'Although I'd heard the story a good 30 times before at previous training sessions, I suddenly heard a *new* message'. You can always find something to learn, so encourage clients to imagine being a novice and let the information in.

- ✔ **Do you know who I am?** Professional experts, senior executives, high earners and high achievers can often let their perceived status block them from learning in a coaching conversation. The person who thinks he's the finished article, who's reached his potential because of a title or qualification, has a cup that's overflowing. Telling him the novice and master story (see the earlier sidebar 'Addressing willingness to learn before teaching') can make the client aware of this blockage.

- ✔ **I don't have time for this.** Everyone is busy. Unless someone values the time and effort involved in coaching, he may be resistant from the start. Being able to demonstrate the return on investment (ROI), and giving metaphors and examples of the benefits of engaging and the costs of non-engagement are great ways to get someone to see the value of the coaching process. Flick to Chapter 2 for the lowdown on making a compelling business case for coaching.

✔ **This is all highly amusing.** Having fun is an integral part of any coaching programme. Fun is a great state for learning. But a distinction exists between having fun and making light of the work. Playing the joker is often a way to camouflage insecurity. When someone is attempting to disengage by using humour for fear of not being good enough, of not being able to learn or of the changes that may come about as a result of the coaching process, humour becomes a problem. In this situation, tell the client that it's okay to have fun and that humour is a good thing, but not to use it as a diversion tactic from fully engaging in the coaching experience.

Making clients aware of the enemies of learning as part of a pre-frame conversation enables them to recognise them and then self-adjust. If they don't recognise when an enemy crops up or don't self-adjust, you can refer back to the pre-frame conversation to remind them. If the client still fails to adjust after the feedback, you now have a topic worthy of coaching around.

Dealing with Roles and Perceptions that Contribute to Blindness

The emotional state a client is in affects how he perceives the world around him and his sense of self-identity. This section helps you to recognise when clients are in a mind-set that is not helpful to coaching, which can blindside them or block coaching, and how to guide them back into optimal coaching states.

This section isn't a how-to guide to identifying and dealing with people who have extreme emotional or mental issues. We focus on business coaching only. Yet you may encounter someone who has an issue that requires therapeutic help. You must be able to recognise clients who have these challenges and know how to assist them to get the right support.

Repositioning the ego state

An *ego* isn't real. It isn't a thing; you can't hold it up for examination. An ego is a set of unconscious, unwritten rules that help you organise your thoughts and behaviours and make sense of the world. Sigmund Freud defined ego as a sense of self. Ego is like walking around with a rule book that you don't even know you have. The book contains all the instructions for how you judge, plan, discover, function, control and test the reality of the world.

In coaching, ego can affect the willingness of the individual to participate in a coaching conversation and block his ability to develop more self-awareness through an

- ✔ Inflated sense of self-worth
- ✔ Undervalued sense of self-worth or lack of self-esteem

Both inflated and undervalued egos block people from making changes. This area of coaching is complex, and a full exploration of the subject is beyond the scope of this book. But the following information and exercise help make your clients more aware of when ego is blocking change and give them tools to change.

Eric Berne, founder of transactional analysis, believed that people have three ego states: parent, adult and child. He developed the theory that when people communicate with others, they do so from one of these ego states. The three different ego states break down as follows:

- ✔ **Parent:**
  - **Nurturing parent ego state:** Represents the more affirming and more pleasant qualities of what parents and society do for a person.
  - **Critical parent ego state:** Represents the corrective behaviours of real parents and the prohibitive messages of society.
- ✔ **Adult ego state:** A single state that can draw on the resources of both parent and child and negotiates between the two.
- ✔ **Child:**
  - **Adapted child ego state:** Represents the human response that has negativity in it – some resistance, some reaction and some deeper hostility.
  - **Free/natural child ego state:** Represents a playful and spontaneous part of human behaviour, from infancy to old age.

These labels help you identify whether a client is in the nurturing parent ego state, the adult ego state or the free/natural child ego state, all of which are optimal for coaching. Alternatively, the labels can help you see whether he's in the critical parent ego state and adapted child ego state, which are states that can restrict or block a client's ability to listen to learn and to function in a more balanced and effective way.

Table 5-1 shows the physical and verbal cues that alert you to which ego state your client is in at that particular time. Pay particular attention to cues that identify either a critical parent or adapted child ego state. These will point to areas where useful coaching work can be done. (After the table, we give you an exercise to help your clients to break out of negative states.)

Table 5-1	Ego Cues to Look For		
	Parent	*Adult*	*Child*
Physical cues	**Critical:** Angry or impatient body language or expressions **Nurturing:** Sincere smiles, nods, relaxed posture	Attentive, interested, non-threatening and non-threatened body language or expressions	**Adapted:** Emotionally sad, tantrums, whining, shrugging shoulders, rolling eyes **Natural:** Laughing, smiling squirming with delight, giggling
Verbal cues	**Critical:** Judgemental, patronising and critical lan-guage: *always, never, for once and for all* **Nurturing:** Soft supportive tones, agreeable and encourag-ing language	Questioning and querying language: *why, what, when, how, where, when, I think, I believe*	**Adapted:** Demanding language: *I want, I need, I don't care, I don't know, it's not my fault* **Natural:** Playful language open to experimenting and willing to make mistakes: *I get it, let's do that again, can I have a go, is it my turn now*

Use this exercise if you feel the client's attitudes and actions suggest that he's in the critical parent ego state or adapted child ego state when dealing with a particular issue. First, explain the definitions of the parent, adult and child ego states, perhaps using Table 5-1. Then choose a particular issue the client is dealing with – for example, struggling to get along with a team member – and lead the client as follows:

1. **Instruct the client to stand up and imagine being in each of the ego states one at a time. Each time he switches ego states, he should move to a different spot to help distinguish them. Have him speak about the subject from the perspective of each, describing what he says, thinks and feels for each of the ego states.**

2. **Ask him which ego state is the most active when he is struggling with his particular issue.**

3. **Instruct the client to re-enact his experience of the adult ego state from Step 1 in the context of the problem once more and to notice the difference.**

4. **Tell him that from now on, he should try to be aware of which ego state he's in whenever he's dealing with the issue and choose to move to the adult ego state.**

After doing this exercise, clients get insights into how their states affect how they see a situation and behave. They also have a more resourceful option as a result of the exercise.

Grounding eccentricity

By *eccentricity* we mean those colourful characters who are often flamboyant, larger than life and always erratic. They're predictably unpredictable, and coaching them can be as challenging as training a cat to fetch a stick.

When you coach an eccentric, agree with him on a clear pre-frame of rules before any coaching begins (see the earlier section 'Pre-framing the Coaching Conversation'). Get him to verbally commit and say out loud to each pre-frame, 'I agree'. Make sure that these are rules and not guidelines, because the eccentric will take advantage of any wriggle room. If the pre-frame is missed, heaven help the coach who tries to pin him down later with a reframe.

Eccentrics see their eccentricity as being a strength (which it is), and their biggest blind spot isn't seeing that their eccentricity can be a blind spot. You get times in business when a little bit of mundane, boring, grounded normality is just what's needed.

Eccentrics often need coaching to combat the following blind spots:

- ✔ **I'm the best.** Eccentrics may not realise that they're not the best people to run certain aspects of their business. You can show them that handing over roles to others allows them to be free to get carried away with their own ideas.

- ✔ **It's all a game.** *Gamification* is the relatively new approach of using game design and technology in other business contexts, such as when creating healthy competition between teams and encouraging customer loyalty. Many tech or science eccentrics are early adopters of this approach. As much as this drives creativity, the attitude of treating business as a game has risks. For example, many tech eccentrics are used to dealing with other people's money, such as large grants, and haven't had to think about money as a commodity that you have to trade with. Coaching them to see when their eccentric attitudes can put the business at risk is essential.

✔ **The world sees what I see.** Working with creative eccentrics who believe in their heart and soul that everyone will want what they have can be difficult. Most eccentrics are passionate about their ideas, but if they can't develop the business sense to turn the dreams into reality, it stays as that – just a dream. Eccentrics often need coaching to ground their ideas in reality – market reality and financial reality beyond the initial budget they have – and in managing their concept to the proof of concept stage. The challenge for the coach is getting them to listen and learn.

Here are a few pointers for working with eccentrics:

✔ Accept their eccentric behaviour. Eccentric behaviour can be a valuable asset; many successful businesses have come from crazy ideas. Don't see your role as telling a client what's possible or what's not – who are you to judge?

✔ If you think that the eccentric is really off track and may damage the business, have the courage and professional integrity to challenge the client.

✔ Allow plenty of time for the client to talk around his ideas and challenge yours – that way he trusts you and begins to listen.

✔ Conducting coaching experiments and coaching games appeals to eccentrics; because you're presenting things as a game, they're more likely to engage in this approach.

Distancing empathy

We can define *empathy* as the ability to understand and even vicariously experience another person's situation and emotional state. Surely empathy is a good thing? Yes, certainly it is – but excessive empathy can have a negative affect on a person's ability to function and to make good decisions.

The reason lies in this part of the definition: *vicariously experience another person's situation and emotional state.* If we share with you an upsetting or traumatic experience and you're empathic, you replay the experience as if it were your own and end up feeling distress. The mind doesn't know the difference between a vividly imagined experience and a real event – just ask any phobic who can terrorise himself just by *thinking about* what he's afraid of. Be empathic for too long and the stress you suffer can lead to burnout or physical illness.

We recommend that you encourage all clients to have *sincere sympathy and compassion* for people but to avoid empathy:

- ✔ **Sympathy** focuses on awareness; it means having care and concern for the person's situation – 'I feel for you'.

- ✔ **Compassion** focuses on action; it means having sympathy for the person's situation and having a desire to help him alleviate it – 'I feel for you. How can I help?'

- ✔ **Empathy** focuses on the experience; it means joining the person in the concern – 'I feel with you'.

In Chapter 10, we explore tools and techniques for being sympathetic and compassionate and not letting empathy be a blind spot for the coach or the client.

The coach or client who's overly empathic also suffers from being too close to a situation to be of real service. He lacks the distance from a situation to see it in perspective. Chapter 2 goes into the value of getting distance from a situation.

Diffusing Dramas that Impede Clear Vision

Have you ever had one of those days when one thing after another went wrong? The alarm didn't go off, someone used the last of the toilet paper and hadn't replaced it, the train was delayed, the afternoon meeting was moved forwards and so on and so on.

Two people can experience the same events and perceive them totally differently. One person is stoical about life and shows up for work calm and relaxed and resourceful; another can be affected by events and turn up for work stressed and in a poor state where he behaves and acts less resourcefully Both reactions to events are choices. The events are not what matters; how you choose to interpret them is what counts – and this interpretation, as we explain, is determined predominantly by the state you're in. (The sidebar 'Creating unnecessary drama with the brain' explains how a negative interpretation can occur.)

Poor resource states are characterised and identified by stress, worry, fear, hesitation, frustration and poor decision making. *Positive* or *optimal resource states* are characterised and identified by someone being calm, relaxed and balanced, thinking clearly and being able to make informed decisions.

Regardless of the day's events, a coach has a professional responsibility to shake it off, breathe and coach in an optimal resource state. The practice of what we call self-care enables you to choose to be in an optimal resource state no matter what and to coach your clients to do the same. Check out Chapter 10 for exercises to access optimal resource states.

In this section, we show you how to coach clients to be in a positive resource state regardless of the day's events, and to avoid getting stuck in what we call the *drama state*, where clients create all sorts of dramas that impede their ability to think clearly. (See the nearby sidebar 'Creating unnecessary drama with the brain'.)

Creating unnecessary drama with the brain

Here are three facts about emotional states:

- What you focus on affects your state and how the brain functions.
- Your state affects what you focus on and see or don't see around you.
- Your state affects how the brain attaches meaning to events and situations.

What you focus on is determined by a part of the brain (located in the brain stem) called the *reticular activating system* (RAS). The RAS operates like a heat-seeking missile, seeking out all the things in the outside world that are of importance to you. The way the RAS operates isn't fixed; it's influenced by your experiences, conscious thoughts and the state you're in at the time you have an experience.

Have you ever bought a new car and then noticed that your make and model is everywhere? That's not because suddenly others rushed out to buy the same car as you; you see them because the RAS has determined that your car has suddenly become significant. It now

points out all the other cars that were always there in the first place. Beforehand, those cars weren't important, and it filtered them out of your awareness (they were a blind spot).

Whatever you focus on, the RAS seeks out. If you're looking for opportunities, it finds them – great! But if you're looking for problems, it finds those too. The result: more problems; more scope for drama.

In addition, the brain then uses a process called *distortion* to twist and exaggerate the information the RAS has found. The exaggeration gives meaning to the information so you pay attention to it. It makes a drama out of any crisis just to ensure that you notice it.

This exaggeration is why the person who experiences events as stressful often interprets this situation as 'The world is out to get me!' Then he sees and experiences other events throughout the day that apparently support this view. By the end of the day, he hears mournful violins playing in the background as a soundtrack to his life.

Moving beyond reactive thinking

Recognising when a client is in the drama state is important because it affects his ability to process information. In technical terms, the drama state stress chemistry changes the way the reticular activating system (RAS) works (see the sidebar 'Creating unnecessary drama with the brain'). The RAS looks around for more potential problems, and the brain becomes sensitive and reactive to potential stresses. This process is like a country going on high alert for a terrorist attack.

One of the biggest challenges for many people when in the drama state is that they experience what's called *reactive thinking*, when they react unconsciously to the outside world. Unconscious reactions happen in milliseconds. Reactive thinking blocks people from being able to calmly, purposefully assess situations and make well-informed decisions; it blinds them to other options.

Coaching clients to slow down and take the time to consciously think is essential. Most people have experienced the value of this. For example, only when they relax, sleep on a problem or simply forget about it do they then get an insight or see the solution. They ask good questions, looking for solutions, and the RAS works away behind the scenes to seek them. Because they're in a good resource state, the brain's neuro-chemistry has changed (awash with neuro-transmitters; see the earlier sidebar 'Valuing EQ more than IQ'), and all their resources are available to them because they have a quiet mind. (Head to Chapter 10 for techniques to quiet the mind and use the RAS purposefully.)

Reactive thinking is the result of a cause/effect relationship. The RAS processes the outside world (cause) and reacts to the information (effect). What's interesting for a coach is when someone becomes aware that he's reacting in a certain way and that other choices exist. Then a gap emerges between the cause and effect where you can explore the other choices available. You can coach the client to react in a new way.

Coaching to make people aware that they have choices and then coaching them on how to react differently is transformational. Equipping a client to make better choices is empowering for him and the organisation he works for. When someone really gets this concept, he switches from living his life at the effect (being reactive) and instead becomes responsible for his own experience (being responsible). You can say he's *living at cause* – he's the cause of his experience *be-cause* he has a new ability to respond in a different way. He has a new *response-ability* when he's discovered the ability to respond in more resourceful ways, and it's then his responsibility to exercise this resource.

Giving up the dramatic roles

When a client sees the outside world (people, places, events) as being the cause of his experience (happy, angry, sad, stressed), he's disempowered. In simple terms, a bad monthly report or poor sales figures means he gets to feel bad, and a good meeting or a smile from the MD means he gets to feel good. He's like a pinball in a machine, being bounced around by the outside world, which determines how he feels. Then how he feels affects how he behaves and the actions and results he achieves. To him, the world is outside-in.

However, the client can see the world in a different way, an empowering way: that the inner environment of how he thinks and feels isn't determined automatically by the external world. He has a choice, and actually the world is inside-out.

A useful way of describing this process so clients understand that they create their own experiences through their thinking is to use the metaphor of *drama role-playing*. People who see the world as an outside-in adopt one of three roles, sometimes switching roles within minutes. These roles prevent them from seeing that they can view a situation in other ways. They're disempowering and create all kinds of blind spots:

- ✔ **Victim role:** When the client chooses to blame the outside world for his experience, he feels sorry for himself and has developed a story to explain why the world is the cause of how he thinks, feels and behaves.

- ✔ **Villain role:** When the client chooses to blame the outside world and points the finger at others: *it's her fault, it's his fault.* His story is evidence that if it wasn't for others, his life would be different.

- ✔ **Hero role:** When the client chooses to blame the outside world because he doesn't trust it. He'll do it alone. He'll go into a bookshop to get a self-help book, and if he can't find it, he won't ask anyone for assistance.

A fourth role exists, experiencing the world as inside-out. This role is empowering and insightful and involves far less drama – the **owner role**. With the awareness that reaction is a choice (see the preceding section), the individual can choose to react in any way he sees fit in any situation. And if he sometimes gets it wrong and gets caught up in dramas and reacts, that's not a problem either, because that's simply being human. (Only a victim would see that as a problem.) He slows down his thinking, is more stoic, takes time to reflect rather than react and makes informed choices.

The owner role seems for many to be too good to be true, a utopia that others can reach but is miles away from where they are. This conversation is worth revisiting, because when someone comes to see that he has a choice in how he reacts, the difference in his professional and personal life is profound. Because he's in a positive resource state, regardless of circumstances, he's less stressed, more creative and a better learner.

Coaxing a client toward the moment of insight

You may have to revisit the subjects in this section over a number of coaching sessions before someone really understands them fully. Many say 'I get this', but they don't yet have an intellectual understanding of how, for example, reactive thinking creates blind spots and puts people into poor resource states. You want the client to really grasp the concepts and make an adjustment by taking personal responsibility and changing how he thinks and behaves. Remember it's not what he says but what he does that's the test for whether he gets concepts.

Profound transformational insights sometimes take time for clients to experience. We tell clients to 'keep in the conversation', 'stay with it' and 'quietly reflect upon the concepts until you recognise when they apply to yourself'. We also use the analogy of the Magic Eye pictures that were popular in the late 1980s. People who didn't see the hidden picture would often strain to look harder. But the skill is relaxing the focus and staring beyond the surface of the page. The harder you try to see the picture, the more elusive it becomes. The knack is to relax and stay with it, and suddenly the 3D picture becomes clear. That's the moment of insight, and with perseverance the client will get there.

Dealing with learned helplessness

Some clients' blind spots are so entrenched that they think it's not worth changing or change won't happen for them. The important word here is *think*. They can change; but they think they can't and have given up. The name for this attitude is *learned helplessness*. Here are a few common causes:

- ✔ Having attempted to change a number of times, the client gives up because he has learned (he thinks) that he can't change.

- ✔ Because of fear of failure, the client isn't even willing to attempt to change.

- ✔ There may be a secondary gain (benefit) in staying stuck or continuing to do something that limits the client and prevents him from attempting something new.

- ✔ He may hold beliefs about what he can or can't do that prevents him from even attempting to change.

Here are some angles you can explore when you're working with a client who has an attitude of learned helplessness:

- ✔ **Thoroughly cover the enemies of learning** (see the earlier section on this subject). Ensure that the client recognises what's stopping him from changing.

✔ **Prevent the learned helpless attitude.** If you can predict a problem or objection ahead of time, the best time to deal with it is before it happens; this situation is called an *inoculation*. An inoculation is preventive rather than curative. A powerful inoculation is to highlight the possible consequences and costs of staying stuck and not attempting to change.

✔ **Consider the gain he must be getting from remaining in a learned helpless state.** What is helplessness doing for him? Giving him? Getting him?

✔ **Treat the learned helplessness as an onion.** Peel away the layers with your work until this helplessness is all gone.

✔ **Challenge the stories that limit him.** Use the Meta Model questions (see Chapter 6) to uncover the deeper meaning behind the stories the client has constructed and believes to be true. These powerful questions enable clients to challenge and question what they think and say.

Dealing with a client's learned helplessness is a great way to flex the coaching muscles and to get really good at what you do. When you can 'un-stick the stuck', the rest seem so much easier. Just keep in mind that you need to be more flexible and creative than the client. If he has five ways to resist learning, you need six to overcome this.

Occasionally, though, learned helplessness is unshakeable, and as a coach you're wasting your breath. If a coach claims to have a 100 per cent track record of success, he probably isn't seeing enough clients. Anyone who has been coaching for any amount of time recognises this statement as truth. You can't make clients follow instructions or use tools and techniques, and nor can you force insight.

Don't take a client slipping through the net as a personal reflection on your ability as a coach. Aim to have 'compassionate indifference': enter each coaching conversation with total commitment to be of service, but with no expectation or attachment to the outcome (because you can't guarantee it). All you can do is show up and do your best. The outcomes tend to take care of themselves when you have this attitude.

Finding the meaning in fear

Perhaps the greatest cause of drama is fear – fear of the known and especially fear of the unknown. In studies of what people fear most, behind the No. 1 fear of public speaking are the fear of death and fear of the unknown. The mind fears the unknown because it could contain anything!

Fear is created in the mind through thinking and is designed to protect you: it stops you from doing potentially harmful or stupid things. Fear quickly creates a bodily reaction designed to save you from the frightening thing, and at the same time, a release of neuro-chemistry affects thinking.

Reacting to fear

Fear reactions come in three commonly recognised types:

- ✔ **Freeze:** Become paralysed and hope the scary thing goes away.
- ✔ **Flight:** Run away.
- ✔ **Fight:** Turn and face the fear (this option has more potential to result in harm than freeze and flight).

In business, you find few instances where freeze, flight or fight responses are needed or useful. Excessive fear channelled into worrying has been proven to affect decision-making processes and creates by its nature blind spots that can harm a business. Studies show that when making a financial decision under conditions of acute stress, people take riskier options.

Think about introducing clients to the idea of the 'flow state' as an option. In the flow state you calm down and make good, quick decisions. Going into a flow state whenever you recognise the potential for stress or fear is a valuable skill to develop. Chapter 10 has the lowdown on this.

Finding the message in the fear

Neuro-Linguistic Programming practitioners make this presupposition: every behaviour serves a purpose in some context and at some level. Fear can serve a useful purpose:

- ✔ In a life-threatening moment (rare in business)
- ✔ As a signal you're about to do or are doing something wrong or stupid
- ✔ As a signal that you're stepping out of a comfort zone and experiencing resistance to the new paradigm

Coaching people to recognise the fear signal and then to distinguish between the three fear contexts radically reduces stress levels and helps them be in a better state for making informed decisions. We advise clients to simply sit quietly with the feeling and ask the reflective question, 'What is the underlying message behind this fear?'

- ✔ If the situation is life threatening, heed the fear and take action.
- ✔ If you're about to do something that with hindsight you'll regret, stop and consider all the consequences and any other options.
- ✔ If you're stepping out of your comfort zone, resistance is a message to let you know you're growing and improving. Use the Well-Formed Goals and Outcomes exercise in Chapter 3 to plan for an easier journey.

Overcoming fear by using your imagination

When Steve was seven years of age, he went to work with his father, who owned a demolition and civil engineering business. The destination was Greenwich power station in South London, which was being dismantled. Most of the floors had been removed, apart from a large section at ground level that could only be accessed by walking across beams about a metre in width.

Steve's father walked across to the platform in the middle and turned around to see Steve frozen to the spot. He was afraid. Steve's father told him to imagine the floors were still there and walk across, staying in the middle. So Steve did. 'Well done', said Steve's father, 'and don't tell your mother you did that!'

From that day forward Steve had no fears of heights, just a healthy respect. Putting a conversation about health and safety aside, the lesson Steve learned that day – to not be fearful simply because of what you imagine – was invaluable.

Distinguishing between imagined fears and valid ones

'There is nothing either good or bad, but thinking makes it so'. So said Hamlet in William Shakespeare's play, and this coaching advice is some of the best anyone can offer. Fear is perpetrated through playing out dramas of the mind, running visual scenarios of what did, could or may happen.

The mind can't distinguish from a vividly imagined scenario and a real event. People with phobias can imagine the thing they're fearful of and be terrified even if what they're fearful of isn't present in reality. A vividly imagined scenario trumps logic every time when it comes to fear.

Shining a Light on Incongruency

Perhaps the most subtle blind spot that limits the ability of clients to change is incongruency.

Have you ever been in a situation where you knew doing something was good for you, you had the ability and resources to do it, and yet for some reason you didn't do it or struggled to take action? This type of internal struggle comes about when you have conscious desires that conflict with unconscious needs. This struggle is *incongruency*.

Incongruency is a blind spot for most people and is often difficult to reveal without honest self-reflection or the assistance of a coach to shine a light on what's really going on.

You can identify that a client is incongruent when he

- ✔ Is clearly in the wrong role or out of his depth but can't see it.
- ✔ Feels something isn't right but can't explain what or why.
- ✔ Is struggling, procrastinating or avoiding.
- ✔ Gives conflicting signals – for example, verbally saying yes but unconsciously shaking his head.

The opposite of incongruency is *congruency*. When conscious and unconscious desires align, walking the walk and talking the talk becomes easy.

Chapter 9 contains exercises that help you discover whether a client is congruent or incongruent. Insights gained through this type of enquiry often end up in big shifts for clients. Many see why things have been a struggle or why they've felt something was wrong, and look to shift roles and responsibilities. They may even decide to move on from a job.

The keys to coaching clients to being congruent are client honesty and courage. Honesty requires vulnerability. When clients are being honest, they have to open up and admit fears and weaknesses all in the name of improvement. Being vulnerable requires courage.

Encourage clients to be honest and vulnerable by being honest and vulnerable yourself. Creating the environment for honesty and courage in the preframe creates a place of trust between you and your clients and enables them to experience deeper, more profound changes. Your coaching will have much more of an impact.

Chapter 6

Telling a Compelling Story in Business

In This Chapter

▶ Knowing why business stories matter

▶ Getting the bones of the story

▶ Separating facts and opinions

▶ Providing feedback on the business story

*E*very business has a story. From the minute someone has a business idea, the story begins, and every day the business exists the story grows. Just think of all the businesspeople communicating messages to staff, shareholders, equity partners, suppliers and customers about change, vision, direction, sales, new products, process changes, acquisitions, mergers and the like. People all over the globe are telling stories to engage about the past, the present and the future of business.

Your clients need to tell their stories well. A compelling story can make a significant difference to a prospective funder, customer or key recruit, and to a journalist who then creates positive publicity. Your job then, in the role of the coach or mentor, is to help clients tell a powerful, genuine story.

In this chapter, we help you understand what a business story is and where its power lies. We give you pointers for co-authoring a client's story, covering how to put the story together and then how to transform a tale by guiding the client to recognise what's fact and what's (possibly incorrect) opinion. Then we round off by giving you some practical techniques for helping clients to frame, develop and challenge their stories

Understanding the Value of the Business Story

Stories in business serve either as a call to action or to inform. Organisations often want people to act as a result of the story information. For example, as a result of a story, people may

✔ Get on board and help build the business.

✔ Invest in the business financially or provide connections that support the business.

✔ Sell products and promote the business.

✔ Deliver new and innovative ways of doing business.

✔ Change their view of a dying market and see new business opportunities or relate to new products.

The following sections give you a grounding in the basics of business storytelling – how businesses tell stories and to whom.

Recognising how a business conveys its story

Telling a compelling story creates a successful business, and coaching can help clients create their current or anticipated story of success to sell an idea, a product or a way of delivering business in the future.

Any organisational story needs to reflect its brand, products and services. It needs a flavour of origin – the story of its founders and the journey that the business has taken from its originating idea to the present day. When the business moves from informing to selling and promoting ideas, products or new directions, the story needs to incorporate more. It needs to paint a picture for the listener or reader, a picture of a compelling future and the journey required to get there.

The way that story is told needs careful consideration. Effective storytelling keeps the audience in mind and relays the story in a way they can hear it. Repetition is key. Where a story impacts the receiver (staff, investors, customers, press), we delete, distort and generalise (see explanations of these concepts later in this chapter), and we need to account for that by getting the story across in several ways. Hearing a story several times reduces deletion, distortion and generalisation, or at least allows those receiving the message to challenge assumptions and check the story.

REAL WORLD EXAMPLE

Stories that have boosted businesses

Stories are powerhouses of information about the nature of a business and can make the difference between survival or failure. Here are some examples from our experience of the impact a compelling story can have on the development of a business.

- Mike, the founder and CEO of a start-up biotech company, needed a sales director and couldn't afford to pay her the market rate. Mike's passion for his business and his story of intended growth persuaded her to get on board, taking a small salary and large share options for the first 18 months.

- Deborah was on the board of several lifestyle businesses. She was well known in the industry. She liked Simon's new concierge and home spa service for busy working parents. Having started her first business with £20, she particularly liked his story of building it with £100 several years ago. She introduced him to a contact who respected her nose for potential investments. Her ability to retell Simon's story helped Deborah point the right investor in Simon's direction and get him the support he needed.

- LAB Inc. purchases lab equipment in bulk and offers it at discount for science-based companies across the UK. Their sales increased when they started to tell their customers the story of how they donate 5 per cent of product sales to schools with targets to improve their science curriculum. Their story of encouraging the next generation of scientists helped them promote their business values and gain sales.

- House Chocs Inc., a UK luxury chocolate company, has ten city stores and a healthy turnover. Their sales peaked at holiday periods, and they identified a gradual increase in corporate client sales. This was accompanied by requests for product customization. 'Can we have our company logo on the gift tag or a logo on an egg?' They decided to innovate and adapt their business model to offer online self-customized ordering for corporate customers. They developed a story of adaptation, one that demonstrated they were listening to customers and working to give them the product they wanted.

- Increasing costs of premises were causing shrinking margins for two High Street retailers – a laundry service and a well-loved café. Both family-run businesses served the local population. They combined their stories and created a new one by leasing a larger premises to create the Soapy Way Café. They combined many operating costs and created a new social hub in the High Street, attracting more customers.

- As mass manufacturing of cheap shoes from the West declined in the late 1990s, Gepetti lost his job of 30 years. With his hand tools, a couple of pieces of equipment and leathers, he created an English handmade shoe business in the garden shed. His story of making and selling artisan shoes to customers in the entertainment business went viral because a sports presenter was asked about her exclusive shoes. Within a month he had a waiting list and investment for a bigger shed because Gepetti changed his approach and created a new story of delivering quality to a particular customer group.

In terms of methods, it is useful to help clients break down their audience groups into the stakeholders they want to target with their story.

Having done that, encourage the client to ask, 'If I were this particular stakeholder or group of stakeholders, how would I choose to access this information?'

Then have the client ask, 'How can I communicate this information in a way that they can hear the message? What story do they want?'

Knowing which stories a business tells

Your client may be developing one, some or all these types of stories:

- **Originating story:** How the business came into existence or how a particular business issue came about
- **Current story:** What's happening in or impacting the business today and why
- **Future story:** Where the business is going, why, with which stakeholders and how it might get there
- **Targeted call-to-action story:** What the business needs from its stakeholders and what it promises to them

Seeing who responds to stories

Customers, suppliers and staff need to understand a business's story before they decide whether to align themselves to it. That story is reflected in its brand, products and services, in its founders and its originating. The following sections explain how all sorts of people in business are affected by a strong, well-told story.

Customers

Customers need to understand a business's story before they decide whether to buy into it. In both business-to-business and business-to-consumer relationships, customers often take decisions to buy based on how they feel about the company. They ask myriad questions in buying decisions: Is the company authentic? Do the products fulfil my needs? Does it treat its people and customers well?

Suppliers

Suppliers want to serve their customers' needs both now and in the future. They need the current and future story to do that effectively and to make sure their products meet or can be adapted to meet current and future needs of their customer.

Understanding the customer is as important for professional coaches and mentors as in any business, and we look at this in Chapter 2. You can't make a case for coaching and pitch for business if you don't understand what your customer wants. Sounds simple, right? You would be amazed at how many coaches can't do this.

Staff

On the whole, people join organisations because they like where the organisation came from or what it does. They stay with organisations to be part of something that gives them work they enjoy and promises to give them appropriate rewards. Staff develop a psychological contract with their employer based on how they feel about the business, its customers, its future direction and the anticipated benefits of staying.

The research indicates that staff don't stay just for the money, so the stories they hear need to be a mixture of all four: the originating story, the current story, the future story and oftentimes the call to action. If organisations want staff to do something different or take a different journey with the employer, they need to be asked to do that explicitly.

Competitors

Competitors would love the fine detail of the future story but no right-thinking business would give them that, would they? They want the overview of the business and the key players who are in it. They want to hear the story of what makes a difference in that competitor's business, whether that's people, secret formulas, patents, intellectual property, location and so on. They want enough of the story to assess if they can duplicate or exceed their competitors in order to win business.

When you're coaching leaders, this is an area where you might help the business check if the story they are about to relay to staff and suppliers might hinder their business by giving away too much information. Transparency is one thing, but giving away a business's detailed recipe for success is another.

Telling the story of what makes a business different, the unique selling point or what value the brand holds is the story your clients want the competition to hear. This is often the originating story and the current story with an overview of the direction of travel in the future without the detailed route plan.

Changing the story in a single sentence

Gerald Ratner wiped £500 million off the value of the family jewellery company with one sentence. When he was asked how Ratners was able to sell something for such a low price, he replied, 'Because it's total crap'. The sentence changed the story of Ratners from that of a successful global high-street chain of more than 1,000 jewellery stores to one of a disgraced and dismissed CEO whose return on sale of shares on leaving was nothing. He lost billions, his children were nicknamed 'the crapners' and the toll was so hard on him personally he spent seven years lying in bed watching daytime TV. It changed his entire fortune and those of everyone engaged in that business.

The bottom line: Whether a business succeeds or fails, it has a story, and that story inevitably follows the business owner or the leadership in that business wherever they may go in the future.

Journalists

Members of the media want whatever will capture the attention of their audience. Developing positive relationships with the press is just common sense for a business with a brand reputation to protect and promote. Acting proactively to ensure the originating story is told often can enhance a brand position with the press over many years. (Think Ben & Jerry's, now owned by Unilever, but the story of their 1970s' origin with two guys who love ice cream is still the story told and retold to maintain the brand.)

Equally for companies with publicly listed stock, the relationship with 'the city' is key, and city journalists want to know the current and future story as this impacts their view of share value. The desire (or not) to tell a future business story more publicly can be a deciding factor when a founder, CEO or Board is deciding whether to issue public shares for sale. Another area for coaching and mentoring.

Helping the Client Create the Basic Story

Supporting a client to relay her story is an art form. Thankfully, businesspeople don't need to be Dickens or J. K. Rowling to express their art. All they need is a little guidance in how to express their stories in an authentic and relevant way. This point is where you, the coach or mentor, come in.

When you're working on stories, give clients the opportunity to practise in a safe place where it's okay to mess up. Their time with you is about getting the message right and delivering the story confidently.

Guiding the client through an exploratory exercise

Here's an easy activity to help clients get really curious about their organisation, their people, the perception of their organisation and what they offer. You can use it to help clients create a specific call-to-action story. You need enough paper and pens to provide one per person or one per group. Follow these steps with your client.

1. **Clear the space.**

   Ensure your client has nothing in front of her: no paper, pens or phone. If it helps her to focus, ask her to close her eyes.

2. **Say to her, 'Consider a business issue or a problem in your business. Think about who is involved in this situation and why'.**

   Give her a minute or two to think about this.

3. **Ask, 'What do you want for the business in this situation?'**

   Guide the client to consider what actions might be necessary to help the business get what it needs right now and in the future.

4. **Play with some ideas.**

   Really play with the client, keeping things light for a few minutes.

5. **Help the client create a metaphor that represents this situation.**

   Use these questions as a guide:

   - If you were in a childhood story, which story would you be in?
   - If you were a character, who would you be?
   - Which characters are others playing internally?
   - Which characters are present in the rest of the story?
   - Where is the conflict or potential for conflict – between whom and for what reason?

   If it helps, invite the client to write or draw the metaphor on a piece of paper.

6. **Ask the client to relay the current story.**

   Asking the client to do it in character may be a step too far, but you can play that one by ear. If it works for her, do that.

7. **Ask her, 'What would be an even bigger and better call to action? What would be a really bold action?'**

   You can keep playing with that until you've exhausted the possibilities or until it just feels like time to stop.

8. **Ask the client to tell the story as if she were talking to the audience she needs to relay the story to.**

   Get her to imagine the audience and key players in that audience; she should notice their reactions and consider what they need from her.

9. **Work with the client to explore the possible responses to the story.**

   Help her consider what questions or objections she might hear. Help her develop responses or incorporate the responses into the story in advance.

10. **Encourage her to consider what the balance of opinion and feeling may be in terms of the overall enthusiasm for this message.**

    Guide the client to make any adjustments necessary.

11. **Play devil's advocate for a minute and help her see any objections or possible misunderstandings that could arise. Help her anticipate the kinds of things people could delete, distort and generalise in the audience.**

12. **Make any final modifications and ask her to tell the story for the last time, imagining the audience.**

This activity can help an individual check her message and get clear on both her story and her call to action. We encourage you to play with this process. Adapt it, notice what comes out of it for the client and modify it. You can also use this in group coaching with teams responsible for conveying a common message or story.

Knowing that 'It's the way you tell it . . .'

The content of the story isn't all that matters; the way the client tells the story is really important in influencing the audience.

Never underestimate the power of a good storyteller to hypnotise and mes-merise clients into believing that the narrative of the story is real. If you've ever been fully engrossed in a novel or a film or a play, you'll recognise how easy it can be to suspend reality and believe in a convincing story.

Elevator speeches (a short, quick description of what a businessperson and a business delivers) can be really predictable and boring. We've heard hun-dreds of them, and they can sound formulaic and monotonous. A business worth talking about needs more attention than a quick pitch. It needs to take the listener on a journey, to get her really curious about what the business is about and what it aims to achieve.

So the storyteller really needs to understand the audience and how they like to hear a story. Do they prefer to hear information in a linear fashion or with more context and visual description?

In telling a story of future change, clients may need some help with getting that message to land with others, particularly where some are winners and some are losers. You may want to help her check the appropriateness of her enthusiasm and passion. For example, she may be enthusiastic about the future, but she still needs to handle her message appropriately with specific audiences. This is particularly important during change. No matter how resilient a person is, no one wants to hear, 'We're acquiring a head office in the Cayman Islands and moving all functions there. Oh, except yours, that is – we're contracting with a shared service provider for HR. So get working on the relocation plan, David. Great news, huh?'

Telling the story as a process

You can tell any story in a linear fashion with a beginning, middle and end like this:

- **Beginning:** Once upon a time, an engineering PhD student had a marvellous idea. He partnered with a business student and shared his idea. They created a vision of a future where replacement hip joints would be lighter than a table-tennis ball.

- **Middle:** They secured funding from an angel investor. They graduated and set up Hips Inc. The business student was a brilliant leader. She recruited a great team, and they took the lightweight hip joint to testing. A large medical supplies company became interested in buying the product and the company. The creator of the hip joint didn't want to sell to the company but secured it as a third-party supplier.

- **End:** Hips Inc. became profitable in year four and grew its market share year on year with new investors on board. All the originating staff became very wealthy. The company became the leading international supplier of lightweight hip joints. Their vision is still: 'We produce the lightest hip joints in the world'.

This is a linear story: this happened, then this, then this. Some people like to hear stories in this way, and some relay stories in this bullet point fashion. Others may tell more of a narrative, with description and links to their story that paint a vivid picture between the beginning, middle and end of a free-flowing story.

It's useful to notice this when you're coaching leaders. Helping them spot their own communication preference and noticing if they communicate in a style that suits their audience can be invaluable. Communicating their story effectively can be either a barrier or success to them. It depends on whom they are communicating it to. Sometimes clients need help in understanding how to get the same message across in different ways to appeal to those who have an opposite preference or where the preference of the audience is unknown.

If you're coaching or mentoring a scientist or technology entrepreneur, she'll probably enjoy describing her business journey like a process. If you're coaching a curator of a fine art gallery, she will more than likely enjoy describing her business journey in visually descriptive terms.

Injecting passion and power

An investor who doesn't regularly think or speak in process terms may find the story in the preceding section difficult to engage with. It just doesn't have enough depth for her. Sometimes you may need to help a client describe her business story in a less linear, more embellished fashion. The audience wants to hear a compelling *why*. They want a sense of power behind the story.

Here's the Hips Inc. example from the preceding section with an injection of passion and power:

> We create the best lightweight hip joints in the world. Our goal is to always innovate to make hip replacement an easy experience with minimal pain for patients. Our founder developed the first lightweight hip joint as a student. His interest originated in his childhood, when he observed five of his family members suffering with arthritic hip joints in their 20s and 30s due to a hereditary condition. He made it his passion to create a long-term business, attracting the best businesspeople, the best scientists and the best developers.

> Our company-funding strategy is simple. We sell large volume through a third-party supplier. We give shares to all staff in the company, from the CEO to the cleaner; we're all investors. We love our product, and we love being the best at what we do. We intend to stay ahead of the curve, always. Want to join us?

This story is more compelling. The language is passionate and punchy and active: 'goal', 'passion', 'attracting the best', 'we love our product', 'being the best at what we do'.

Which would get your attention, this story or the one in the preceding section? The description is for the same company; all that's different is the way the story is told.

Describing a business in different ways, like the Hips Inc. example, increases the possibility that the story appeals to all. For maximum impact across a wide audience, both approaches need to be incorporated into the story.

Condensing a story into a sound bite

In the 21st century, people relay stories fast, in summarised sentences or a few sound bites. Why not help your client tell her story succinctly in a metaphorical way? Help the client play with her story and tell it in terms that everyone can identify with. Here are some examples:

✔ Poor, striving farmer makes a castle in the sky from scattering a few beans: how a self-made guy called Jack created Beanstalk and Co. Fabulous self-made entrepreneur seeks investment for amazing business development. CV available on request.

✔ A Snow White revolutionises the lives of manual labourers with her range of handmade bedding and wholesome lunchtime takeaways. Bianca B diversifies into specialised products for working-class men who post-recession have increasing disposal incomes and demand more from their lunch and their lie-down. Join the wholesome crew today.

If you had a giggle reading these stories, great. Reframing stories to incorporate metaphors is a fun exercise to do with your clients, individually or in group coaching. Creativity often starts with play in organisations, and we encourage lots of that.

Distinguishing Fact from Opinion

People see the world differently. Sometimes, worldviews collide and overlap and people agree with each other. Other times, you think you understand what someone means and then later discover what you heard was not what she meant. It's as if two different conversations were going on at the same time.

In any business coaching or mentoring conversation, you must be able to find the truth behind the words and to distinguish facts from opinions:

> ✔ **Facts** are something that can be verified with evidence. They're things *you know for certain* exist, are true or have happened.
>
> ✔ **Opinions** are personal interpretations based on belief and perspective. They're things *you believe* exist, are true or have happened.

As well as coaching people to create compelling stories, you need to help them delve beyond opinions to see the facts. For example, you listen to stories of being hard done by poverty, striving, lack and limitation. You look for opinions disguised as facts so you can rewrite the story into an epic tale with a happy ending.

To be of true service to the client, don't simply buy into her story, whether the story is one of the business or of the individual. Great coaches are willing to ask great questions and to challenge assumptions. Start this process at the beginning of any coaching or mentoring conversation when you ask a client, 'What do you want?'

Helping your client to distinguish fact from fiction makes both of you

- Better listeners
- More persuasive communicators
- More open to new ideas
- Able to avoid confusion and misunderstandings
- Less limited by beliefs about what may be possible

The following sections help you think about fact and opinion from various angles.

Thinking in terms of maps of reality

Everyone has an individualistic unconscious way of assessing facts and then formulating opinions. You experience life through your five senses: visual, auditory, kinaesthetic, olfactory and gustatory. You assess experiences and make sense of them. Some are referenced as good, some bad, some simply neutral. You give order to the world around you by what you learn from it; not just from your own personal experiences but also by what you learn from the experiences of others. From these accumulated experiences, you create unconscious maps of reality that you store in the mind and then use to navigate your way through the world.

Dipping into Neuro-Linguistic Programming

A presupposition exists in Neuro-Linguistic Programming (NLP): 'The meaning of the communication is the response you get'. This phrase is used to explain that if through your communication you aren't getting a desired result, it may be because the listener heard a different story to the one that you meant to express. So the response you get is determined by the perspective and interpretation of the listener. Therefore, having a better understanding of how people create their perspectives and make interpretations is integral to effective communication.

Alfred Korzybski, who studied human potential by understanding language and the nervous system, famously said, 'The map is not the territory'. The maps of reality are simply unconscious models of how the mind perceives the world to be. Like all models, they're simplifications of reality. Equally, the territory is not the map. The maps we all create are our own versions of our interpretations of experiences and are not the experiences themselves.

Imagine that we hand you a map showing you how to get from London to New York. The map is a sheet of white paper with two dots on it. This isn't a useful map – it lacks information. If we draw a line between the two points, you now have more information, but probably still not enough. As we add more information, there comes a point where you have enough for it to be a useful guide. The map is enriched.

When clients express ideas, explore concepts and develop opinions, they have accessed their map of reality based on their interpretation of the information they have at a point in time. But what if their map of reality is never or rarely challenged? This is often what coaches do. You challenge the client's map of reality to help her see and check her map or see an alternative interpretation of the reality she has created. She must understand that the lens she's looking through may not be experienced in the same way as other people. This is key in effective storytelling.

Imagine you're in a meeting coaching a project team. A member of the team, Jane, says, 'We've investigated all the possible choices available, and the research shows that the targets for next year will be challenging to meet'. On the surface, this sounds reasonable. Yet Jane is simply expressing an opinion based on a whole lot of information that she's not verbally expressing. What Jane says is *surface structure expression*. What she doesn't say, and is as yet unavailable to the team because it's stored at the deeper level in Jane's map, is referred to as the *deeper structure*.

In order for you to really understand what Jane is saying, you need to dig deeper into her map to find her reality and the story she's telling herself. You can do so by asking Jane some good-quality questions, which we present in the next section.

Asking good-quality questions

In the preceding section, we introduce the example of Jane, who tells her team, 'We've investigated all the possible choices available, and the research shows that the targets for next year will be challenging to meet'. Here are some good questions for Jane – or anyone presenting an opinion as fact:

- ✔ Have you investigated all possible choices?
- ✔ How did you investigate?

✔ Are there other ways to investigate the choices?

✔ How did you evaluate the research?

✔ How did you reach the conclusion that targets would be challenging to meet?

✔ What do you mean by 'challenging'?

Such simple, good-quality questions can help separate fact from opinions and reveal many deletions, distortions and generalisations (see the next section, 'Weeding out deletions, distortions and generalisation patterns').

Here are a few pointers for questioning clients:

✔ **Don't overdo it.** Be judicious about when to ask questions that build on the words expressed by a client. Not every statement a client makes needs to be questioned; otherwise it can feel like interrogation rather than conversation. When a coach first begins to notice that people mean more than what they say, she can overdo the questioning and challenge everything someone says. This attitude can lead to lost friends, arguments with loved ones, frustrated clients and death by meetings. When first practising the skill of digging deeper into the map, remember that it's only worth digging where you think you're going to find treasure.

✔ **Watch your demeanour.** When asking questions, remember that your demeanour affects how the client receives the communication. Avoid interrogating your clients. Always consider your tone, have a twinkle in the eye and use softener phrases:

• *'I'm curious*, what do you mean by . . .?'

• *'I hear what you say*, and I was wondering . . .?'

• *'Okay, I think I understand*, but . . .'

A calm, curious and caring demeanour ensures you come across as simply seeking information and not wanting to catch a client out or disbelieving her. In Chapter 10 we explore managing your inner world and how you can come from a place of curiosity to help your client.

✔ **Be willing to be ask.** Be smart enough to appear to be stupid and to appear naïve. Be willing to ask for clarification if you really aren't sure what the other person means.

✔ **Ask the 'golden question'.** One simple, all-encompassing question gets to the facts and helps you recover deleted information and highlight what information has been distorted or generalised in the story: 'What do you mean?' When you ask this question, you see clients really think. Their eyes often flit around as they search their map of reality for an answer (in technical jargon they're doing a *trans-derivational search*). They search in the deeper structure for more information and then explain it with more specific detail.

Drawing out details to drill down to facts

When coaching a business that wanted to expand and grow with the view to sell in five years, we conducted an organisational audit to find out what was working and what wasn't. We wanted to understand what specifically the business meant by 'expand and grow'. During an interview with the head of sales, Steve asked a deliberately general and vague question:

'So how are things?'

'Oh, great. Everything's fine', he said.

'What do you mean by that?'

'Everything's going really well'.

'I'm curious: What do you mean specifically by "going really well"?'

As the head of sales explained his version of 'going really well', it became clear that it was different to the version the directors of the company had described earlier. Accepting his story that 'everything's going really well' as a fact would have been a mistake because the sales department had skill and process gaps that needed to be addressed before any growth could be considered. By implementing any growth plan, we'd have been building a castle on sand, and the problems would have been compounded and become major resource drains for the business.

It wasn't that the head of sales was lying or deceitful or negligent; he simply had his own worldview, his opinion of the facts, which he expressed in vague terms. Asking good questions allowed us to distinguish fact from opinion.

Weeding out deletions, distortions and generalisation patterns

All communication goes through three unconscious filtering systems in the mind:

- ✔ **Deletions:** The information is filtered out. It's just not heard.

- ✔ **Distortions:** The information is heard but reworked quickly by the unconscious into something that changes its original meaning.

- ✔ **Generalisations:** The information is reinterpreted into a generalised statement of fact by the unconscious based on the person's worldview.

Ask any two people to recount the minutes of a business meeting, and the filtering processes of deletions, distortions and generalisations of a shared experience become apparent: no two sets of minutes are the same.

These filters determine:

- How you take in and store information
- How you come to conclusions about the information
- How the information affects your behaviour
- How you share and express the information

To find deletions, distortions and generalisation in your clients, you need to act like a detective (think more Columbo in style than CSI):

- Ask questions.
- Listen for the communication behind the communication.
- Listen for what isn't spoken and missing.
- Be less influenced by what is said and more by what is really meant.

The three filtering processes of distortions, deletions and generalisations leave patterns in language. Like footprints in sand, they're clues as to how someone is navigating with her map. As you become more familiar with recognising the patterns and how they show up in communication, you begin to see the questions to ask. The elusive obvious becomes the really obvious.

These language patterns and accompanying questions form a meta model. The *meta model* is simply a description of how you might ask questions to help a person make sense of her experience; in effect, to challenge a client's thinking and assumptions to help her notice her deletions, distortions and generalisations.

The following sections give you the lowdown on deletions, distortions and generalisation, showing you the patterns to spot and the questions to ask.

Deletions

Your brain is never going to be able to process every piece of information you receive; you'd be overloaded. So you delete and filter out information that you unconsciously deem to be unimportant to you. When you communicate, you also leave data out, and yet communication still makes sense because people are good at predicting what has to be there for something to make sense.

Table 6-1 explains deletion patterns and includes examples and questions that you can use for each.

Table 6-1	Meta-Model Patterns: Deletion	
Pattern	**Examples**	**Questions You Can Ask**
Simple: Where the client leaves out an important element, object, person or event.	We're right about this decision.	How, specifically, are you right?
		What decision, specifically, are you right about?
Comparative: When the client makes a comparison. If the comparison is implied, it may be valuable to establish fact from opinion.	This product is better/quicker/easier/worse.	How is this product better/quicker/easier/worse?
	The way things were before was better.	How, specifically, were things better before?
Lack of referential index: When the client hasn't specified a noun, object, person or event.	People aren't buying this new product range.	Which people, specifically, are not buying?
Unspecified verb: Where the client hasn't clearly defined a verb.	Things are moving slowly.	How, specifically, are things moving slowly?

Distortions

The process of deletions and simplification leads to distortions. People change and twist information in a creative way, often using analogy and metaphor to explain or describe something. Distortions are the creativity filter, enabling you to come up with new ideas, concepts and perceptions, and they allow you to create belief systems that can limit or empower you. So identifying and questioning distortions is particularly valuable.

Table 6-2 explains distortion patterns.

Table 6-2	Meta-Model Patterns: Distortions	
Pattern	**Examples**	**Questions You Can Ask**
Cause and effect: When a client has implied a casual relationship.	His actions make me mad.	How, specifically, are his actions making you mad?
		What, specifically, are his actions that are making you mad?

(continued)

Table 6-2 *(continued)*

Pattern	Examples	Questions You Can Ask
Mind reading: When someone claims to know what someone else is thinking.	I know they will agree to this. She thinks I'm not up to the job.	How do you know they will agree to this? How do you know that she thinks you're not up to the job?
Complex equivalence: When a client says that two different experiences are the same.	He was unhappy with that report; I'm a failure. That market research was a success. The project will be a success.	How does him being unhappy with one report mean that you're a failure? How does the success of the market research mean the project will succeed?
Lost performative: A client doesn't reference the person expressing an opinion as a fact.	It's not right to ask a boy to do a man's job.	Not right according to whom? Who says it's not right to ask a boy to do a man's job?
Nominalisations: A client has made a verb into a noun.	There's not enough motivation in the team.	How is it that the team is not motivating itself?

Generalisations

Humans unconsciously pattern match, forever judging and assessing and looking for similarities and comparisons – 'Is this like this?', 'Is this like that?' They do this because they feel comfortable with what's the same and also because generalisations help people to learn. You find out how to tie one shoelace and generalise that all shoelaces work the same way. You achieve one success and generalise that you'll succeed in similar situations. You fail at something and generalise that you'll fail in similar situations. Generalisation patterns are often extreme examples of black-and-white, all-or-nothing thinking caused by experience.

Table 6-3 outlines generalisation patterns.

Table 6-3	Meta-Model Patterns: Generalisations	
Pattern	*Examples*	*Questions You Can Ask*
Universal quantifiers: Words that show a broad generalisation; for example *all, every, never, always.*	He never gets his reports in on time.	What not ever, not once?
Modal operator: Statements and words that define people's beliefs about the possibility of behaviour; for example *like, could, should.*	I should be getting on with this. I have to go ahead with this.	If you should be, what's stopping you? What makes it so you have to?
Presuppositions: The client implies a relationship between two things, and one is required from the other to be true and accepted.	If the business really cared, they would be doing things differently.	How do you know they don't care for you? What specifically would they be doing differently?

Playing master sleuth to separate opinion and reality

Sometimes coaches need to play detective, applying an enquiring mind to a problem. We all fail to see the obvious, and the role of a coach can be to help a client see the assumptions they and others may be making in order to support them to communicate clearly.

Sherlock Holmes and Dr Watson were investigating a mystery out on the moors late one evening. They set up camp, and in the middle of the night, Holmes stirred and said to Watson, 'Watson, are you awake?'

'Yes, Holmes. Why do you ask?'

'When you look up, Watson, what do you see?'

'Holmes, I see the night sky, the Plough, the North Star and all the Milky Way. I see the universe and all of creation. What do you see, Holmes?'

'Elementary, my dear Watson: I see someone has stolen our tent'.

Being a master sleuth means seeing what's elementary. It means noticing deletions, distortions and generalisations and asking quality questions (see the preceding sections), which leads to better communication with your clients and helps them create compelling stories beyond the limitations of their current thinking.

Getting the story behind the story

Here's an example of the experiment in action. Marie asked a coaching client a simple question: 'Jean, what's the biggest single problem you currently face that when addressed would make life easier for you?'

'It's Graham, the managing director', replied Jean. 'He doesn't like *me [mind reading]*'.

'What do you mean?' Marie asked.

'Well, whenever *[universal quantifier]* he sees me, he has an angry look on his face. He quickly mumbles hello and then walks off, and I'm left feeling awful *[cause and effect]*. I don't think he's happy with the job I'm doing *[mind reading]*. I've lost all my confidence *[nominalisation]*, and I'm just waiting for him to start looking for someone better *[comparative deletion]* than me to do my job'.

From the Sherlock Holmes Business Robot perspective, Jean has stated four facts:

✔ The managing director is called Graham.

✔ He had a look on his face.

✔ He said hello.

✔ He walked off.

Everything else Jeans said is assumption, opinion and story, even if it seemed convincing to Jean.

A few of the deletion, distortion and generalisation patterns in Jean's statement are marked to help you see what's really going on behind the story and distinguish facts from opinion. Here are just a few questions Marie asked Jean:

✔ **Universal quantifier:** 'I'm curious when you say that whenever he sees you he has an angry look. Has he never ever seen you and not had an angry look?'

✔ **Cause and effect:** 'How does his mumbling hello mean you get to feel awful?'

✔ **Mind reading:** 'How do you know specifically that he's not happy with the work you're doing?'

✔ **Nominalisation:** 'I'm wondering how his appearing to be angry and mumbling mean that you get to lose confidence?'

✔ **Comparative deletion:** '*Better?* What do you mean by *better*?'

After answering these questions, Jean began to doubt what until then she'd believed to be true. This short story ends happily. It didn't take long to reveal that Graham was not angry; in fact he was happy with Jean's performance and had total confidence in her. For a few weeks, he had been experiencing severe gastric problems and was in a lot of pain and worried. Jean had been interpreting the facts and making many assumptions and opinions. As often happens, the map isn't the territory and the story isn't the melodrama it is often perceived to be.

What Jean's company came to realise from this experience was the power of

✔ Open and honest communication

✔ Asking good questions

✔ Challenging assumptions

✔ Discerning facts from opinions

Now you can turn the Meta-Model patterns from the preceding section into a living, breathing tool that helps you to see the story behind the story. Imagine you're a Sherlock Holmes Business Robot. Wearing a deerstalker hat and pipe is optional, but having a curious attitude is obligatory. Remember to have a calm, caring, curious demeanour. The world around you is a laboratory full of clients, customers, CEOs, suppliers and coffee-shop sales assistants who are unsuspecting, unpaid lab rats for you to experiment with.

Choose a language pattern for the day from Tables 6-1, 6-2 and 6-3, and listen for it when in everyday conversation with people. Notice how often people use it and notice how easily you could have assumed you understood what someone meant at face value. Try things out and learn lots.

Next, you can experiment with separating fact from opinion and see what emerges. Listen to the client's story and find the facts: what's there, what's verifiable, what you can see, hear, feel, smell or taste.

Everything else is opinion or assumption that you can flag up as a story to be examined and questioned. Use Tables 6-1, 6-2 and 6-3 to help you spot the patterns in the client's language that are masking the facts.

Giving Feedback on the Business Story

Business has never been so publicly exposed as it is today. The opportunity to give real-time feedback through the eyes of a customer is instantaneous and ever present. Leaders sometimes need support through the coaching and mentoring process to respond (or not) to rapid feedback, to adapt their story or to stay with their story.

How leaders choose to hear feedback and what they do with it is critical. The leadership of public stories can make or break a brand,. The business response can wipe percentage points off share value overnight. Leaders who disregard critique and view feedback as personal criticism do so at their peril.

How people feel at any time about an organisation feeds forward into the story that's being told tomorrow. It impacts how the various stakeholders experience the organisation and its leaders. Helping a leader develop the story they tell by paying attention to their vision and previous stories rather than simply reacting without thinking is an important role in coaching and mentoring. Sometimes a coach is the only objective observer who can help a business leader keep it real and maintain perspective. Supporting a client to consider how she wants her response to be experienced by others and holding the space for her in that place until they can do that is key.

An example from the Luxury Goods market illustrates this point.

Business brands have generated considerable significance in the 21st-century. Who could have guessed 100 years ago that today one of the top 20 brands in the world, with an estimated brand value of just under £25 billion, would be a luxury bag and watch retailer? Louis Vuitton sells luxury goods, and although it may be one of the most counterfeited brands in the world, its story of exclusivity and quality keeps it in the top-20-brand list.

The LV story in the last 15 years could be 'brand diluted by increasing production of counterfeit goods in Asia'. But although its work to challenge the counterfeiting through legislative change is successful and ongoing, it's background noise. The really interesting brand news is LV's ability to sell its craftsmanship and its ability to customise goods as a result. In a world where the LV brand is potentially seriously compromised, LV has developed a niche within a niche.

Depending on your view of the facts and your own good opinion, your feedback to LV ten years ago could have been one of doom and gloom. 'Your logo and leather goods are available in every street market in Thailand and China. 'You're finished, the logo is becoming commonplace' or 'You are affected by counterfeit products. How might you diversify to keep your high-end niche customers happy"?

How you frame what you observe says a great deal about your own orientation. It can serve coaches well to remember that in business, feedback is often simply opinion based on a set of filters. Advisors to LV no doubt developed grey hair thinking about the counterfeit issue and the associated risks to brand; yet the key strategy seems to have been to focus on dominating the very highest-end luxury goods market. It is bizarre and brilliant that in a world where the sale of lightweight luggage with swivel wheel action is on the increase, LV is selling a luxury leather trunk at £170,000. A trunk! And we thought they went out with the Victorians.

The role of a coach in helping business leaders develop and rework their stories requires that she steps up and sticks her neck out a bit. As a coach, you must pose difficult questions to help clients see alternative strategies for their business and sometimes help them change the story. It can be one of the most powerful things coaches help clients do – get their story straight, be congruent and create a storytelling powerhouse.

Chapter 7

Mentoring to Assess Business without Rose-tinted Spectacles

*G*inni Rometty, the first female CEO and president of IBM, tells a story about being successful and relates her success to learning and taking risks. She describes risk-taking as the times when she learned the most; when she has been in the zone of not knowing, it has kept her fresh and on form. She says, 'Someone once told me growth and comfort do not co-exist. And I think it's a really good thing to remember'.

So do we, because successful business leaders are not created by sitting on the sidelines watching others. They're created when they move towards complexity and uncertainty and know at some level that being able to work with ambiguity is the real work of a strategist.

Without a high level of ambiguity and an element of risk, relatively little strategy and tactics are needed. A need for resource coordination for management of tasks and output is apparent, but that can be done at the level of operations. Business growth and development happen when leaders know that the foundations of the business are robust enough to tolerate risk. So while leaders are hanging out in the land of ambiguity, the clever ones have already checked that the rug isn't going to be pulled out from underneath them. They have a high level of confidence in base camp.

In this chapter, we discuss how to help clients take an objective view of their business and outline some techniques that mentors can use to help leaders create a successful business.

Testing the Foundations of the Business

You want to mentor your client to find out how to 'observe' his business as impartially and dispassionately as possible. By doing so, you help develop his strategic perspective and work on the business rather than in the business, looking at the business and the picture it presents in all of its complexity.

Like houses, if the foundations aren't solid in a business, one day – sometimes with little warning – three little pigs may just blow your dwelling down. Normally the pigs would be heavily disguised as bankers, asset strippers or receivers appointed by the court, and they would have no problem looking at the business dispassionately. Best to discover how to do this task yourself if you're a business owner or executive leader responsible for helping to keep the house upright.

Applying Strategic Thinking

You almost certainly know that a significant difference exists between task-level thinking and strategic thinking. Unfortunately, in our experience, a number of leaders who believe they're highly strategic just aren't. In fact, what they're really good at is *task-level thinking* – handling and delegating tasks. They're great, brilliant even, at managing complicated tasks or leading a high volume of activity in the business.

Strategic thinking and strategic leadership is more about handling the complexity that cuts horizontally and vertically through the business. Strategic thinking is multidimensional – more like Neo and Morpheus handling The Matrix than Frodo and Gandalf chasing a ring around Middle Earth.

Put simply, *strategy* is the direction of travel that an organisation plans for over the long term. It relates to how the organisation creates advantage in the marketplace that it operates in and how it organises its resources to deliver. Some of the questions that a mentor may work through with a leader may be those strategy-level questions a potential investor may ponder when considering investment.

Do the executives have:

- ✔ The right skill mix to deliver the mission and vision
- ✔ The confidence of investors and non-executive directors on the board
- ✔ A strategic big-picture focus

✔ The ability to proactively lead people, manage resources and create followers who will do the same

✔ A hungry desire to drive for results

Do the executives understand:

✔ Their marketplace

✔ The industry and product offering

✔ The cultural norms in their area of business in the markets they operate in

Can the executives:

✔ Anticipate economic trends and how these trends may impact the industry and specifically their business

✔ Translate strategic intention into realisable organisation-level outcomes and objectives

✔ Think and act strategically

✔ Spot trends and understand the impact of those (can they look up the hill and over the hill too)

✔ Handle unanticipated consequences and risk-taking

✔ Take decisions that align with anticipated trends and their identified strategy

✔ Define a clear vision, mission and values that are in alignment

You can ask your client to rate themselves on a scale of 1 to 10 against each of these factors. Then, share your experience and knowledge of each area with them. Share what you have done in the past to develop yourself in each key area, where you have created success and where you came unstuck.

Help your client to take each point on their scale and develop their own planned activity for improving their skills, knowledge and experience across these dimensions. You can find an outline format for a mentoring learning plan in Chapter 11 (or feel free to create your own). Work with your clients to help them see the gap between where they are on the scale right now, where they would like to get to and what sits in between the two.

You then ask clients to summarise and identify the first step. Do the same for each area where the clients feel they have a development need and then take an overview to identify how to handle the development plan as a whole to check you have a plan that is realistic.

REAL WORLD EXAMPLE

Assessing the situation before developing a plan

Scaling can be used to help clients see the gap between the reality of their current situation and the required actions to help them move towards their desired result. This case example walks you through the first part of a process to the first action step. After you reach the first step with your client, keep working with the process until all the steps are explored and the client has a defined set of sequential actions.

Mentor: So where do you think you are on a scale of 1 to 10 right now in relation to understanding your industry and products?

Client: Well, I understand the biotech supplies industry really well, I've been in it for 25 years, but I don't really understand all the products we sell – only the ones my company brought with us in the merger.

Mentor: So, on a scale of 1 to 10, where would you place yourself on the scale in relation to this?

Client: 7.

Mentor: Let me share my experience of getting to understand the products of a business I acquired and how I went about doing that in the first year . . .

Client: I can see that some of the same elements would apply here. I need to talk to the operational managers in the merged business.

Mentor: Where would you like to get to on the scale in six months' time?

Client: I'd like to be fully conversant with the products and know about their functionality and which customer segments we were selling into. I'd want to know what revenues have been created and where we may have product alignment post-merger; where we may be able to increase revenue by offering more to the market; where we can upsell with specific product combinations. I'd like to know Ashley's strategy on that in some detail. I'd like to be at 9.

Mentor: You've articulated a great list of what you would like to understand and whom you would like briefing from. How specifically can you achieve that do you think? What sits between 7 and 9 for you?

Client: I need to get on the floor with the supplies team and warehousing in particular. I may spend a day in each in the next month and work alongside Geoff. I'd like to see the workflows in operation, and I want to speak to Jacqui and review any customer data for those products and maybe view a couple of the focus group meetings. I may actually ring a couple of high-value customers to hear what they have to say. I think I should attend the supply conference too to increase my profile with others in the specialist supply side of the industry. I'm more well known in the product design and marketing sectors.

Mentor: Anything else? Could I just reiterate that I talked about engaging staff in generating ideas around product synergies and innovation in relation to new products or adaptation?

Client: Yes. I think I would do that after I've done this groundwork. That would be the difference for me between 9 and 10. I'd be asking Geoff to create some process for ideas sharing and testing ideas out as you describe.

Mentor: Okay, let's recap on what you're going to do overall and then tell me what your first step will be on this one.

You can get your client to draw a scale line for each element. Take a piece of paper with the development areas down the left side. Against each one write 1, 2, 3, all the way to 10. As you work through, get your client to mark his scaling assessment. Mark the current scale point and desired scale point for each element and write the bullet point actions in between the two scale points. Your client creates a visual record of his actions and can readily see the elements in his development programme and can quickly identify any overlaps, making adjustments at the end before determining the first action steps.

Making the Complicated Simple

As a mentor, you want to help the business leader look objectively at his business; to helicopter above it as though he was observing it rather than being in it; to take the rose-coloured spectacles off and put on those rather less attractive glasses the opticians use when they change the lenses until you get to one that makes you say, 'I can see clearer with than without'.

Using a framework to walk around the business

Many business frameworks are available for you to use. The logical levels format in Chapter 8 works well here. At its simplest level, you can work with a business plan to assess whether everything was well thought out and clearly articulated.

Your objective as the mentor is to help your client to stop, reflect on the business and describe it by talking about it out loud. Then, tap into your wisdom about leading in business to see what may need to be reviewed, tweaked or radically changed. You want to encourage your client to use and develop his strategic thinking by 'looking in', to avoid getting caught up in his task-based thinking long enough to identify an appropriate series of actions rather than identifying and taking action in a piecemeal fashion.

If you're working in location and it helps to physically walk around the business with your client, you may want to try that too. Marie once had a CEO walk around his building with her to do a 'sensing sweep', and at the entrance to each department I asked him, 'What do the people deliver in here, and how do the people on this floor relate to each other? What do you notice here – how does it feel on this floor?' You would be amazed by how much he knew about the six floors and even more amazed by what he didn't know.

He knew a great deal about the artwork, the renovations and adjustments that had been made to the structure of the building. He understood where the departments were and the names of some staff, but he didn't know which functions related to which or who led the functions. He had a sense that it was a beautiful environment to work in and that staff seemed hard working and dedicated. What he didn't see was that as he entered each area of the building, all the employees looked down at their desks – no one looked up to make eye contact with him or greet him. When I asked him some questions to help him see beyond his surface impressions, he could see where he had gaps in understanding the cross-functional roles people had and where he had difficulty connecting with more junior staff. This became part of his coaching objectives.

By simply walking around and getting the visual picture of people working, the feel of the building, its branded walls and artefacts, the dialogue with a client can be richer. His ability to create a picture of what needs to change can be much easier to access walking around, particularly if the leader isn't a particularly visual person who can create mind pictures easily.

Working in plain lens spectacles

Use the 'Organisational factors' matrix in Figure 7-1 to metaphorically walk around the organisation and help your client review the business. You can use the sample questions or develop your own depending on the business. You should ask the key overarching question in italics and use some of the others to probe and help him develop his picture. Treat this exercise as an elicitation and be careful not to ask too many questions; otherwise it can feel like interrogation.

Organisational factors

Governance	Quality & monitoring	Culture	Strategy
Finance	Revenue	Expenditure	Cash management
People	Customers	Staff	Stakeholders
Marketing	Product	Pricing	Sales & distribution
Analysis	Consumer	Market	Competitors

Figure 7-1: Organisational factors matrix.

Illustration by John Wiley & Sons, Ltd.

You can do the walk around the business as physical practice. Lay out pieces of cards on the floor with the headline words of the framework you're using on them. As you deal with each element, ask your client to stand on the relevant card while he talks through his responses. Help your client relax and get into a high visual state because this state is where people do their best big-picture thinking and where they can think about complexity more easily.

In this exercise, you are checking that the rose-coloured spectacles have been taken off and that your client can use objective information to see his business reality clearly.

1. **Ask your client to sit quietly for two or three minutes, to breathe into the diaphragm and just focus on the breathing and slow it down.**

   It can help if he closes his eyes.

2. **Ask him to imagine that he is the lens of a pair of spectacles looking into his business and that he is going to take a big-picture look at the different aspects of the business with fresh eyes to assess what is working well in the organisation and what may need attention.**

3. **Ask him to step (physically or in his mind's eye) into the space of business analysis and product marketing and answer the following questions:**

   'Is there a demand for your product now and in the future?'

   - *What are you selling?* This question doesn't just refer to the product (for example, a face cream for men) but the value proposition. The answer should include the problem that it promises to solve for your customer (moisturises the skin while reducing the five o'clock shadow and shaving rash) and what this answer means for the customer (skin like a baby's bottom and making him so irresistible that every woman he passes in the street will want to race towards him and kiss his cheek with pure abandon).

   - *How do you market it?* Do you sell under one brand or several? How do you promote your product? Advertising, trade fair promotions, where and to whom?

   - *How do you sell and distribute the product?* How do you get the product to the customer and is that efficient? Are you selling business to business or direct to the consumer? How is it sold? Online, off-shelf, a mix? How do you find customers – through a sales team, advertising, via a partner product? Is the product sold on its own or with another item? How is it distributed? What transport methods do you use? Is it taken direct or through a third-party distributor? Where do you hold stock, or is the product an on-demand product?

- *How do you price it?* What is your pricing strategy? What margin are you working on? What costs need to be loaded into pricing? What product volume do you need to sell? Do you give discounts? Do you destroy product rather than discount in order to hold the price? Do you sell at different price points to different customer groups? What currency do you trade in? What factors impact price and therefore influence where the product is made, stored and distributed from?

- *Where's your research and development?* Have you done your homework? Is this an identified problem? (How many men in the market you're in are worried about their skin, stubble and shaving rash?) Is there a gap in the market for your product or room to capture existing purchasers from the competition? What is the competition doing in the market? Can you do it better or cheaper for an existing customer group, or is there untapped potential in the market for a different segment? Can you create a higher-value product or same value but better packaging and distribution channels and target higher-value customers in the luxury goods market, for example? Can you secure a decent margin given your costs? Is it a product that people want to buy?

4. **Ask him to step (physically or in his mind's eye) into the space where people impact and contribute to the business and answer the following questions.**

Exploring the people elements:

- *Who is involved in your business?* Who are your key stakeholders? What roles do they occupy? What do they add to your business? How do you manage relationships with your investors and keep them on board? If you have non-executive directors, how do you utilise their expertise and knowledge? How do you relate with your bank, insurers, accountants, legal advisors and so on – is there a natural cycle of communication with them?

- *How do you lead your people?* What staff do you employ or what contractors do you work with? What is the mix of skills and knowledge in your business? What is the structure? How do you attract, develop and retain talent? What policies and procedures do you have to manage people and ensure that they have safe working conditions and that your employment liabilities are met? What culture are you creating through your people?

- *How do you relate to customers?* Who are your key customers and who consumes your product? How do you communicate with them? Do you use social media, phone, online offers? How do you involve them in feeding back on your products and product development? Do you use focus groups or product panels?

5. **Direct him to step (physically or in his mind's eye) into the space where he can imagine pound signs and can turn his attention to the finance aspects of the business.**

'Is the business financially robust?'

- *What revenue streams are there in the business?* Are there multiple products? Which create the most revenue? Which create the most revenue when you combine them or partner with another seller? Which create steady, even revenue, and how do you look after those revenue streams?

- *What are your costs made up of?* What are your core costs and what are variable costs? How do you control costs across the business? What controls are in place to ensure that wastage is minimised? What controls are in place in terms of the number of budget holders and sign-off authority?

- *What is the financial and legal structure of the business?* What loans, capital assets and shareholding agreements exist? What form does the business take and where are the risks in the business that may need legal or other agreements to protect your assets such as intellectual property agreements or non-disclosure agreements?

- *How do you ensure that you don't run out of cash?* Who tracks the numbers daily in your business? What processes do you have in place for billing, collection and debt recovery? How quickly do your sales generate income versus the flow of expenditure out of the business? What kind of interest do you pay on overdrafts, and what interest do you get on monies in the bank account? If you're dealing with foreign currencies, how do you manage those income and expenditure flows as currencies shift around? How do you hang onto reserve cash? If the business is growing, how are you managing cash coming in at a rate to support increased sales of product and expenditure to fund that?

6. **Direct him to step (physically or in his mind's eye) into the space where he can imagine turning his attention to the governance aspects of the business.**

'Are you creating the conditions for a sustainable business?'

- *How does accountability work?* How does your Board hold the executive team to account? What assurance measures (key performance indicators [KPIs], risk registers, governance measures such as external regulation and auditing) are in place for your Board? How does the Executive Team hold operational management to account for delivering against objectives and assessing the quality of work, products and leadership? What ethical practices are in place? What standards do you hold dear? How are expectations communicated and cascaded through the organisation?

- ***What kind of culture are you creating?*** What stories do people tell in the organisation? Does your work environment and the spaces where you meet and greet your stakeholders match the brand image you want to create? Are people clear about 'how we do things around here', and do they know how to navigate their way around the organisation to get what they need? Do the systems and controls you have match the articulated values and the vision for the organisation? Is it obvious where decision-taking and power is held, and do people use that appropriately?

- ***Are the strategies and tactics designed to get the results you want?*** Are key strategies agreed between the board and executive team? Do the agreed tactics (mini strategies) align? Is there a sense of organisational congruence? Does it all add up?

7. **Ask your client to summarise what he has noticed.**

   'What is working well across the organisation and down through the organisation? Highlight what needs your attention. What needs the attention of other stakeholders?'

   You could share some of your experience of handling the key issues that need attention. Help your client think about how he can draw on your experience sharing to generate ideas to improve his own strategic picture. Elicit what he needs to do more of or less of and how he can translate some of what you have shared and adapt it for his own business situation. Help him to develop his action plan.

   In this process, as a mentor you're asking yourself: has my client done the analysis to check that he has something people want to buy, and is there room for it in the current market or can he create one? Are the relationships being well managed, and is the business thinking about these proactively? Do the finances look healthy, and are there checks in place to ensure that the money flows cover the costs of running the business, leave enough cash and make the required return? Are risks managed, and is there room to innovate and take opportunities if they arise? Are the arrangements for ensuring that the business is well managed in place and sufficient? Overall, does the business present congruently?

Determining Where the Best Mentoring Work Begins and Ends

A risk is apparent in mentoring around strategy and business assessment, in particular for those who have successfully or unsuccessfully led as an owner or executive in business. The problem of opinion creeps in disguised as feedback. Watch for this situation because mentors can unwittingly transfer their unresolved business angst or previously tamed risk-driven ringmaster by overly identifying with the client's business. You know you have reached this point if you hear yourself saying 'If I was you . . . ' or 'You should . . . ' Recognise that you've now stopped using the coaching skill set to help the client take his own path and have unwittingly slipped into becoming a business advisor. We suggest that you notice this change and self-correct.

If you don't understand the distinction between a business adviser and mentor, you can read about it in Chapter 1. If you find yourself advising more than mentoring, you should consider developing your coaching skill set further.

Developing Trust and Honest Appraisal through Feedback

Business has never been so publicly exposed as it is today. The opportunity to give real-time customer feedback on social media is ever present. Leaders sometimes need support through the coaching and mentoring process to adapt to that reality because failing to adapt can seriously compromise business and personal success.

Be careful with your words. It really isn't appropriate to give lots of feedback to a client on what you've observed about him and his organisation in the first session. Doing so can create a degree of defensiveness at a time when you're looking to build trust. Remember, business is highly personal; the founder, CEO, leaders, board members and loyal employees are emotionally and financially invested in it. So give the feedback in a coaching style to help him see an alternative view.

The difference is between

> 'This business plan is just awful. Little wonder no one beyond your immediate team understands what they're supposed to be doing'.

and

> 'I'm wondering if you have any thoughts on why the whole of your operations team, the finance group and the sales team are finding it difficult to articulate how their month-to-month activity relates to the business plan?'

If you're plugging away and he still doesn't get it, try giving an example of something similar from your own experience and ask the client how your story may relate to his current situation. Alternatively, you can give him carefully worded feedback after asking 'Can I offer you some feedback?'

Encouraging clients to be open to regular feedback

The leadership of key issues becomes an organisational story that can make or break a business. The business response to negative feedback can wipe percentage points off share value overnight. Leaders who disregard critique and view feedback as personal criticism may need to ask themselves whether they're sitting in the right seat.

Helping business leaders to welcome the feedback, to genuinely thank stakeholders for their comments and to act on the ones that point to missteps is a real differentiator in business. It requires a real ability to help your client cut through the assumptions, distortions and generalisations; to depersonalise and consider what message or story he wants to give out in response.

Using feedback to feed forward

A world of difference exists between a leader who primarily focuses on the company's real-time information and one who focuses on historical analysis.

In some sectors, such as the leisure and entertainment industry, people's bonuses are linked to how many positive Twitter and Facebook hits they get for their business. Whole departments are dedicated to providing a customer response to issues raised in social media in real time. This data provides a wealth of potential stories. It can be helpful for leaders to ask what is coming through in real time and experience the customer journey as it plays out rather than in retrospect. A business can take corrective action and mitigate risk of adverse publicity quite quickly with careful handling.

In general, a focus on real-time stakeholder experience indicates a desire to find quick solutions and mitigate current risk, and a retrospective look may suggest a focus on identifying how to avoid similar instances in the future. Great leaders pay attention to both.

Helping a leader develop the future story he tells by paying attention to his vision and the threads of previous stories rather than simply reacting to current feedback is an important role in coaching and mentoring. Sometimes a coach or mentor is the only objective observer who can help a business leader keep it real and maintain perspective. Supporting a client to consider how he wants his response to be experienced by others and holding the space for him in that place until he can do that may be in order.

Learning from the Spectacular Success of Others

Never underestimate the power of modelling. Not your 'dripping in Armani' trip down the runway, but rather identifying what the person does, why he does it and how. In coaching and mentoring, you can help your clients by showing them how to emulate the qualities, behaviours, physiology and thinking strategies of a successful entrepreneur that they want to identify with. Because they can't ask the person they want to emulate any direct questions, this activity is a kind of mini-modelling where they need to really use their imagination.

When children are small, parents sow the seeds of this technique when they encourage them to use imaginative play. They do this particularly when they suggest things like, 'Imagine you're Superman (or Wonder Woman). What would he (or she) do?' If your client has ever imagined that he was someone else as a child, he can discover how to 'be success' easily now too. He doesn't need to reinvent success through trial and error when he can identify a successful person or two and find out how to do what she does, act how she acts and think how she thinks. If your client play-acted in this way as a child, he's already halfway there.

Mentoring Inside a Small Organisation

Not everyone is mentoring inside a large organisation or has a weighty board of advisors to draw on. If you're mentoring inside a small organisation (and you can use this activity if you're in a larger organisation too), you can use a technique called 'creating your virtual genius team'.

As a mentor, you work with your client on the process. Make sure you have pens and paper handy.

1. **Consider what qualities you would like that you don't have at the moment and create a list or a mind map of him.**

   A *mind map* is simply a drawing of images or circles naming the key qualities with a series of sub-elements that flow from them.

2. **When you have your list, relax, go inside and ask yourself a simple question: 'Who do you know of or admire in business who already has these qualities? Choose someone whose work you know and understand, someone you admire and see as a role model. Name him'.**

3. **Get clear on what it is in this person that you would like to emulate.**

   Be really specific.

4. **Imagine that he's on your Board or part of your advisory dream team, and get specific about the role you would like him to play and what you would like him to contribute.**

   You could imagine **him** as a potential investor in your business, for example.

   The next step is seemingly 'woo woo' but is the really cool part.

5. **Imagine that you are him.**

   Imagine that you're inside his body and have the potential of his whole experience and his thinking at your disposal. Really use your imagination to see the world through his eyes. Imagine that you have the person's physiology and are really him (just like you did with your favourite character when you were a child).

6. **Ask your question. Whatever you want his help with, ask.**

   You can say something such as, 'As I sit in the body of Warren Buffett, I want to know how I create a business in the next five to ten years that he would want to invest in. What would I look for if I am Warren Buffett? What would I look for in the history of the business in its first five to ten years?

   Notice what comes up in the response you get.

7. **Continue exploring further.**

   Ask what specifically would he do to track the business? What would he look for in the results you have achieved, perhaps about the way the share price has moved? What would he look for in the management team? In the products? What would make him say yes to investing?

   Now, you aren't necessarily looking to call Buffett tomorrow. You're looking to replicate what he would see in your business. You'll have a rich picture and some ideas.

8. **Keep going with this exploration for as long as you're getting data and insight.**

   Who else would you have on your virtual Board? If you wanted to create a successful brand, you could call on Jo Malone.

9. **Go through the process again, following the steps.**

   Your mind map on being Jo Malone and creativity in brand development may look something like Figure 7-2.

10. **When you have elicited all the qualities you're looking for, consider how you can apply these qualities in your specific context.**

    Have fun with it!

Be true to the qualities you want to be known for

Shirley Chisholm made history by becoming the United States' first African-American congresswoman in the 1960s. She was appointed to the Forestry Department and asked to be reassigned (unusual for a newly appointed person in Congress to question the role offered). She was given a far more interesting portfolio in Veteran Affairs. Chisholm was the first major-party African-American candidate to stand for the Democratic nomination for presidency in 1972. She served in the US House of Representatives for seven terms, which was a record at the time.

She wrote a book titled *Unbought and Unbossed*. Are we surprised? No.

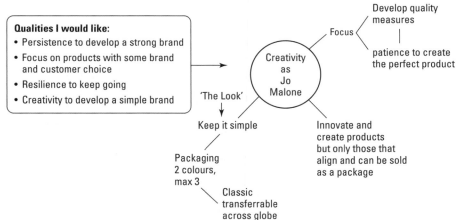

Modelling Jo Malone brand development

Qualities I would like:
- Persistence to develop a strong brand
- Focus on products with some brand and customer choice
- Resilience to keep going
- Creativity to develop a simple brand

Figure 7-2:
A sample mind map.

Illustration by John Wiley & Sons, Ltd.

People wear their qualities for all to see and demonstrate them through their values, their behaviours and in what they pay attention to. Assessing a business is about looking at whether it's robust, congruent and does what it says on the tin. A bit like being a robust, congruent organisational leader. Successful leaders create successful organisations. That's just fact. Don't underestimate the value of working on yourself and on how you show up while working on the business.

Chapter 8

Developing Vision, Mission and Values Using Simple Coaching Methods

In This Chapter

▶ Developing congruence and confidence in you and the business

▶ Getting clear on what you want

▶ Using tools to help you define and refine your business proposition

*I*t would be nice if words like 'mission' and 'vision' could be replaced with whole sentences like 'Why are you here?' and 'Where does your ambition want to take us next?' That kind of everyday language makes the whole planning and strategy piece in organisations far more inviting. It would mean that we could do without the need for explanation, definitions and reinvention of this particular terminology. Clients would be less likely to confuse and conflate their mission with their vision.

Coaching is all about helping clients find clarity. Developing and describing a business proposition that makes sense and aligns with what the business aims to deliver is an area where a good coach can get her toolkit out and add real value.

Aligning Who You Are with the Business You're In

Business is personal. Business owners, leaders and coaches do what they do because it satisfies a need. When that need isn't satisfied, they become demotivated, their performance suffers and their business can be affected. Aligning their needs and wants with the way they do business is sometimes overlooked. When they do that, they create and run businesses as though they're something outside of them – something 'over there' and separate.

People have been confused by the notion of work-life balance looking like something that demands they separate their personal identity and work identity. In truth, it's just not realistic.

We encourage you to bring your whole selves into your work. If you're an owner, doing so is probably easy – you created the business, and it reflects your values and your purpose. For leaders employed in business and for coaches, it's about choice. The choice about where to work and who to work with is more fruitful when you choose to be in organisations that align with your personal values and desires.

Revealing What's Really Important

People often confuse the terms mission statement, vision statement and values. Make sure you understand the difference so you can help your clients understand the difference and see the value you bring as a coach.

- ✔ The *mission statement* sets out the purpose of the organisation and sometimes the approach it uses to deliver on that purpose.
- ✔ A *vision statement* is aspirational – an articulation of the desired future of the company.
- ✔ *Values* are about the behavioural qualities that the organisation holds dear. They set out standards of conduct for stakeholders in the business.

You can see the articulation of vision, mission and values as a management tool required for the annual report, or you can view them as key leadership tools that encourage followership. They're an indicator of purpose and passion, an explanation that inspires people to turn up for work every day and their customers to buy from them.

Defining the how and why of your business

Having a mission and vision isn't optional. You'll find it hard to sell the benefits of what you do without stating them clearly and with passion. You need to sell yourself to current and prospective stakeholders, particularly investors and staff. If people can't see the benefit, it's hard for them to invest their money or themselves.

> *It is hard to trust in the leadership of someone who is half-hearted about their purpose, or only sporadic in focus or enthusiasm.*
>
> —Sebastain Coe, President, International Association of Athletics Federations

Often, mission and vision statements are combined and are sometimes used interchangeably. This doesn't really matter so long as you articulate the why and how of your business clearly.

- ✔ The mission describes the core purpose behind the company that doesn't change much over time. It articulates why the business exists and
    - Applies to the whole organisation
    - Is clear, compelling and easy to retain and repeat to others
    - Aligns with the values of the organisation
- ✔ The vision is about the why and how of the business. It's about the delivery of the mission. It sets out what the business is looking to deliver in a bite-sized statement.
- ✔ Values are a 'how' of delivering the vision. They:
    - Provide a direction of travel
    - Underpin strategy generation and planning

Stakeholders look at mission and vision; potential investors look to them in deciding whether to invest or not; and people decide whether to apply to work for organisations based on how they feel about the statements that are made. You're asking people to buy into you and your business and it's important to get them right.

Stopping your history from holding you back

Many business owners do well in business because they want to prove something to themselves and others. They're escaping from something they fear, or they have made mistakes, turned a corner and want to make a difference. Some people have grown up in family businesses and choose to do something different or would like to run the family business in a different way. Some people enter the business world with a long family history of business, and some are the business pioneers.

Wherever you're starting from, coaching is often about helping owners and leaders leave the limitations of their less than useful thinking behind. Coaching is often about handling limiting beliefs about what clients think they are not capable of or about helping them see that to grow or change a business they may need to challenge their own thinking. You must help them question what other people expected of them and what they want and expect for themselves.

Checking your locus of control

We all have a *locus of control* — a set of beliefs about where control lies in relation to ourselves. We believe that what happens to us is primarily invested in and determined by others (external locus of control), or we believe that we are where we are largely by our own efforts (internal locus of control).

If people have an external locus of control, they may get frustrated if they're given pieces of work that need independent action or require them to think and decide without consulting others. This frustration sometimes shows up in people who resist taking on new challenges at work or things that involve autonomy in decision making for example.

Most business owners and many business leaders operate from an internal locus of control. They've a high need for independence and a desire to participate in decisions that affect them. There's also a suggestion that work satisfaction, resilience and risk taking are enhanced in those with an internal locus of control.

Desire drives the locus of your focus as a leader

The World Wide Web is the most profitable free product ever distributed to humankind. Sir Tim Berners-Lee, who invented the World Wide Web, didn't create it because he wanted a means to hack into other people's confidential data. He invented it because that is what he is – a solution creator, a scientist. At the level of identity, scientists normally want to create solutions that help us understand how things work and can make a difference to our world. He invented it because he could see how to create a means of connecting people across the world.

While Berners-Lee is wealthy by most people's standards, it isn't wealth creation that drove him. It was a desire to use his mathematical talent to create something useful for society. His wealth is a tiny fraction of Mark Zuckerberg or Larry Page and Sergey Brin. He could probably have created the platform and coding for Facebook and Google. Instead, he has spent time establishing things like the World Wide Web Foundation, whose mission is to ensure that the web serves humanity by 'establishing it (the web) as a global public good and basic right'. He is a founder member of the World Wide Web consortium, whose vision for the web involves 'participation, sharing knowledge, and thereby building trust on a global scale'.

What do you think drives his desire? It's deeper than the money and the kudos. In an interview in the *Guardian* newspaper, he talked about his early career and how his mind-set was not on his career; it was on 'what was necessary for the web'. If he'd wanted to create it for his own adulation, if his values had been driven only by making a personal mark and creating a platform for profit and economic wealth creation rather than altruism and a recognition of his scientific genius, he'd have called it MMW (Money Making Web), wouldn't he?

Understanding locus of control can help a management team be realistic and ambitious about what they can influence. It helps them ascertain how much they can influence through their actions and commitment to act in certain agreed ways.

Here are a few questions worth asking:

- ✔ **Where is your locus of control?** This question links to desire and to how much control you feel you have over what you want. What you want impacts what you value about life and business. If you're developing a business or re-evaluating the business that you're in, exploring what you want is fundamentally important. If you don't place any focus of attention here, you simply end up living someone else's life and being in business that doesn't float your boat.

- ✔ **Where do you place your control?** Do you believe that you have the power to control the majority of your life, or is life mostly determined by other people, other sources of power and influences outside of yourself?

Sometimes when a coaching client begins to explore what he believes he can control, limiting beliefs can pop up. You may hear a client say, 'I couldn't do that/have that/be that'. You can address limiting beliefs with a client in a number of ways. A simple, structured way is to question and explore whether the limiting beliefs are true or not (see Chapter 12).

Getting clear on what you value and what you want

'What do you want?' can be a challenging question. The only expert on this conundrum is you. No one else can answer this question. When Marie first asks it on the retreats she runs for successful leaders, the answers are invariably head-based answers. They fall out in a list: 'I want to do good work', or 'I want to earn enough to have a nice home', 'I want to be successful', 'I want to have enough to feed my family and take care of the kids', and the list goes on.

Truth is, these wants are often fear-based and 'away from' in orientation, generated from what we don't want – the fear of not being seen as competent at work, of living in scarcity, of being seen as less than, or going hungry and losing the house or losing the children. These fears are often rooted somewhere in our history and don't even belong to us.

In the simplest terms, if somewhere in your ancestry you have relatives who were poor, lost everything and ended up in the workhouse, that dialogue told you by granny is somewhere in your story-making DNA. Your story-making thoughts can influence and restrict what you think you want. It begs the question, is what you think you want and what you really want the same thing?

Finding your heart-based desire

The questions 'What do you want?' or 'What do you value?' can be answered at different levels. It's an area that people rarely explore and, when they do, it can provide surprising results.

When people are externally referenced, they can sometimes place desire in terms of what they think other people expect of them. This attitude normally shows up as a 'should', an 'ought to' or has a moral tone behind it. This kind of referencing doesn't come from a deep sense of self or of real self-knowledge. We've seen this problem in established family businesses where someone inherits a business and leads it in fear of losing it, of mucking it up and ruining family reputation and significance.

So to get beyond that head-level response, the question becomes, 'What do you really want?' This question is searching for a feeling – a felt response to what looks like a head-based question. The answer comes from the heart rather than off the top of your head.

If you ask a leader 'What do you really want?' and leave plenty, and we mean plenty, of room for her to answer, you know you're getting to desire when the feelings-based words come up. Things like 'I want to feel that I matter, that I've made a difference in this world', 'I want to create a business selling games products that I love and other people want to buy', 'I want to create community where I live by providing wholesome food in a nice setting at a price where everyone can come together and talk', 'I want to be appreciated by my peers for creating the best hairdressing business in Ireland'. (These statements are from real people leading business.)

Whatever the response is, notice that it's dynamic and future-focused. It has action behind it and a sense of orientation towards a felt sense of something.

Going deeper to find the source of all wanting

Do you ever have that feeling of just knowing that something is instinctively right, wrong or not for now? Coaches call this place all sorts of things – soul-level knowing, wisdom, deep desire. However it's framed, the response is coming from the deep instinct, from the gut, and it doesn't always make sense to the individual when it pops out either. Whatever you call it, it's the real deal.

In the business context, this response is where the juice is – the thing that drives individuals to make products and provide services that make the world a better place or not. Whatever the drivers are, they're personal to each person. Two people may get to the same outcome or be in the same kind of business, yet value and believe in different things. We can't see those drivers by simply looking at what business leaders create but those creations are value laden.

So how do you get to that deep desire? Take yourself to a quiet darkened room and ask yourself slowly, 'What do I really, really want?' Don't do this task in a 1990s pop-song jingle-and-jiggle-around-the-dining-room kind of way; do it in more of a zen meditation, sitting-on-a-mat way. Marie first saw Deepak Chopra doing a version of part of this process in 2007 with 1,200 people. Step by step, the three-stage process works like this:

1. **Sit quietly and comfortably with no distractions, and set a timer for 2 minutes. Breathe deeply and slowly. Then ask yourself, 'What do I want?' When the alarm goes, stop.**

   Answer internally or out loud with statements that start with 'I want. . .' If you want to, jot down a few notes.

   Make sure the alarm on the timer is a gentle one to suit a reflective mood, not the theme from *Batman*.

2. **Set the timer again for 3 minutes and re-create the environment as in Step 1. Then ask yourself, 'What do I *really* want?'**

   If you get stuck, repeat the question and wait for the answers to come. Again, make some notes when the alarm goes off if you wish.

3. **Set the timer for 4 minutes. Relax and breathe deeply in the belly and ask yourself, 'What do I really *really* want?'**

   Wait for the answers to come and repeat the question as you need to. Make a few notes when the alarm goes off and notice the difference in your responses to the questions.

Notice what pops up when you just listen for the answers. Things like 'freedom', 'self-determination', 'connection', 'recognition', 'happiness'.

When you're looking at personal and business values, the meaning you make of your nominalisations is important – really, really important. Whatever pops out in this exercise is worth exploring because it helps you determine how your version of 'freedom', 'self-determination' and so on get played out. Work with these nominalisations to define your values. This stage is where a coach can really help.

If you were using this process to coach a client, you might ask her to consider one of her nominalisations such as freedom. You might ask. 'So what do you value about freedom? What does freedom look like to you in your business? In your life? What does your business look like if a guiding principle were freedom?' and so forth. These questions are deep. They need to help the client create her picture and plan and develop the business or her contribution in an organisation by creating a role that meets her deep desire.

Checking that your head, heart and gut all agree

It can be useful for you (and your client) to check that your personal, business and organisational values are aligned. You can do this by checking how you experience them when you speak them out loud. What do you think about them, feel about them and experience them in the body?

If working with a client, get her to stand up. Ask her to imagine a thread from the top of her head to her gut with words and sentences she's generated written along the line of thread. Ask her to quietly reflect and consider how the responses line up in the following three areas:

- ✔ **Head:** Say to your client 'When I speak your words to you, notice how you hear them and what you think about them'. Replay your client's articulated wants at a storytelling pace so she can hear and absorb them. Listen for positive, affirmative responses from your client. Do they sound in line with what she says she wants? If her response to what she hears isn't positive, there's something for you to explore here.

- ✔ **Heart:** Say to your client, 'Focus your attention around the heart. When I repeat your words, feel them in the heart and notice what you feel'. Let your client be quiet and reflect internally as you repeat her words. Encourage her to let the words sink in so she notices how it feels to hear them. If her response is anything other than wholly positive, explore why that might be with her.

- ✔ **Gut:** Say to your client, 'Focus your attention towards the belly and to the edges of your skin. When I repeat your words for the last time, notice your response and how you experience them deep in your gut. Notice if the words encourage you to act, if they feel right. Is there a yes or a no response deep in your gut?' If her response is anything other than affirmative or if you see a confused expression, explore that.

You're looking for a high degree of alignment between the head, heart and gut response. If it isn't there, there's work for the client to do with your help. If the head, heart and gut agree, great. If not, ask the client to see whether she has anything to add or change to increase alignment. Keep checking until the client feels that her head, heart and gut responses are lined up internally and feel true for her.

Helping a Business Create Operating Values

Values are about how individuals behave in a business, individually and collectively. They are a key component in terms of business ethics, social responsibility, corporate governance and reputation. Although they're more than just attitudes, they need to be consistent with the attitudes the business presents.

Attitudes flow from values, and misalignment can create real business problems. When customers, staff, investors and the general public experience a mismatch, they complain, take out grievances and hold the organisation to account.

If in doubt, just open a newspaper and look at the compensation claims for employees who have taken their employers to court and won claims of mistreatment, and then take a look at their organisational values statements. We can guarantee you will find a mismatch, and that incongruity doesn't come cheap.

When working with companies on values, be clear about what they're signing up to. Make sure they're prepared to be held accountable for the behaviours that flow from their values statements.

Coaching business leaders to identify values

Here's a process for coaching a group of business leaders to identify values:

1. **Identify the locus of control (see the earlier 'Checking your locus of control' section in this chapter).**

   Ask the group, 'Where do you place your control? Do you believe that you have the power to control the majority of this business, or is the business mostly determined by other people, by other sources of power and influences outside of this room?'

   If members of the group don't believe they have the control over most of what they do and how the business conducts itself, either you are with the wrong group of leaders or the leaders you are with see themselves as followers not leaders.

   Assuming they do recognise that they have control over how the business relates to the world, you want to help them articulate the limits of their control and understand who holds them to account and how. You might use a stakeholder mapping exercise to help them here (see Chapter 14).

   You want to explore the locus of control to help the client determine what her boundaries are and what she feels she has control over.

2. **Walk the group through the three-part 'what do you want' elicitation, which focuses on the business.**

   Do it slowly by asking the following three questions repeatedly, leaving lots of room for the group to answer:

   - 'What do you want for this business?' Repeat this question periodically over a 10- to 15-minute period.

     Record the group's answers on a whiteboard, flip chart or laptop linked to a projector – somewhere visual so everyone can see it. Then ask the second question.

   - 'What do you really want for this business?' Repeat this question periodically over about a 20-minute period, depending on the group size and the time you have.

     Again, record the answers as they emerge. Finally, ask the third question.

   - 'What do you really, really want for this business?' Repeat this question periodically over about a 20-minute period.

     Continue to record the answers. If you need to, prompt the group with specific follow-up questions such as, 'What do you want for the people in this business? For your staff? Your customers? Your shareholders? The end users of your goods and services?'

   Take the answers in this elicitation without commenting on them or having the group discuss them – just share. It's important to get the responses out on the table before you coach the group around them.

3. **After you have elicited as many answers from the group as possible, work to consolidate the content with the group. Coach them through the range of responses, get them to talk about their answers and ask them to agree on five to ten nominalisations.**

   You're going to work with these nominalisation to create a set of values.

   For example, these might be the answers for a client:

   - We want:

     To be the best cinema café in Devon

     To have top, current films that make customers want to make a night of it and buy cocktails and a meal

     Repeat visitors who are loyal

   - We really want:

     For people to love our theme nights

     To create a beautiful experience that is accessible to everyone

     To be recognised by the industry as a top venue

     To create more cinema café venues across the Southwest

- We really, really want:

  Recognition

  Heart

  Creativity

4. **Take the nominalisations one by one and explore them with group questions.**

   The idea is to flesh out some values statements. (See the next section to find out how to do so.)

5. **Keep going across all the nominalisations, then refine them into five to seven values statements.**

You can adapt this elicitation process if you want to walk around different aspects of the business or focus in one area or on one stakeholder group. For example, you can ask:

✔ What do you want for your customers?

✔ What do you want for your products?

✔ What do you want for this marketing team?

✔ What do you want for this new work environment?

Fleshing out values statements

You want to flesh out values statements that articulate how clients will do business and meet those aspects of what they really, really want to create. For example, you may ask on recognition:

✔ What do you want to be recognised for? *(the quality of the customer experience, the creativity of the building and the retention of our customers)*

✔ What does recognition look like to others? *(for customers and staff, internal rewards; for the business, the Small Cinema award, the Leisure award for the Southwest region, the Devon 4-star restaurant rating)*

✔ How would you know that the business was being recognised? Specifically, what would you notice? *(staff photos in reception, local PR stories reporting staff and customer awards, award trophy, Southwest certificate and local PR)*

✔ Who and what would be recognised? *(the whole experience that customers enjoy, the chef and restaurant for the quality of our food)*

 ✔ How will you recognise staff and customers? *(create a staff-member-of-the-month scheme and give public acknowledgment – photo in reception and additional staff discount for the month; give loyal customers upfront discount – buy five tickets, get a sixth free; create theme nights and give a free meal for two to the winner)*

You can then generate some values that might support those outcomes. For example:

 ✔ We create a great quality experience for our customers from when they arrive to beyond their leaving.

 ✔ Our customers are our community, and we exist to serve them.

 ✔ We create a fun place to work where staff are acknowledged publicly for creating a service people love.

Articulating values in the brand and the employee experience

One highly successful Idaho-based consultancy supports purpose-driven companies to develop and build their brand. Oliver Russell (www.oliverrussell.com) is a B corporation, a company that works hard to meet the exacting ethical, environmental and transparent business requirements of B Corp certification (www.bcorporation.net).

Russ Stoddard, president and founder, describes the company values as 'creative, collaborative, progressive and socially responsible'.

He ensures that the company values align with the way the company engages with and treats staff. He established the company because he likes to help others and figured that if he was going to be spending significant time at work, he wanted to do something he enjoys. He and his people enjoy working with others to create brands that support purpose-led business. If you look at their website, you'll see their creativity, even in the way they describe themselves as a team. They look like they're having fun.

Collaboration shines through in the volunteer work they engage in and the 'change maker' relationships they highlight. They're one of just 1,500 corporations that have met the B corp standards. Inside the company, their staff enjoy free health insurance, receive generous maternity and paternity leave and get $50 a month to spend on their own development, whether that be a health club membership or a massage. We'd call that progressive; wouldn't you?

As for their social responsibility record, the company regularly supports good causes through its social impact grants, use of fair trade and local products wherever possible and reduction of its carbon footprint by educating staff to be conscious of their environment. This can be as simple as turning the lights off regularly!

Transparent oranisations that are prepared to be accountable will increasingly be employers of choice for generation Y talent (those born in the early 1980s to early 2000s) who tend to be looking for a clearer alignment with values and purpose than previous generations. Enabling organizational leadership to create these environments and coaching leaders to engage talent seems to be a growing area.

Organisations don't just create a set of values and philosophy in a one-hour business meeting. They go through a process to get everything right. Marie once spent three full days with a management team working on two questions – who are we, and what do we want to create going forward?

Get familiar with the issue of developing values/principles/philosophy from nominalisations by looking at organisations you regard as successful. See how they describe themselves and work backwards to see whether you can guess the words they might elicit if they did the preceding exercise.

Check out what a company you like says it values. If you're a customer, you might check that your experience aligns with what the company says.

Designing an Inspiring Vision with the Logical Levels Model

The Logical Levels model (see Figure 8-1) was created by Robert Dilts building on the work of Gregory Bateson. This model is widely used in personal development and business coaching. You can use it both as a diagnostic to help clients consider where the business is currently and also as a planning tool to elicit rich data to support the development of mission and vision. It can also be useful when coaching leaders who are planning for change.

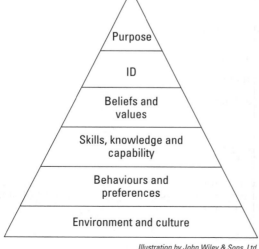

Figure 8-1: Logical Levels model, developed by Robert Dilts.

Illustration by John Wiley & Sons, Ltd.

The following are adapted descriptions from the original model that you can use if helping a business leader or team diagnose their business and spot the gaps. Dilts recognised the importance of helping individuals and teams understand the various levels at which they operate. We have adapted the model for use in a business context.

The interplay between the six levels in the model is important. We can create more sustainable business by paying attention to all the levels and how they relate. You might notice that the higher you go up the pyramid, the more invisible the factors become. They're harder to change and harder to assess, but this level is where the really powerful work is. Lots of organisations spend too much time at the lower levels of the model fiddling around with the environment. This focus may take the form of changing the organisation chart, reorganising the office or restructuring roles.

The place where leaders and coaches can make the most impact is working at the top of the logical levels model: on purpose, identity, and values and beliefs. If those are robust, everything else is relatively easy. This level is where mission, vision and values are developed. However, you need to work through all six levels with a new business, and we explore that next.

Environment level

The environment level describes the physical layout of the business, its offices, factory floor, retail unit, warehouse – where the business operates. It relates to its range of stakeholders and relationships – the operating environment.

The questions you can ask include:

- ✔ Where do you do business?
- ✔ When do you do business?
- ✔ Whom do you do business with?

Behaviour level

The behaviour level relates to the specific actions in the business: what behaviours are evident in the business explicitly, and what behaviours are set down by the leadership.

The questions you can ask include:

- ✔ How do you expect people to behave with each other?
- ✔ What specific behaviours do you want to see in this business or specific business scenario (for example, change, merger, acquisition)?

Capabilities level

The capabilities (or competencies) level includes the requisite skills and knowledge that impact the way people behave in the environment they work in.

The questions you can ask include:

- ✔ How does the work get done?
- ✔ How does the operations team relate to the delivery team?
- ✔ How do you train and develop people to make sure that they've the right skills and knowledge?
- ✔ How do you assess their competence from time to time?

Beliefs and values level

The beliefs and values level encompasses those things that the business and people in it consider to be important – the emotional, heart-based drivers that explain why the team works here rather than in the business next door.

The questions you can ask include:

- ✔ Why do you do what you do?
- ✔ Why is it important to you to be here?
- ✔ Why is teamwork/commitment/balance important around here?

Identity level

The identity level is about how the organisation thinks about itself: how it describes itself, its purpose and how the teams in it describe themselves and their roles collectively – in other words, who it is.

The questions you can ask include:

- ✔ What is the identity of those working in your business? (Describe the roles.)
- ✔ Who are you? (Describe your purpose in the world you operate in.)

Purpose level

The purpose level is about the wider connection beyond the business: how the business connects to something outside itself, its reason for being there and its relationship to something bigger.

The questions you can ask include:

- ✔ What are your services and products here for?
- ✔ Whom do they serve?
- ✔ Beyond that, what's the impact of those products and services?
- ✔ What else do they reach, wider than that?

Using the Logical Levels model

The levels influence each other in both directions, but a change at a higher level in the model always has a greater impact on the lower levels.

To step a client through the Logical Levels model, have your client relax in a chair and do this activity as an eyes-closed process, or use a Logical Levels diagram (see Figure 8-1) on the floor, or get your client to colour in it as you go along. Add lots of encouragement as you move between the levels. You want to encourage a bit of playfulness and fantasy-type thinking. If you're working with a team, engage them in creating a picture or infographic for each level. At each stage of the process, you're building on what the client generates. Use her language and descriptions, and keep building a rich picture of her new world.

Using the model works well with clients who like a structured way of thinking about things and may need some encouragement to be creative and flesh out their ideas so others can understand their business proposition.

You can start anywhere in the model depending on what your client is working on in her coaching. If her concerns are about staff competency, you can explore at that level. If you see a need to look at the behaviours she needs for a specific project, go to behaviours. Then do a check. Whatever you elicit and whatever actions she decides on, walk her through the model and check the impact of those decisions and whether they're congruent with other aspects in each level of the model.

Coaching a new entrepreneur on developing a business identity

Marie worked with a new entrepreneur looking at the development of her stem cell testing company. They used the Logical Levels model as it can really help a business owner starting from a clean sheet to get into a planning habit. The two simply worked through the levels in a logical order (funny that).

✔ *Level of the environment: What are you standing in or what virtual structure is required?* Start with the future environment, the place you want to do business. Develop a really rich picture of the offices and the laboratory. Imagine an environment you would love to work in and describe that in detail.

✔ *Level of behaviour: What do people in and around the business need to do?* Imagine you were filming in the offices and laboratory you described. What can you see people doing there? How are they behaving in their work and with each other? What different stakeholders are involved? What are they doing?

✔ *Level of capability: What do you need by way of skills and competency to deliver?* If you were in the environment you have described, noticing what you noted about what people are doing, what new capabilities and skills would you need to establish Scientific Testing Labs Inc? What technical skills? What management skills? What support team skills?

✔ *Level of values and beliefs: What do you believe in and what drives you?* Now imagine that you have created a great place to work. You have the skills and capabilities you need, and people are doing what you need them to do. What values would you need in the business? What do you need to believe as the leader in this business to be motivated and create this great business? What is your goal? What values do you have as a human being?

✔ *Level of identity: Who are you and how do you describe your identity in the future?* You have all the artefacts of the business sorted except the big story. But who are you, and how do you describe yourselves? What's the position that Scientific Testing Labs Inc holds? If you were to go inside yourself and see whether you can find a metaphor or an image that describes your identity, what would it be? What would you compare yourself to? If you were to feel and breathe in the identity of your future business, how do you describe that? What defines how you show up as a business?

✔ *Level of purpose: What else is in your universe? How and where will you make a wider contribution?* What else do you exist for? Whom do Scientific Testing Labs Inc exist for? Whom and what do you serve? In the wider world, what will you add?

For example, learning a new skill (capability level), such as how to do business in China, might open her up both to the importance of other cultures (values level) and her identity – 'I am in the world and I am part of it' (identity level). It changes her behaviour because she can potentially relate to people whom she may not have related to before (behaviour level). There might even be a dramatic change in her environment – she may move to China for a while (environment level).

If the belief level is changed first, the power of that belief change is enormous as it impacts through all the levels. For example, if your client had a limiting belief that sounded like, 'I can't learn how to do business in China', and you can change that to 'I can learn how to do business in China or any other country if I choose to', the shift will affect every other level of the Logical Levels.

Reverse engineering the future

After you explore every level, go back down through the levels and check whether those levels feel aligned for the client. Ask, 'What do you think about what you have generated? How do you feel about it? If you were to check in with your inner wisdom, your gut, does it all seem right to you?'(Help your client make adjustments as necessary.) You have probably been taking notes, and it's a good idea at this stage to give your client time to write down this story/strategy in her own words.

Now ask your client to work backwards. You may ask her to imagine she was in retirement looking back, imagining that she had lived up to her defined purpose. Ask, 'How did you get there?' Start at the purpose and end at environment, making the last sentence 'I had an idea for a business'.

When you work in this way with clients, you're helping them double-check their broad plan, helping them to see it as though they've already delivered it and working it backwards to spot any gaps.

Notice what it's like for your client to start on purpose achieved. If it doesn't light her up, there's more work to do on defining purpose.

Communicating the Vision

When a clear vision has been formulated, it needs to be shared with other current and potential stakeholders in order to make the vision a reality. You can use the stakeholder map (see Chapter 14) to determine whom you might want to share the vision with.

The vision needs to be clearly articulated to engage stakeholders and promote the actions that the business needs from each stakeholder group. It must align with the mission.

Simon Sinek, author of *Start with Why* (Portfolio), has a great way of explaining how to communicate vision. He challenges businesses to think of 'why' as the starting point rather than 'what'. People don't buy what we do, they buy why we do it; they align with our purpose and beliefs in making buying decisions. He starts with 'why', then moves to 'how' and 'what'. A why-based statement may sound something like this:

> 'We like the buzz of successful business and exist to create winners in the leadership game. The way we do that is through individually crafted programs using closely guarded ninja-like methods. We create C suite winners through executive coaching and lifestyle support. If you want to play in the game not just stay in the game . . .'

 After you have the statement, consider the who, why, how and where of communicating it. Who needs to know? Why do they need to know? How will you communicate it (in writing, verbally), and where will you communicate it (social media, press, website, staff meetings, shareholder AGM)? State it frequently and with the passion it deserves. Passion creates followers, and businesses need those to do business.

Examples of Mission and Vision Statements

Following are some examples of mission and vision. Notice where the passion is and where the vision story supports the mission.

International Federation of the Red Cross

Mission: 'The International Federation of Red Cross and Red Crescent Societies (IFRC) is the world's largest humanitarian organisation, providing assistance without discrimination as to nationality, race, religious beliefs, class or political opinions'.

Vision: 'To inspire, encourage, facilitate and promote at all times all forms of humanitarian activities by National Societies, with a view to preventing and alleviating human suffering, and thereby contributing to the maintenance and promotion of human dignity and peace in the world'.

Fusion Optix

Mission: 'Delivering the perfect beam of light'

Vision: 'Fusion Optix is one of the world's leading optical and LED technology companies. We are focused on solving the problems in LED lighting that hold up mass adoption of this important light source. Our LED engines and optics are designed to work together to save energy, improve performance and lower the costs of next-generation LED lighting products'.

JP Morgan Chase and Co

Mission: 'First-class business . . . in a first-class way. In everything we do, excellence and integrity are the guiding principles. Excellence means more than 170 years of experience and knowledge that comes from focusing on the complexities of significant wealth, day in and day out. We augment this knowledge with some of the boldest, most innovative thinking today. Integrity means keeping your interests front and center always, and carrying out our work with utter discretion'.

Vision: 'You can expect dedicated guidance for each key area of wealth management–investments, liquidity and credit management, wealth planning and banking. Equally important, we have the experience, organisational structure and commitment to integrate these separate strands into a unified and comprehensive plan aligned with your particular vision'.

Chapter 9

Coaching to Transform Visions into Workable Plans

In This Chapter

▶ Creating a creative mind-set for project planning

▶ Walking clients through the stages of a plan

▶ Keeping going and adjusting the plan as it evolves

*O*n 12 November 2014, the European Space Agency (ESA) successfully landed a space probe from the Rosetta spacecraft onto the surface of Comet67P/Chryumov-Gerasimenko. Rosetta's ten-year epic expedition began in March 2004 and involved three fly-by encounters with Earth and one with Mars. The spacecraft went into deep space hibernation for over two years and travelled over 4 billion miles before culminating in landing on a moving comet 251 million miles from Earth.

All went to plan until the last minutes when the harpoons designed to anchor the Philae landing probe to the surface failed to fire properly, and the lander rebounded before finally coming to rest one kilometre from the selected landing site. A £1 billion project with teams of the smartest rocket scientists on the planet still didn't cater for the comet's surface being harder than expected.

Few coaches are involved in such epic grand-scale projects, but whether you're coaching a start-up business launch, a new product development, a sales campaign or a space project, you work with clients to create robust plans where the odds are stacked on the side of success, knowing that even the best-made plans can't cater for every eventuality.

The maxim that states 'proper prior planning prevents poor performance' is all too often the reality in business. Plans and projects are undertaken without a robust enquiry or duty of care.

This chapter introduces ideas, tools and techniques you can use to enable clients to appraise visions, ensuring that options have been thoroughly explored so they can create workable plans. These can be used with individuals, teams (projects) and organisations.

Creating a Plan Fit for Purpose

Some people would like it to happen, some wish it would happen and others make it happen.

–Anonymous

Steve's friend Emma is a big-picture visionary trailblazer of a person and, although able to go into detail if required, she finds herself often overwhelmed just by the thought of it. She has learned to outsource or delegate the detail to someone who loves doing this type of work. By working with a team, she gets amazing results. (See Chapter 3 for details on working in our zone of Genius.)

You need to ask two important questions of your coaching clients before engaging in any coaching around the subject of project planning.

- ✔ Do they feel more comfortable and prefer to work with big-picture concepts or are they comfortable with going into detail?
- ✔ How much detail do they need to go into at this stage?

When planning, there is a comfortable sweet spot between careless work (avoiding detail) and over analytical (going into fine detail). This Goldilocks Point is where the depth and detail of the planning will be just right, for now, for the client. The devil is always in the detail of any plan, but if detail work is outside the comfort zone of your client, he must recognise this limitation from the outset and recruit or outsource this work to someone who loves detail work and is great at it.

Both careless work and over-analytical work are often driven by the emotion of fear. Careless work comes from desperation for a project to work and an unwillingness to look into too much detail in case the vision is unattainable. It shows up as overwhelm and procrastination. Over-analytical work comes from the fear of getting it wrong and wanting to get it perfect. Perfection planning can paralyse an individual or a team and stop a worthwhile vision from ever getting started. If your client demonstrates either of these traits, Chapter 10 has tools and techniques enabling you to coach him to deal with this.

You're not coaching to pour cold water on a project plan or to give your client the green light that the plan is fit-for-purpose. Nor is your role as a coach to have a pre-cognitive, crystal-ball reading view of the future. Your role is to work with a client so he has undertaken a sufficient enquiry and he is comfortable that he has done a good and robust job in creating a plan, based on the information that is to hand at this point in time. It's not your vision, nor your business, and the ultimate decision to execute a plan must remain with the client.

Planning mind-set rules

The grim reality of business is that grand visions often end in failure, new products are unsuccessful and new ventures fail to live up to their expectations. In the UK, 20 per cent of businesses fail in the first year of trading, and by year three that number rises to 50 per cent. You can probably think of many stories where blind enthusiasm and perseverance led to business success, but these stories are the exceptions to the rules.

A successful venture is more likely to be achieved by following the right processes; enthusiasm and perseverance on their own just aren't enough. What you need are strategies that move a business in the general direction of success. The rapidly changing economic landscape also means that businesses have the added pressure of having to innovate, plan and execute plans quicker than ever.

Companies now realise the benefits of having a plan which is 'good enough for now', launching a project and gathering feedback and adjusting to the feedback as the plan evolves. A new paradigm for change is evident in product and service development and how visions are transformed into successful realities.

This paradigm for change is:

1. **Having a vision (get clarity)**

2. **Having a strategic plan (good enough for now)**

3. **Executing the plan (without it being perfect)**

4. **Measuring results and getting feedback (from customers, team, suppliers)**

5. **Adjusting the plan according to the feedback received (making sure that everyone is on board and clear about his responsibilities)**

6. **Testing that the plan is progressing in the right direction**

Before coaching on planning options, you need to set in place certain attitudes and rules, whether working with an individual, team or organisation. These are the *Planning Mind-Set Rules*.

Clients must be

> ✔ **In a calm, relaxed state before any planning or appraisal:** Avoid over-enthusiasm because it can distort perceptions leading to blind enthusiasm. Avoid negativity because it can lead to ideas being dismissed before properly assessed. (See Chapter 10 for state management.)

✔ **Open-minded to all options and have a willingness to explore and play:** Many great ideas come from 'out of the box' or 'blue-sky thinking'.

✔ **Honest and vulnerable with a willingness to hear, contribute and welcome all feedback:** Being precious about an idea or a way to achieve something can prevent clients seeing a quicker, easier or better way. Fear of offering a comment, idea or asking a question can mean that a valuable insight may be missed.

✔ **Neutrally detached from the outcomes of the plan:** Separating any attachment from the outcomes of a project means that the plan can be appraised from an unbiased perspective, without any neediness or desperateness for the plan to work.

✔ **Committed to engaging and contributing to the planning process:** Clients sometimes detach from the planning process for reasons they may not always be able to voice. Gain a willingness to engage, setting aside all personal reservations about the vision.

The Planning Mind-Set Rules set the conditions for successful, creative and worthwhile coaching sessions. Always set out these conditions and get clients' willingness and verbal agreement to adhere to these rules before starting. If there is reluctance to engage, this reluctance must be immediately addressed (this situation is covered in the 'Gaining honest commitment and buy-in' section). Neutralising any objections or resistance in advance sets the session up for success. Write the rules up on the wall as reminders.

Exploring options

With the Planning Mind-Set Rules in place (see the preceding section), you now need to explore and appraise options.

Always start a planning session with the following two exercises. The time they take depends on the scale and detail of the project. They're best done in one session or workshop; dedicating focused time enables momentum and the opportunity to stop, have breaks and let the client have moments to reflect on his findings.

Exercise 1: Well-Formed Goals and Outcomes

In Chapter 3, we cover the Neuro-Linguistic Programming process for defining Well-Formed Goals and Outcomes. This process is a series of questions that reveal whether a goal or vision is likely to happen. It reveals potential obstacles from the outset of any project. Having completed the enquiry into Well-Formed Goals and Outcomes and assuming that the conclusions are still that the vision is great and looks achievable, you now need to really explore and experiment and get creative.

If the conclusion at the end of the exercise is that the project is unlikely to succeed, then a lot of valuable time, money and effort has been saved. Although people may be disappointed with this conclusion, they need to focus on what they've saved by not following up on the vision.

Exercise 2: Detached Perspectives

In 1956, George Miller published 'The Magical Number Seven, Plus or Minus Two: Some Limits on Our Capacity for Processing Information'. Miller demonstrated the limits of our mental ability to retain and process discrete bits of information beyond that of 7 (+/– 2). Demonstrate this phenomena by asking clients to listen to your voice, become aware of the chair they're sitting in, notice the temperature of the room, listen to their own internal dialogue, become aware of the light in the room, recall what they had for breakfast that morning, scan their body to notice which part of them is the most comfortable and to then notice how many of those seven tasks they had forgotten or were unable to track all at the same time.

This task is the mental equivalent of a juggler spinning plates on a stick. We are all mentally limited to how many things we can concentrate on at any one time, including those who believe they can multitask.

The relevance of this concept when planning is important. You will witness a client one moment enthused and excited about the vision; then he shifts his thinking to the planning, perhaps criticising or doubting it as he goes into detail, at which point he forgets about his enthusiastic vision. Then when he goes back to the vision, he forgets about the detail that has to happen to make the plan real. Mentally spinning the plates, he swings from enthused to doubtful and back again. People can't mentally process all the information needed to transform a vision into a plan at one time. This common process of shifting perceptions from the vision to the plan is mentally draining and often ends up in paralysis with visions that would be worthy of time, money and effort being put aside or procrastinated over.

The following exercise can help your client form a plan for the vision without experiencing overwhelm or procrastination.

You need:

- ✔ Large sheets of flip-chart paper or a large white board and pens
- ✔ Lots of sticky notes and index cards
- ✔ Some space (If working with a team, ideally use three different rooms. If an individual, you need three distinct spaces for them to stand in.)

Throughout this exercise we reference working with a team, but the exercise works equally well with an individual. Use Figure 9-1 to guide you through the various perspectives.

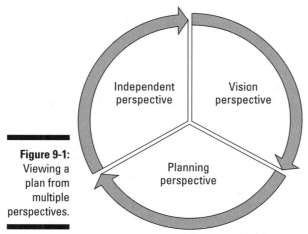

Illustration by John Wiley & Sons, Ltd.

Figure 9-1:
Viewing a plan from multiple perspectives.

Remind the team of the Planning Mind-Set Rules and get them to openly commit to follow the rules. If they violate the rules, you then have permission to point this out to them and get them to 'STOP IT'.

1. **Get the team into the Vision Perspective.**

    Select a part of a room or a separate room and in this space ask the team to *only* think about the vision. They should not be concerned whatsoever when in this space about how the vision is to be achieved or whether it's realistic or doable. Get them into the physiology of a vision-ary, looking upwards and outwards, perhaps with arms outstretched and bold gestures and in the mind-set of blue-sky no-limits thinking.

    The importance of physiology and how it influences our thinking and behaviours is covered in Chapter 10. Playing some great uplifting instrumental music gently in the background can help get them into the right perspective as can having an inspirational view or being in an inspirational location.

    Invite them to describe the vision:

    • What can you see? What can you hear? What do you feel?

    • If the vision was better, what would it look like?

    • If you could create anything, describe what you would create.

    • Is this vision really the best? Dream no small dreams, and so on.

From the Vision Perspective no limits exist. Use this perspective and encourage the team to push beyond boundaries and thresholds they may have about what's possible. As they describe the vision, use the cards to write keywords down. You're looking to get the vision out of their heads and bypass the limitation of the magic number 7, +/– 2. There will be more than seven aspects of the vision for them to describe. Keep the descriptions flowing, encourage them to keep talking and describe the vision in positive terms. Do not allow them to stop and reflect on what they've written because it stalls the creative process.

During this process, observe how people participate. You may notice team members who are not 'on board' with the vision; they will be disengaged, withdrawn or simply playing along nicely. This knowledge is valuable. It's best to have any reluctance or reservations about a project revealed at the start. Disengagement leads to sabotage or failure to meet deadlines.

When the answer to the question 'Is this vision really the best it can be?' is a 'yes', then the time has come to stop the exercise and take a break.

Debrief the group. Remember to keep the conversation away from how this vision is to be achieved. Ensure that you engage those who seemed detached in the activity. Keep an open mind about what gets revealed during this step.

2. **Step into the Planning Perspective.**

   Again select a different space or room, ideally with lots of white board or flip-chart space. This space is where the planning department resides. Get the team into the physiology of planners (they're to act as if they're planners), adopt a quizzical, curious look on their faces, perhaps hand stroking of the chins. Instruct them to imagine where they sit to do their personal accounts or update their diaries and get into the same physiology.

A blue-sky perspective

Marie conducted this exercise with a corporate client who fitted tracking devices into car fleets so clients could monitor and manage their mobile resources. They had booked a penthouse conference suite in a hotel in London for the project planning exercises. The directors were gazing out across the landscape while talking about the vision they had for the company, when one of them stopped and looked out at the thousands of cars driving below. He turned to the others and said, 'Look at all these cars. We have hardly scratched the surface with our business. I can't believe we have been thinking so small'. This was a paradigm shift in perspective, which resulted in the vision becoming bigger and the next four years dedicated to a worthwhile blue-sky venture.

In this space they're planners, external consultants who have one mission and one mission only: to explore options and create plans to achieve the vision.

As the ideas flow, let them write keywords on the index cards and drop them to the ground. At this planning stage they're *only* interested in high-level concepts. You want to create the framework of a plan, not necessarily all the finer details of the plan. If you get a sense some planners are going too much into detail with processes or systems than others may feel comfortable with at this stage, ask them to make a note that more detail is required for that part of the plan; the finer details will be addressed later.

Prompt the planners by continually asking good questions (while ensuring not to interrupt their flow). In the next section of this chapter, you find the Information Grid. Use this grid to ensure that planners review and assess key areas that make up a robust plan. Keep prompting and asking questions until you get a sense that the planners have exhausted all high-level ideas, then take a break.

Return to the Planning Perspective area (get clients into the physiology) and instruct them to lay out the pile of cards with keywords and group them. They will start to see patterns emerge with logical steps and sequences. When they're happy that the cards have been sorted into logical patterns and steps, transfer what has been produced onto the flip charts or white boards.

A plan will start to reveal itself. Allow the planners time to reorganise the plan. Look for and mark up for further consideration:

- Streamlining (where sequences can be improved)

- Overlap (avoid repetition)

- Redundancy (some steps may, upon review, seem unnecessary)

- Milestones (points where the plan can be measured for progress and celebrated if on track)

- Pinch points (gaps in knowledge or where failure to deliver can hold up the progress of the rest of the plan)

There comes a point where the planners want to go into too much detail for this stage, or they feel that they've done a good job. At this point, stop and have a break.

3. **Now instruct them to take an Independent Perspective about the job the planners have done.**

Move into the third space or room and ask the team to imagine that they're external auditors whose role isn't to question the vision but to examine whether the planners have done a thorough job. If they were presented with an invoice from the planners, would they pay it?

A fascinating thing happens with this stage of the exercise: The same people who created the plan now point out flaws or gaps that, when they were in the planners perspective, they were unable to see. This change is the magic number 7 phenomena at work and highlights the value of a third-party perspective discussed in Chapter 2, even when the third-party perspective comes from the same people. When all constructive feedback has been exhausted, take a break.

4. **Return to Step 2, and from the Planning Perspective take on board all the constructive feedback from the Independent Perspective and adjust the plan accordingly.**

   When the planners again feel they've done a good job, move to Step 5.

5. **Return to the Independent Perspective and ask the same questions in Step 3. Feed this information back to the planners.**

   Keep going between Independent Perspective to Planning Perspective to Independent Perspective until the independent consultants are satisfied that a good job has been done for now and they're willing to pay the planners invoice. Take a break.

6. **With a high-level plan in place, return to the Vision Perspective and review the vision but now with a plan designed to make it a reality and see what happens.**

   The question to ask the team is, 'What does the vision look like now in comparison to before you had a plan?'

   Step 6 is an exciting and nervy moment for clients and coach alike. Most clients, when they return to the vision with a robust high-level plan in place, comment that the vision has changed. For some, it seems clearer and more achievable. For some, it no longer appears to be the same: they often describe it as distant, less clear or even uninspiring. The first time Steve had this experience with a client, his first thoughts were 'Oops, what have we done wrong?' but the client turned to him and said, 'Now I realise that if this is the plan that will get me the vision – and it is a great plan – it's not worth the time and effort working on this project. I would rather not do it'.

How often have businesses undertaken a project that with hindsight they wish they had never started? This experiment helps clients have the advantage of hindsight ahead of time.

Assuming that the vision is still inspiring and the plan is robust, you can look at some of the common causes why a great plan can fail.

Revealing what may stop or derail the plan

The exercise in the preceding section prompts clients by asking good questions, which reveal what has to be there for a plan to work. For this, use the Information Grid, shown in Figure 9-2. Plans fail for common reasons; just as patterns for success are apparent, so are patterns for failure. By highlighting potential problems before they arise, you can enable a plan to run smoothly.

Time	Money	Effort	People
Beliefs & values	Skills	Capabilities	Environment (PEST)
Ecology	Legal	Feedback (KPIs)	Feed forwards (adaptability)
Strengths	Weaknesses	Opportunities	Threats

Figure 9-2: The Information Grid.

Illustration by John Wiley & Sons, Ltd.

The Information Grid has 16 categories, each with a series of questions that the client is asked. The questions highlight any potential problems as well as direct the thinking in the direction of a solution.

Use these questions to get your clients really thinking about what information and resources are needed to create a robust plan and make it a reality. Consider what's there and what's missing. During this exercise, remember there are no dumb questions, so if something comes to mind, ask it and encourage clients to speak up and do the same. If people feel a question may be stupid or the answer obvious, they may be reluctant to ask it. What you will find is if one person has the question, someone else may also have it. The seemingly obvious questions often reveal valuable information that would be overlooked if it were not asked.

You can methodically work through the grid one category at a time or see where the conversations takes you and address the categories ad-hoc. Whichever way you choose to work, be sure to address all the categories.

- ✔ **Time:** What are the timeframes for the project? Do you have the resources to allocate the time needed? When are the key project milestones? How will you deal with project slippage or missed deadlines?

- ✔ **Money:** What will this cost? Do you have the resources/cash flow? How will you fund this?

✔ **Effort:** Have you correctly factored in the workloads required to achieve the plan? Will this remove resources from other parts of the business? How will you deal with this?

✔ **People:** Who will do specific tasks? How do you know that they're the best people for the tasks? Have you considered outsourcing to people better suited to do specific project tasks?

✔ **Beliefs & values:** What do you believe about this project that is empowering and supportive? What do you believe about this project that may limit or affect the project negatively? What do you believe that may stop you from honestly committing to the project fully? What would you need to believe to commit fully? Why is the project important to you? How do you ensure that actions taken all meet your values?

✔ **Skills (what we do):** Do you have the skills to undertake the project? Are there skill gaps? If so, when and how can they be bridged?

✔ **Capabilities (how we do it):** Do you have the personal and organisational capability to do the project tasks? If capability gaps are apparent, who by, when and how will they be bridged?

✔ **Environment:** Where will this all happen? Do you have the right environmental setting to complete the tasks?

✔ **PEST (Political, Economic, Social, Technology):** The PEST model is an assessment of microeconomic factors that may affect a project plan. Ask these questions for each PEST category:

- What is the current situation?

- What can you foresee that may change over the time of the project, and how would it affect your plan?

- What actions can you take knowing this?

The categories are:

- **Political:** Tax policy, political stability, labour laws, trade rules and restrictions, trade tariffs and embargoes, environmental laws

- **Economic:** Economic climate, interest rates, exchange rates, inflation rates, funding and grants

- **Social:** Cultural idiosyncrasies, population statistics, educational and career trends

- **Technology:** Technological limits (limited capacity), new ways to automate (the effect on costs, pricing and demand), outsourcing and delivery options (new suppliers or emerging platforms)

✔ **Ecology:** By implementing this plan, what might also be affected by it?

✔ **Legal:** How do you know that you understand the legal implications of this project plan? Do you have the knowledge to comply with the legislation?

✔ **Feedback (key performance indicators):** What are you going to measure to ensure you're on track? How do you know that you're measuring the correct performance indicators? How, when and to whom are you going to present your findings?

✔ **Feed forwards (adaptability):** What are the action steps if you find you're off-track? Who is responsible for taking the decisions and ensuring that they're actioned?

✔ **SWOT:** Examining the strengths, weaknesses, opportunities and threats a business faces is known as a SWOT analysis. It has become a standard section in any business plan presented to investors and is also a useful diagnostic framework when creating a process plan. Each of the components gets its own box in the last row of the Information Grid in Figure 9-2:

- **Strengths:** What is the project's unique selling point? What advantages does the business have over its competitors? What do you do better than anyone else? What do your customers and competitors see as your strengths? How does this project strengthen the business?

- **Weaknesses:** What can you improve? What should you avoid? Where do you perform poorly? What loses business? What is a drain on time, money and effort?

- **Opportunities:** What are the easy opportunities (low-hanging fruit)? What are the opportunities that you haven't even considered yet? What are the opportunities that you may have considered in the past that may now be relevant? What trends are there that may lead to new opportunities?

- **Threats:** What obvious obstacles do you face? What are your plans to address them? What are competitors doing that may be a threat? What are the mission-critical threats that may seriously damage the business, and how will you deal with this? What are the external conditions that may affect the project plan (PEST)?

When considering opportunities and threats, go back through and ask the questions in the PEST categories. Often microeconomic changes lead to problems and potential threats. If clients can foresee a threat, not only can they plan accordingly, but if they can offer a solution to a problem, there is the possibility of a new business opportunity.

The degree of depth that you go into with a client with your coaching questions depends on the scale of vision and complexity of the project plan that delivers the vision. The Information Grid provides a robust enquiry, but of course you're not limited to the questions listed here.

The only thing that never changes is that things constantly change. What may have seemed a great plan at one moment in time may need revision or abandoning. Scheduling in a regular coaching audit and revisiting the plan with the Information Grid as a guide enables clients to assess where are they now, where are they going and how they will get there.

Gaining honest commitment and buy-in

Have you ever been in a meeting where steps were put in place for a project and at the next meeting not much had changed? Of course there could be genuine reasons why targets and objectives had not been met, but it's these project slippages that have knock-on effects and can cause a plan to stall or miss key milestones. For many businesses and projects, this theme is all too common. Often the cause is people's failure to disclose concerns before a project starts.

At the end of each planning meeting, check with clients that:

- ✔ All involved individuals are aware of their allocated tasks and when they're to be delivered.
- ✔ Everyone has voiced a positive commitment and support for the plan.
- ✔ Everyone has voiced any concerns or resistance to the plan.

The questions in the Information Grid (see the preceding section) that reveal factors that may affect the commitment of an individual to honestly and fully engage in a project are 'What do you believe that may stop you from honestly committing to the project fully?' And 'What would you need to believe to commit fully?'

The business has to create the safe environment where individuals feel free to speak up and express themselves, to realise there are no smart or dumb questions and give genuine reasons if they have any beliefs that may stop them from honestly committing to a project.

Pinpointing when NOW is the right time

With a robust high-level plan in place and an honest commitment from all involved, the question is, when do executives do what their name implies – execute decisions and take action? When is the right time to pull the trigger on a project?

Treat this stage as you would going on any journey. Do a last check with your client to ensure that everything is in place, and pay particular attention to the resources needed for the journey. In Chapter 10, we discuss packing for the journey.

One indication that *now* is the right time is when the client demonstrates a sense of frustration, a desire to get on with it. The role of the coach is then to step aside and let the business get on with it.

Assuming that the client is inspired with the vision and has a good plan in place, we suggest adding a little momentum before he starts. Ask the questions, 'Are you really up for this? Are you sure this is right and you wouldn't be better off just letting this go?' A little chiding and provocation and pushing the client back (verbally only) will get pushback, and that's the time to step aside.

It's reasonable for the client to have some apprehension before starting this grand venture, so you need to check whether the apprehension is excitement or a genuine signal that something's missing or has been overlooked. If he's made a thorough check and if all is in place, then *now* is the right time.

Resourcing the Plan

After your client has a solid plan to achieve his vision, you can help him determine the specific details of the plan and what supports need to be in place to carry it out. In this section, we explore techniques for walking and talking through simulations of a plan, looking for where and when resources will be needed and what to do when not all goes according to plan.

When the best resourced plans go wrong (and they will), stop, breathe and calmly look for the silver lining in the situation. Sometimes it's good not to understand the full effects of a crisis and instead have a different perspective to all those around you.

Packing the luggage for the journey

The word 'timelines' refers to our mental ability to code time so we can distinguish between past, present and future events. Patterns are apparent to how people code and represent time in their thinking. This exercise is a great coaching tool to enable clients to explore this phenomena and use it to plan and resource a plan.

Use this Walking through the Plan exercise to literally walk your client through a plan to the ultimate vision. You can break down the plan into smaller chunks and walk him through it in smaller sections. Although this exercise can be done sitting down and in the imagination, it is best done standing up and with plenty of space.

Turning an oversight into a silver lining

In 1997, Steve was directing a project to dismantle a two-track railway that crossed over another two railway lines, underneath which was a two-lane road. Having spent weeks examining the original Victorian construction drawings and hours visualising different scenarios, he finally had a project plan in place. There was a three-day window to dismantle and reconstruct the ageing bridge. Calculations had been made for the quantity of material that had to be removed, the manpower needed and the resources to ensure that the project came in on time.

These projects often come with penalties for non-performance because missing a deadline can have knock-on financial consequences with other contractors standing idle. In this case, there was a £50,000 per hour (or part of) penalty. In these scenarios, Steve always negotiates a performance bonus if he completes his contract early. In this instance, there was a £10,000 bonus for every half hour reduced from the eight-hour contract time.

The vision was to hand over a clean space. The plan was in place as were men, equipment, cranes, excavators and lorries, plus backup in case of breakdowns. Everyone knew their roles and were ready to go. An hour before the railway line was shut down and handed over, one of the lorry drivers approached and casually asked Steve where they were taking all the gravel, iron and brickwork. 'To the usual waste transfer yard', he replied. 'It's a bank holiday. They're closed for three days and aren't open again until Tuesday morning', the driver said.

While calmly walking and thinking what to do next, Steve noticed someone locking the gates of a builders merchant just down the road from the bridge site. He approached the man, who turned out to be the owner, and explained his problem. The owner had a large open yard that was in need of repair, so Steve negotiated to rent the yard over the weekend to temporarily store the materials from the bridge, to clear the yard by Monday and resurface the yard. The result was that the project was completed nearly an hour ahead of time, earning a performance bonus that more than covered the cost of the yard hire, handling the materials twice and resurfacing the yard. It also not only greatly impressed the clients but led to future contracts.

Use the specific language written in the following instructions. Some sentences may seem grammatically incorrect at first glance, but they've been written to create temporal and spatial shifts in the listener's perspective. They come from hypnotic language patterns and, although this experiment does not mean you're hypnotising your clients, the specific words cause them to experience an altered shift in their perceptions of time. Most will feel they've been travelling through time, and for many, their experiences of the time markers when they walk through the steps of the exercise will seem surprisingly real

   1. **Instruct your client to stand and face the open space and to imagine that the spot he's standing on represents the present moment, the now; point behind him and instruct him to imagine that the past is a**

line on the ground running off into the past and then point in front and ask him to imagine that the future extends off ahead of him.

Some people imagine a line, some a road. Allow the client to represent these timelines as he deems fit.

2. **Stand 1 metre in front and just off to the side of his future timeline and ask him to imagine a pleasant event in the future, say one week.**

   It need not be related to the plan. It may be, for example, going out with friends. Always preface this instruction with 'a pleasant event'. You don't want clients to imagine anything challenging or unpleasant at the start of a planning exercise – doing so may put them in an unresourceful state and affect the exercise.

3. **Gesture with your hand and ask him, 'Where do you get a sense that a week in the future is?'**

   He will get you to move farther away or move closer. You'll be surprised when you first do this how exact some people are when instructing you to make adjustments because you're too close or too far away. Make a mental note of the distance along the imaginary timeline (or if there is a carpet on the floor, mark it with your shoe as a reference).

4. **Repeat this exercise for other time markers that are relevant to the project duration.**

   For example, one month, three months, one year, and so on. Choose no more than five time markers.

5. **Instruct him to close his eyes and to relax. Let him know that in a moment you will be touching him on the shoulder or arm and gently walking him with his eyes closed into the future to the first time marker.**

   When you do an exercise that involves asking someone to close his eyes and then touching him, get his permission to do so first.

6. **Gently place a hand on his shoulder or arm and walk him to the first marker.**

   Tell him to imagine he is now one week in the future (or whatever the first time marker is), the project is underway, and ask him to describe what's happening.

7. **Instruct him to notice where he is, what's happening and describe out loud how the project is progressing, to 'say what you see, describe what you hear and to feel what it feels like'.**

   Instructing him to see, hear and feel engages three of the five senses (visual, auditory and kinaesthetic). This sensory prompt will trigger a rich and often vivid imaginary experience for the client. Allow him to speak and jot down notes of keywords to review after the exercise.

8. **Prompt him with other questions and instructions such as:**

   - Notice what's working to plan.

   - What's not working and why?

   - What resources are you using?

   - What could you do with having more of?

   When they have described this first time marker in detail, clients often just go quiet, so prompt with one last question. 'Is there anything else of value you can notice now?' Use the word 'now' because you want them to represent and imagine the 'future-present'.

   Mentally put yourself in the same time marker as the client and use the temporal language you would use if it was a week in the future – keep in the present tense.

9. **Repeat Steps 6, 7 and 8 for each time marker until he reaches the vision or the end of the part of the project selected for the exercise.**

10. **Instruct your client that in a moment you will guide him to take one more step off into one month after the last time marker. You will then turn him around, and with his eyes still closed, he can imagine look-ing back at the end result, the vision, and describe it.**

11. **Walk the client one month after the end of the project, turn him around and ask him to describe how it all went.**

    Let him talk and take notes. Then prompt by asking:

    - What worked?

    - What didn't?

    - What additional resources would you have allocated to the project and when?

    - With hindsight, what would you do differently if you had the chance to go back and do it again?

12. **Instruct your client that in a moment you will walk him back through time, bringing back all the new insights and understandings he has gained with hindsight.**

13. **Walk him slowly back down the timeline, stopping at each time marker and asking him to make any adjustments based on his hind-sight and to nod his head when he is ready to move on.**

    Repeat this process until you get him back to the original starting point, the present, the now. Turn him around to face the future timeline once more and ask him to open his eyes.

14. **Ask him to 'look off into the future now, having had made those adjustments, and notice what's different'.**

    Keep quiet and let him speak.

Common responses from doing this exercise are that firstly people say 'that was weird'; and many feel they've actually lived and walked through the project. Some things to look out for in regard to such responses when taking notes for your client are:

- ✔ **Timeframe changes for the project:** We could have done it quicker, sooner. We need to take longer and give ourselves more time.

- ✔ **Obstacles and roadblocks:** We were stuck, this is how we dealt with it, it was unresolved.

- ✔ **Gaps in knowledge:** We didn't have the skills, capabilities or resources – we would have been better outsourcing to experts or people with more experience.

- ✔ **Changes in motivation:** The vision seems more alluring now or less compelling. If less, then explore why it is less compelling.

Knowing the route and moving in the right direction

During the Independent Perspective exercise in the previous section 'Exercise 2: Detached Perspectives', what commonly comes to light are areas where more detailed planning is required and where obvious milestones or check points exist. We suggest you do the Perspective exercise before going into any detailed planning. Putting the notes generated from the exercise onto a wall chart or white board is a simple and effective way to create a detailed project plan, highlighting options and choices and the milestones for the project.

By breaking any journey down (whether travelling or journeying through a project) into small chunks with checkpoints, it makes what may seem an insurmountable task seem possible. This method is essential for ensuring that you remain on course; and even if you're off course by a few degrees, you're always generally heading in the right direction. Small course corrections along the project journey are easier to make than big adjustments.

The intelligent business also factors key performance indicators (KPIs) into their plans, measuring and evaluating what's working as well as having a strategy for adjusting to the feedback received. Infinite KPIs exist for a business to measure, so selecting which are the most useful is important. The selection will be idiosyncratic to the business you're coaching.

Useful common KPIs to consider are

- ✔ Revenue generated from specific marketing

- ✔ Customer satisfaction

- ✔ Customer lifecycle (paying attention to when and why customers leave)

✔ Measuring procurement and acquisition

✔ Measuring business and project deliverables

Scheduling when to rest and refuel

Even a high-performance Formula One car racing at top speed has to come in for regular pit stops to refuel and repair. During any project lifecycle, the people involved may experience project fatigue unless given the chance to step away from the project. Factor into clients project plans rest and refresh time. Most people report that insights and breakthroughs in ideas happen when they've stopped thinking about an idea or when they're most relaxed, on holiday or have a shower.

Recommend to clients that they schedule in workshops (often unrelated directly to the project) or project breaks so their people can slow down, move to a different environment and get a new perspective on the project. In Chapter 2, we address the value of a third-party perspective and being able to see the woods for the trees.

A great time to stop and rest and refuel is if something goes wrong.

Have you ever been a passenger in a car when the driver has missed a turning? What do most drivers do? They tend to speed up, so now they are heading even quicker in the wrong direction. In business if a project takes a wrong turn, instead of panicking or reacting, you have the opportunity to slow down, rest, refresh, get a clear mind and re-assess the situation.

Use the acronym STADAC as a prompt to

✔ **Stop:** Take some time out to get a clear mind.

✔ **Think:** Enjoy clarity from having a calm mind (head to Chapter 10 for some effective coaching techniques for achieving this).

✔ **Assess:** Review the choices available.

✔ **Decide:** Make the best choice at that moment in time.

✔ **Action:** Take action and get commitment from all involved.

✔ **Check:** Ensure you're getting the results you desire.

Actioning and Reviewing the Plan

What we pay attention to we notice. Scheduling regular project meetings and checking performance against project plans and reviewing KPIs must happen in a regular, structured way for this valuable feedback to be of benefit.

Gathering feedback and feeding forwards

Avoid project meetings being simply a nice time to catch up. You need to ensure that they're productive and coach your clients to use this meeting framework to set the stage for actioning and reviewing a plan throughout its lifecycle.

Structure your project meetings to address the following (see Figure 9-3):

Figure 9-3: Build effective meetings on a solid foundation.

Actions

Realism

Attitude

Clarity

Illustration by John Wiley & Sons, Ltd.

1. **Clarity:** Remind the team of the vision and the values, the 'why' they are there.

2. **Attitude:** Create the space for open, honest, truthful, committed dialogue.

3. **Realism:** Get the facts first, then the opinions afterwards.

4. **Actions:** Ensure that everyone is fully accountable and takes responsibility for his part of the project and the action steps taken after the meeting.

Committing to the action steps is the key to turning feedback into the adjustments that keep a plan on track.

Checking that the plan is on track

In addition to using the meeting framework as an opportunity to coach your clients to test and check the status of a project, ask the questions in Chapter 19 to test and challenge an individual or team to see whether they're on track. Regular checks enable minor course adjustments to be made as the plan unfolds and evolves. Three key indicators to pay attention to are:

  ✔ Time

  ✔ Money

  ✔ Effort

Anyone who has ever had building works done has probably had a negative personal experience of the fact that, of the things humans are notoriously poor at estimating, the worst are the time it takes to complete tasks, the costs involved and the amount of work involved. Allowing contingencies for time, money and effort usually caters for such slippages, but knowing where overruns can seriously damage a business is mission critical.

Knowing when quitting is good

Nick Jenkins, founder of moonpig.com – an online greeting card business – was the owner of a company that made losses for its first five years of trading. He eventually sold the business in 2011 to Photobox for £120 million. All business owners and entrepreneurs recognise the importance of resilience, yet many examples are evident where perseverance and throwing more time, money and effort at a plan does not have a happy ending.

Use Figure 9-4 and the following sailing metaphor to coach individuals, teams and organisations to evaluate when is the right time to change direction or to call it a day. When sailing you have an end destination in mind (vision), you have a course calculated (plan A), which takes into account ever-changing conditions such as wind, weather, tides and currents (represented by the Information Grid).

A sailor is constantly navigating and making course corrections with the destination in mind. There come times when, despite the best will in the world, conditions have changed or are so against him that a course change is needed (a new vision, plan B). If a sailor fails to listen to the feedback, he risks entering danger zone waters when he's too late to change course and may encounter a time when the only option left is the life raft (plan C).

When a business decision is made to alter course, make plan B the new plan A and use all the techniques in this chapter to make sure that the plan is robust and fit for purpose.

A coach's role isn't to make these hard decisions for a client. However, as a coach, you have a moral and professional responsibility to point out to clients if their dogged perseverance may end in them hitting the rocks and sinking the business.

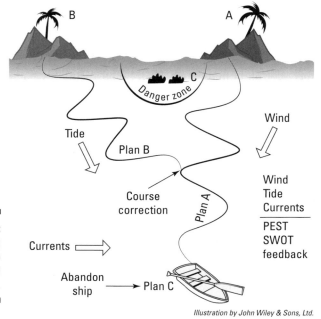

Figure 9-4:
Navigating
your way to
your final
destination.

Acknowledging a job well done

Has anyone ever told you that you were doing a good coaching job? Did you have a spring in your step and a refreshed vigour for your work? Have you ever done some great coaching work and had it gone unnoticed – after all, you're simply doing your job, aren't you?

We are all at times internally referenced, and we check with ourselves that we are doing a good job or making a good decision or are falling short of the mark. We are all at times externally referenced where we check with others whether we are doing a good job or making a good decision.

Even self-starting independent people occasionally need an external verification that they're doing a good job and are on-track. Otherwise, they run the risk of being so internally referenced that they ignore external feedback.

Coach your clients to value external acknowledgement about how they're performing and to sincerely recognise and acknowledge the work done by their colleagues. Keep the team on board; even if they're predominantly internally referenced, let them know that they're valued.

Part III

Tools to Develop the Business Leader's Mind-set

Considering the Definition of Success

What does success mean to you?

- ✔ **Is it stuff?** Stuff is the property you have, the car you drive, the brand of clothes you wear, the watch on your wrist, the credit cards in your wallet.

- ✔ **Is it symbols?** Symbols include the school your children go to, the university you attended, the postcode where you live, the clubs you can get into.

- ✔ **Is it experiences?** Experiences include where you take holidays, the kind of sport you're involved in, the restaurants you go to, the amount of personal grooming you can afford.

What is *your* measure of personal success?

The free article at www.dummies.com/extras/businesscoaching mentoring explains why professionals take on the role of mentor and what benefits they gain from doing so.

In this part . . .

✔ Learn how to develop self-awareness as the first step to self-management, personal growth and performance excellence.

✔ Explore the inner world of thinking and behaviours and how to change them.

✔ Look at how to coach clients to adapt to changing circumstances and explain how to think outside the box and learn from the experience and mind-set of others.

✔ Examine definitions of success and leadership in business and how to coach clients to be more empowered personally and professionally.

Chapter 10

Managing the Inner World of Thoughts and Emotions

*T*he common denominator between all leaders is that they have followers, people are inspired by them and they lead by example. The new thinking around leadership is to encourage individuals to work autonomously as empowered leaders – to be self-starters and self-managers. Among the many qualities that define empowered leaders that we explore in this chapter are their abilities to

✔ Remain calm in challenging situations

✔ Get over setbacks quickly

✔ Be creative and see solutions where others see problems

The abilities to remain calm, creative, and able to see solutions help leaders make well-thought-out decisions. These abilities may come naturally to some, but these qualities and skills can also be coached and taught to others. With practice, they become natural and habitual.

Coaching clients to become more self-aware about how they think and the impact this has on their emotions and behaviours empowers them to manage their inner world and be the leaders that businesses need. In this chapter, you discover how to do just that.

 Think of the techniques in this chapter as lifesaving devices. If a client is struggling to keep afloat, you can throw her a lifeline and give her immediate aid. Remember, though, that if people are struggling to swim, all they need to do is relax and they will naturally float.

Coaches who are new to the profession often go looking for problems to fix. Don't go looking for what's not there – that's making coaching about your own personal needs and not the needs of the client.

Understanding How Humans Think

Understanding the foundations of human thinking and the many factors that influence human information processing is a complex subject. To simplify this subject, here are five concepts that are relevant to the techniques throughout this chapter:

- **The mind stores information holographically.** The brain requires adequate supplies of blood, oxygen and water to access and transmit information. If the brain lacks any of these materials, it affects brain functioning, impairing memory recall and retention and performance. To operate holographically, the brain uses neuro-chemicals, enabling information to be transmitted through the synapses. Neural transmitters such as dopamine and serotonin – which are generated by things like activities that make us happy, regular exercise and exposure to bright light – aid in the flow of information; neuro-inhibiters such as adrenaline and cortisol – which are generated by positive and negative stressors – restrict the information flow.

- **The body cannot distinguish between the mind playing out a vividly imagined experience and having a real one.** Humans can imagine things and experience a wide range of emotional responses related to their thoughts, even though the event may never have happened or are past events. The degree to which someone can vividly imagine may vary from a daydream to a vivid hallucination or anything in between, the emotional response experienced by the body is caused by what neurologists call *synesthesia patterns*, discussed in the next point.

- **The mind overlaps the senses creating synesthesia patterns.** *Synesthesia* is where the brain converts one sense into another. The five senses through which we experience and make sense of the world are visual, auditory, *kinaesthetic* (touch and feel), *olfactory* (smell) and *gustatory* (taste). The senses do not work in isolation. The brain overlaps the senses to create rich experiences of the world. Synesthesia enables humans to feel, hear, taste or smell a visual image, for example, or for a sound to create a kinaesthetic response in the body. Imagine biting into a lemon and you experience the taste and smell. Imagine someone scratching a blackboard with her nails – you experience a feeling.

Fantasy and reality are the same in the brain

Charlie owned a small start-up business and was terrified at the thought of having to pitch his business to clients. During a session, it came to light that Charlie had only presented once before, and it had been a complete disaster because of his nerves.

In the coaching session, Steve asked Charlie in the safety of the coaching room to imagine presenting sometime in the future and to grade his emotions from 0 to 10, where 0 is calm and 10 is terror. Charlie was able to experience a 10

within seconds, just by thinking about presenting. As far as Charlie was concerned, there was no difference between the physical experience and terror of the real event, his recollection of the past event or his imagining what he would experience in any future event.

After coaching Charlie to change the way he thought of the original event, he was able to successfully present to a client with calm, relaxed confidence.

✔ **The mind and body are in a psycho-cybernetic loop.** This term comes from the field of cybernetics, which is the study of how systems interact and regulate themselves. In the context of coaching and specifically managing the world of thinking and emotions, the key principle to remember is that thinking affects the body, and the experience in the body affects the thinking. If this feedback loop is negative, it can lead to a downward spiral. For example, worry leads to the release of stress chemicals and stress and tension in the body; stress in the body leads to worrying. The psycho-cybernetic loop can also be a positive feedback loop where recalling joyful events makes people feel wonderful (releases good-feeling neuro chemistry), and the wonderful feelings make them think that life is great. This is known as a *virtuous circle*.

✔ **Actions are preceded by thought.** If you get up to make a drink, you first have the thought about doing so; otherwise you would sit in your chair and take no action. These thoughts are quick, elusive and seemingly unconscious, yet they happen. The thoughts that pop into your head getting you to take the action are in the form of visual images and internal dialogue, which will be discussed in detail later in the chapter. The quality of your thinking (whether visual or internal dialogue) determines the quality of your actions and what you do or don't do. An extreme example of this process is someone who is an obsessive-compulsive. She thinks the thoughts and then feels compelled to do the activity; the thought loops over, seemingly out of control, compelling the individual to repeat actions. Without the thoughts, she would not do the actions.

We are what we think

A relatively new science called *psycho-neuro-immunology* has appeared on the block, which studies the interaction between thinking and the chemistry of the body in relation to illness and disease. If you remove all the water from yourself and your clients, you will be two piles of chemicals having a coaching session.

Thoughts become chemistry. If a client has a happy thought, she creates a particular chemical cocktail different to when she has depressed, stressed or angry thoughts. The quality of her thinking changes not only the chemistry of her mind and body but her ability to process information.

We become what we practise

How do you get to Royal Albert Hall? The answer is to practise, practise and practise more. Every human behaviour that is practised consciously becomes an unconscious habit at some point. Practice is the 'mother of skill', and every human behaviour is an accomplished skill brought about through repetition.

Self-awareness teaches a client to have a greater range of flexibility and self-management about how she thinks and feels, enabling her to be more creative and resilient.

Regard every human behaviour as a learned skill, whether that's playing the piano, procrastinating, stressful thinking or being resourceful. If a client has practised the skill of depression or worrying, she has clocked up many hours doing negative thinking and simply become good at it. People can't unlearn a skill, just like they can't forget to learn how to play the piano, or to read or tie a shoelace. What you coach her to do is to become aware of what she is doing and, if negative, coach her how to stop doing it. Then replace the old habitual way of thinking with a new more resourceful way of thinking until the new practice becomes habitual.

Coaching a client to become self-aware and to manage her own internal world is truly transformational. Before coaching others to be congruent, 'go there first'. Practise the techniques in this section on yourself so you can lead by example.

Choosing the Most Appropriate State in the Moment

Imagine waking up Monday morning with an exciting day of coaching ahead of you. However, the boiler plays up, so you have a cold shower, the milk is off and no breakfast is available, the train is delayed due to unforeseen leaves on the tracks. You arrive to find that your first client has been called into an emergency meeting and will be 30 minutes late, which has a knock-on effect to the rest of your sessions. While waiting, you check emails and notice a tax demand for money that you know isn't due, and just before you start coaching, you receive a call from the school telling you not to worry, your child isn't badly hurt, but they have taken her to hospital just to be sure. In you go, carrying all this mental baggage with you, prepared to coach a client on dealing with work-related stress and how it affects decisions and performance.

Before coaching any clients, be professional and leave your own emotional baggage outside the coaching room and get into a calm, resourceful state (use the techniques in this chapter to achieve that state). Then check that your client is in a calm, resourceful state before coaching. Appearances can be deceptive. Don't rely on how calm someone appears. Ask her on a stress scale of 0 to 10 (0 being totally calm and 10 being aaaaaargh!), where are you? If her answer is anything over a 2 or 3, coach her to change it; otherwise her state has a negative impact on her ability to fully participate and profit from the coaching session.

We use the term *state* to define both emotions and moods. Emotions tend to be short-lived, often changing within minutes, while moods are emotional states that have been practised over time so they become habitual and sometimes chronic. Good or bad emotions or moods do not exist – in particular contexts, they all serve a useful purpose. Only when they negatively affect behaviours and performance do they become an issue.

Noticing the effects of a negative emotional state

The negative effects of stress on judgement, decision-making, health and performance is well researched and documented. It has a huge cost to business. In the UK, 10.4 million working days are lost to work-related stress, costing £460 million a day due to employee absence and affecting the UK economy by £15.1 billion a year. Making bad decisions and mistakes and stress costs business money and has a toll on an organisation's most valuable asset – its human capital.

What's not so clearly researched are the costs to individuals and businesses of other emotional states that affect performance: depression, procrastination, worry, doubt and the impact that small daily stressful events of life can have a on people. Never underestimate the effect a delayed train can have on performance.

Our emotional state has an effect on how we perceive and react to the world around us and how we behave. A depressed or stressed person sees the world as a depressing or stressful place and acts differently to the same situations and circumstances to the same person when in a happy state. Our ability to perform is said to be 'state dependent'.

Looking at the State Behavioural Model

The State Behavioural Model, shown in Figure 10-1, provides a framework for evaluating how individuals create the quality of their thinking and generate their states (emotions and moods). It provides the basis of a self-awareness and self-care plan. The techniques in this chapter all relate back to this model.

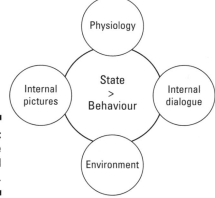

Figure 10-1:
The State
Behavioural
Model.

Illustration by John Wiley & Sons, Ltd.

The model has four parts to explore with clients:

✔ **Physiology:** The impact on posture – how they sit, stand, move and breathe. The next section explains how changing physiology affects thinking and states.

✔ **Internal dialogue:** The impact that self-talk has on states is profound; talk to yourself in nice tonality, and you will feel good; talk to yourself in abusive tones, and you will feel bad. The 'Changing Internal Self-Talk' section later in the chapter explains how we have the power and ability to change our internal dialogue and change the way we feel.

✔ **Internal pictures:** The images and movies people play in their minds have a large impact on their states. These visuals range from idle daydreaming to catastrophic traumatic thinking of an epic proportion. In the later in the section 'Making Mind Pictures That Matter', we explore how you can become the script writer, director and producer of the internal pictures and movies you make in your mind.

✔ **Environment:** External factors such as noise, light, motion, food, drink and drugs affect emotional and mood states. Many people use external environmental means to change internal states, often in unhealthy and dysfunctional ways. Throughout this chapter, we explore ways to manage the inner world of thoughts and emotions so clients need not change the environment in order to feel good.

Always separate the behaviour from the identity of the individual. For example, ask 'What's the problem?' rather than 'What's your problem?' Then find out what clients are saying or imagining to create their experience. They can then be coached to change it.

Your role isn't to coach a client to eliminate or manage all thoughts and emotions like Mr Spock from *Star Trek*. Firstly, make her aware that it's okay to experience the full range of human moods and emotions. Doing so normalises her experience. Then use the State Behavioural Model and the techniques to coach her to see that she has a wide range of choices as to how she thinks and feels at any given moment.

Working with the four F's of flight or fight

Most people recognise the story of others who have studied for an exam. They have read all the texts, done the practice papers and know their subject matter. They enter the exam room, and their mind goes a complete blank. As soon as they leave the exam environment, they give a sigh of relief, and all the information and answers they needed in the exam room come flooding back to them.

This phenomena happens to businesspeople during meetings, networking events, presentations and in the middle of taxing or emergency tasks. It's caused by neuro-endocrine changes in the brain brought about by stress that affects thinking and then behaviour. The phenomena is part of the flight-or-fight survival pattern:

- ✔ **Flight:** Identified by raised breathing levels, increased adrenaline and cortisol levels and heart rates, sweaty palms and a dry mouth as the body prepares to run for the hills.

- ✔ **Fight:** The same physiological indicators as with flight. However, the decision and reaction isn't to run but to confront the perceived threat.

Most people are aware of flight-or-fight patterns, but two lesser-known yet equally impactful patterns are:

- ✔ **Freeze:** In the freeze state, breathing becomes shallow or hyperventilated. Blood and oxygen flow is restricted to the brain, the thinking capacity is reduced and problem thoughts seem to run on an automatic loop.

- ✔ **Flow:** Indicated by a calm, relaxed state and the ability to assess a situation quickly and to make a quick, informed decision and take appropriate action. (Later in the 'Using mindfulness, meditation and the mysterious to support business' section, you discover how to access the state of flow on demand.)

In business (and in most people's private lives) which warrants freeze, flight or fight is quite rare. However, we all have these unconscious programmes available to us if we should ever need them. If you're confronted by a sabre-toothed tiger, you will be thankful for them. The sequence is first to freeze, then flight; fight holds more risk of damage, so for most people fight is an option of last resort. These three patterns can all be triggered by a buildup of smaller events rather than one big trauma or drama; this accumulative effect is what is often overlooked.

Under stress, the brain switches off parts that aren't relevant to dealing with anything other than the immediate perceived problem, which is perfectly fine for dealing with a sabre-toothed tiger, but not for reviewing and coming up with creative solutions to a business problem. Only when the problem is over can people breathe and neuro-endocrine levels return to normal and thinking comes back online, enabling it to make creative solutions.

Coaching clients to recognise whether they're already in or are accessing freeze, flight or fight patterns and training them to change to the state of flow may take some time and practice but is worth it. (See the sidebar 'What does it cost to replace a burnt-out executive' for a real-life example.)

What does it cost to replace a burnt-out executive?

Marie was coaching Adam, a manager for an IT company, to deal with excessive stress and high workload. These things were affecting Adam's performance at work and having an impact on his home life. He was finding it difficult to sleep, had begun to drink too much after work and was taking sleeping pills at night. Adam revealed that his boss was a self-proclaimed 'workaholic' who 'thrived on pressure'. Any expression of being stressed or unable to cope was regarded as a sign of weakness by his boss.

Marie explained the State Behavioural Model to Adam and taught him coping skills to release built-up stress and tensions and to have a quieter mind and calmer body. Over a few weeks Adam noticed he seemed more relaxed, was dealing with the same workload but no longer felt anxious about his work and had cut down on his drinking.

A month after Adam began his programme of self-care, he reported that his boss was off work indefinitely, suffering from 'executive burn-out'.

Knowing that breathing is a better choice than not

The first place to start coaching anyone who is in an unresourceful state is to change her physiology. Most people find changing physiology easy to do, and they notice an immediate change in the way they feel.

To identify the freeze pattern, follow these steps. Where the instructions are to do an action slowly, read *very slowly*. If a client fails to notice any change during the exercise, she did the actions too quickly.

1. **Sit comfortably with your feet flat on the floor and arms by your side facing forwards. Take a moment to relax and notice how you feel inside your body.**

   What you're looking to assess is how awake and aware you feel. Grade this with 0 being completely switched off and 10 being wide awake and aware.

2. **Slowly and carefully, lower your head centimetre by centimetre and notice what happens to the feeling of awareness as you do this.**

   Most people experience a sense of switching off, and as their chin lowers to their chest, breathing becomes shallow. This sensation is often described as 'feeling like shutting down'. Grade the experience again 0 to 10 so you can compare this to the starting assessment.

3. Then, slowly, lift your head back up and notice what happens.

As you do this, you probably experience a sense of being awake, aware of being switched on. You get to a critical point where it feels like a switch has been flicked. People often say something like 'it's like coming back online'.

By lowering the head, you're restricting the breathing and blood supply to the brain and effectively changing your physiology and, by doing so, going into the posture of the freeze pattern. Simply by adjusting your head, you're changing your neuro-chemistry and your state.

Consider how many people work all day, looking down at a screen or keyboard and are inadvertently accessing a stressed state just by their physiology and breathing.

In the section 'If things aren't looking up, looking up helps' is a stress reset technique that you can teach clients to use to come out of switched-off states and access more awake, alert states on demand.

Looking downright depressed is a dismal choice

In Neuro-Linguistic Programming, you find physiological patterns called the eye-accessing cues. The direction and positioning of the eyes enable a trained observer to identify if someone is:

REAL WORLD EXAMPLE

Practise feeling enthused just because you can

During stress management workshops, Steve asks the group to sit as they would if they were depressed. Everyone drops her head and slumps forwards with shallow breathing. They have glum looks on their faces, and they naturally and unconsciously adopt the physiology of the freeze pattern.

Then they're instructed to sit how they would sit and how they would breathe if they were enthused and about to experience the most joyous training experience ever. Everyone unconsciously knows the physiology and posture of enthused excitement. The group all lift their heads, they all put smiles on their faces and they all breathe again. While they're in the enthused excited state, they're instructed to stay in that physiology and try to feel depressed. They cannot do so without changing the physiology.

They're then instructed to sit in the enthused excited state for the rest of the workshop.

✔ Accessing recalled visual (VR) images – imagining a remembered past event

✔ Accessing constructed visual (VC) images – imagining a constructed future or past event (constructing does not necessarily mean someone is lying)

✔ Accessing recalled auditory (AR) information – for example, recalling a piece of music or a conversation

✔ Accessing constructed auditory (AC) information – imagining a conversation that's not happened

✔ Engaging in auditory digital (AD) behaviour – talking to self

✔ Kinaesthetic (K) – accessing internal feelings

Figure 10-2 is shown from the position of the observer looking at the client. The eye-accessing cues appear like this.

Figure 10-2:
The NLP eye-accessing cues.

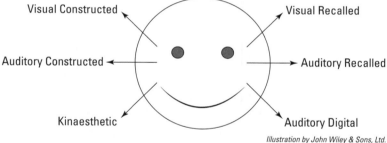

Visual Constructed Visual Recalled
Auditory Constructed Auditory Recalled
Kinaesthetic Auditory Digital

Illustration by John Wiley & Sons, Ltd.

You may have heard the phrase 'I feel downright depressed' or 'I feel downright happy'. These descriptions of the experience are literal where most people (predominantly right-handed people; for left-handed people this may be reversed) look down and to the right to access the feelings inside the body. If they're accessing positive states, such actions are not an issue. Only if clients are accessing unresourceful states do they need to be aware of the importance of changing their physiology.

Make the client aware of the impact that her posture, breathing and where she looks have on her states and behaviours. Awareness is the start of being able to change a habit; as she becomes more aware, she can then interrupt her habitual patterns.

If things aren't looking up, looking up helps

The 7/11 stress reset is a technique developed by Steve Crabb. Steve specialised in coaching clients with therapy-related issues, particularly depression, anxiety, fears, phobias, stress and emotional overload. The technique is designed to be fast-acting and requires little training for it to be effective. It incorporates changes to physiology, breathing and eye direction, which have all been discussed in this section.

The benefits of doing this technique as part of a regular self-care plan are multiple. As a result, clients spend less time in stress-related states, become calmer, clearer-headed, more resourceful and resilient. They begin to experience better sleep patterns, and an extra bonus is that if they practise the technique on public transport, when they roll their eyes upwards they will also be guaranteed a seat on their own!

Follow these steps to try the 7/11 stress reset.

1. **Instruct the client to sit comfortably in a chair, feet flat on the floor and hands relaxed by her side. Ask her to notice whether she has any physical or emotional stress in her body and grade it 0 to 10 with 0 being none whatsoever and 10 being the top amount possible.**

2. **Instruct her to imagine a candle in front of her and to breathe out completely and empty her lungs as if blowing out the candle.**

3. **Then, instruct her to smoothly and easily breathe in fully and deeply through her mouth while pushing the tummy out to the count of seven.**

   This step ensures that the breathing is diaphragmatic and the lungs fully inflate.

4. **When her lungs are full, tell her to hold her breath for a second or two.**

5. **Instruct her to roll her eyes up to the ceiling.**

   Ask her to imagine that she has a pair of sunglasses on top of her head and is attempting to look through them while avoiding tipping her head or neck back.

6. **Tell her to relax and close her eyelids.**

7. **Ask her to softly and smoothly breathe out through her mouth to the count of 11.**

8. **As she breathes out, remind her to relax her jaw and let it hang loose.**

9. **Then, have her relax her body completely loose and limp like a rag doll, starting from the top of her head down to the tips of her toes.**

10. **Ask her to become aware of the difference in her body and grade it 0 to 10.**

    She will almost certainly report a significant shift after doing this technique once. Get her to practise this exercise on an hourly basis.

What happens during the different stages of the technique is the following:

✔ By breathing deeply, the client is coming out of any freeze, flight or fight pattern. The heart monitors the oxygen supply in the blood, and the elevated oxygen triggers a feedback signal to the brain, basically saying to the brain, 'She is breathing again, the sabre-toothed tiger must have left, so switch off the adrenaline. All is well'.

✔ The eye roll upwards stimulates theta waves in the brain, taking the client into a relaxed state.

✔ The jawbone is one of the strongest bones in the body, but during times of stress or threat, the joint can be vulnerable, so stressed people often hold their jaw tight. By relaxing the jaw, the neck muscles and surrounding muscles also relax, releasing tensions.

Coach clients to do this technique hourly for a few days. It has an accumulatively positive effect on the body's neuro-chemistry. Once a day isn't enough for it to have a chemical impact. Use the setup of saying, 'It's a technique that will enable you to feel good for no particular reason, just because you can'.

Changing Internal Self-Talk

We all have internal dialogues. We all talk to ourselves, and there's nothing wrong or weird with that, yet few people appreciate the impact that internal self-talk can have on emotional states, behaviours and results that people get in life.

Try a simple thought experiment. Talk to yourself in a positive, confident voice, motivating yourself to do something positive that will be good for you once done, and notice how it feels when you have done that. Rate how motivated you feel on a motivation scale, 0 being totally apathetic and 10 being totally motivated.

Now use the same words as before, but change the tonality of the internal dialogue to sleepy, tired and bored. Do this for a minute and now notice the difference and grade on the motivation scale 0 to 10.

Now go back to the positive, confident, motivating voice. You will notice that simply changing the tone of voice has an effect on the feelings. This is a synesthesia pattern where the auditory voice creates a kinaesthetic feeling in the body.

Leaders demonstrate confidence and motivation when taking action. A common coaching theme is clients wanting more confidence and motivation when what they're really doing is demotivating themselves or undermining themselves with their own internal self-talk.

In Chapter 6, we discuss language patterns and describe when someone converts a verb action into a noun; these patterns are called *nominalisations*. Motivation and confidence are examples of nominalisations. When someone says, 'I lack motivation' or 'I don't have enough confidence', she's turned the verbs into nouns; the first thing to do is revert them back into verbs – doing so gives clients ownership of the experience. They can now take personal responsibility for what they're doing and do something about it, rather than thinking of motivation and confidence as things (nouns) over which they've no control. To denominalise the nouns, ask the client, 'What is it you're saying or imagining to demotivate yourself?' or 'If you were to do things confidently, what would you be saying or imagining to yourself?'

This process works the same for other common coaching issues such as stress, procrastination, fears and doubts, which are also nominalisations. They're all things people do – people don't have them. People don't have stress, it's not a thing – they do it. Once a client has a new self-awareness of how she talks to herself, she's then in a position to change what she does.

Understanding that it's not what you say, it's the way you say it

In the 1960s and 1970s, it became popular to practise the power of positive thinking and to use positive affirmations; yet for many people, this failed to change the way they felt. Although they were using positive words, many were saying them with a negative tonality and doubting what they said.

Whether the words come from someone else or from our own self-talk, what is said has less of an impact on the mind and body than how it's said. Consider your own life experiences when maybe someone said something where the words meant one thing but the tonality conveyed a completely different message. For example, if someone says, 'Oh, well done' yet the tone is sarcasm, the tonality has the greater impact, not the words.

Many qualities of the internal self-talk can affect the feelings that are created. The following are four to listen out for:

✔ **Volume of voice (or voices):** From a quiet whisper to a bellowing shout

✔ **Speed of voice:** Ranging from slow to fast

✔ **Location:** Whether the voice comes from the front of the head, the back, sides or top of the head has an effect

✔ **Tonality:** Including a wide range from calm, worried, sleepy or angry to sarcastic, happy, irate or loving

To identify your internal self-talk, simply experiment and begin to become aware of the distinctions between the different internal self-talk voices that you use and how these different voices make you feel.

1. **Remember a time when you felt confident about doing an activity.**

   Choose a subject that is also good for you to do. Talk to yourself inside your head in the way you spoke to yourself back then.

2. **Notice how it feels and grade it 0 to 10, with 0 being no confidence and 10 being totally confident.**

3. **Once graded, become aware of the volume and the speed of the self-talk, its location (point to where the voice is located) and tonality of the voice. Make a note of the qualities you use.**

4. **When you have finished the exercise, stand up, walk around, shake your head and break out of the state of confidence.**

Repeat the preceding steps for:

✔ Doubt followed by certainty

✔ Hesitation followed by desire

✔ Stressed followed by calm

You can experiment with other combinations.

After you know how you talk to yourself in a range of internal self-talk voices and how it affects the way you feel, consider where using this knowledge would be useful. Consider the applications for your clients – where they can choose how they talk to themselves in a way that supports the behaviour they want to have.

Making the ridiculous sound ridiculous

Here are two simple yet powerful techniques you can use for yourself and clients to change any negative or limiting internal self-talk by changing the qualities of the voices used.

Ask a client who is unduly stressing herself to first identify how she talks to herself:

1. **Get her to remember a time she was stressing and talking inside her head and tell her to talk to herself in the same way now.**

2. **Ask her to grade the stress 0 to 10.**

   Even when not actually going through the events, people can still experience stress because of the power of their internal dialogue.

3. **Ask her to note the volume, speed, location and tonality of the stress voice.**

   She should change the qualities of the internal dialogue one at a time, as follows:

   • **Volume:** Turn the volume up slightly. (She may experience more stress when doing this.) Then turn it down to a whisper, and then put it back the way it was.

   • **Speed:** Speed up the voice so it's talking so fast she can't make out the words. Then slow it down like a record played at a slow speed, and then put it back the way it was.

   • **Location:** Hold out an arm with thumb pointing upwards, then tell her to imagine moving the voice down the arm till eventually the voice is coming from the thumb talking towards her.

   • **Tonality:** With the voice now coming from the thumb, change the tonality to that of a cartoon character such as Donald Duck or Sylvester the Cat.

4. **Instruct her to stop, break state, stand up and shake her head. Then say, 'Now, try in vain to talk to yourself in the same old stressed voice, but notice what's different now'.**

   You need to use these exact words because they almost guarantee that she will be unable to get the old stressed voice back.

5. **Have her grade how it now feels and compare to when she started the exercise.**

   Some people experience just a slight shift, in which case you can do the exercise once more and the shift will happen.

Many experience a complete change in the voice. People often say, 'It sounds ridiculous now and has no effect'. The brain has the ability to rewire and reorganise itself – scientists call this process neuro-plasticity. With this exercise, you're working with the client to scramble the old neural pathways, making it difficult and sometimes impossible for someone to again talk to herself using the stressed internal voice.

If clients are used to saying ridiculous things to themselves, have them do it in a ridiculous voice and it won't feel the same anymore.

This exercise involves scrambling the internal self-talk. Follow Steps 1 through 3 in the previous exercise so you can identify the negative or limiting internal self-talk. Then instruct your client to do the following:

1. **Slow down the internal voice, saying one . . . word . . . at . . . a . . . time . . . with . . . gaps . . . between . . . each . . . word.**

2. **Say the same things this time with the gaps and streeetch . . . oooo-out . . . eeeeevry . . . siiiiingle . . . wooooord.**

3. **Spaaace . . . aaaand . . . streeeeetch and give every word a cartoon-like tonality.**

4. **Stop, break state, stand up, shake her head.**

5. **Then say to your client, 'Now try to talk to yourself in the same old voice but notice what's different'.**

Again, clients find it virtually impossible to talk to themselves in the old negative way simply because they've given instructions to the brain to reorganise.

Explain to clients that what they've been doing is the equivalent of taking a CD and scratching it so it's difficult to play it the way they used to.

Being kinder and nicer matters

The above techniques are all about changing negative self-talk. Here is a simple technique that can enable a client to find out how to talk to herself in nicer tonalities. We recommend you only do this technique on a one-to-one basis unless you're experienced in dealing with someone possibly becoming emotional in front of others.

This exercise is about being nice to yourself:

1. **Scramble the negative self-talk using either (or both) of the two techniques just given.**

2. **Tell the client to imagine sitting in front of her is a young woman who is stressed/lacks confidence/lacks motivation, whatever the negative self-talk is that you're working with.**

3. **Instruct her to talk inside her head nicely and kindly to this woman in a way she would if she were sincerely encouraging and supporting someone she cared deeply for.**

4. **Tell her to point to where the kind, loving, supportive self-talk is, and notice the volume, speed and tonality.**

    When she does this, ask her how it feels hearing this voice? The answer is always in the positive.

5. **Then say, 'Now I want you to realise that the person sitting in front of you is you. So keep talking to yourself with kind, loving support and perhaps this is something for you to practise on a daily basis'.**

If someone does get emotional, let her have her moment, sit quietly, remain calm and when she is done, ask what happened. For many people, this may be the first time they have spoken to themselves in this way, and it can cause an emotional release. Later in the chapter, we discuss what to do should a client want to discuss (or demonstrate) therapeutic issues beyond your coaching skills or remit.

Making Mind Pictures That Matter

You have probably heard people say these phrases:

- ✔ 'I can't see the future clearly. I need some clarity'.
- ✔ 'Things are overwhelming me. I can't see the way forwards'.
- ✔ 'I keep dwelling on the past. I can't seem to put it behind me'.
- ✔ 'I don't see myself doing that or I see myself doing that'.

Take what people say as a literal description of their experience and you start to see how people are thinking inside their minds. These phrases mean what they literally say. When people say, 'I don't see myself doing that', they're unable (yet) to make a picture in their mind of themselves doing the activity.

We all make pictures in our minds, holographically projecting these images outside so we can see them. Some are called *cue pictures* because they instruct us to do activities. For example, when someone says, 'Oh, I've just remembered I have to call someone', the mind has presented an image, almost as if a to-do reminder on a computer pops up to prompt the person to make the call.

The following are characteristic of the pictures we make in the mind:

- ✔ The images can for most people be distinguished from reality. Some emotionally charged images can feel real. However, there are people whose mind images appear as hallucinations and seem as real as reality.
- ✔ Some people are more aware of their mind images than others, and some are better at manipulating and managing than others. Consider

brilliant architects or designers. They're able to conceive how a space would look after they've constructed a building or laid out furniture in a particular way.

✔ The images are often short-lived and fleeting because the nerves in the eye are constantly vibrating in order to process incoming light and to make sense of the world. The projected images also flicker on and off and seem transitory.

This exercise is about becoming aware of your internal mind pictures. Imagine your front door and now point to where the key goes. Give the projected image a number based upon how real it seems (0 being unreal and 10 as real as if you had your door in front of you). The answer isn't right or wrong as to how real it seems. Now imagine the texture of the door and notice what this does to your perception and measure of reality. Most people experience it becoming more real. Then imagine the door's just been painted (or varnished if you have a wooden door) and again reassess the measure. By adding in extra senses (kinaesthetic and olfactory), images tend to seem more real.

What you're observing is a holographic image projected out. When you do this exercise with clients, you're giving them an experience of what is meant by mind pictures. They aren't real, are ephemeral, are projected out and have a profound effect on how people behave and feel.

Getting distance from the situation

Mind pictures come with picture qualities that affect the impact they have on people's feelings. These qualities are known as submodalities. Here are a few key visual submodalities:

✔ Location in space, size and distance from the observer

✔ Associated (in the image) or disassociated (being an observer of the image)

✔ Still picture or moving

✔ Colour or black and white

✔ Two-dimensional (2D) or three-dimensional (3D)

Here are two simple techniques to enable clients to manage their own mind pictures. Empowered leaders can put things out of their mind so they can see the bigger picture. These techniques can be used to get over poor performance, bad experiences, mistakes and stress.

Practise these exercises on yourself first, working with good feelings, before using them with clients so you have a personal experience of the effects of changing submodalities.

Follow these instructions to feel amazing for no particular reason:

1. **Remember a time when you really enjoyed a pleasurable experience.**

   See what you saw, hear what you heard and notice how you feel now and give it a number. On a scale of 0 to 10, choose something 8 or higher to work with. Even though you aren't in the experience, you'll still recall and experience some of the positive emotions associated with the event. You will feel good.

2. **Point to where the image is and notice its location, its distance from you and its size.**

   Are you associated or dissociated? Is it still or moving? Is it colour or black and white? Is it 2D or 3D? Now, let's experiment and notice what happens to the feelings when you do each of these changes.

3. **Reduce the size and move it farther away.**

   If an associated image, step out and see the event as an observer would; if colour or black and white, drain the image so it becomes translucent; if a movie, make it still; if 3D, make it 2D. Notice what happens to the emotions. They will have reduced.

4. **Put the submodalities back to the original.**

5. **Increase the size slightly, step into the image, become associated with the experience, turn up the colour (if black and white, add colour), make sure it's a movie.**

   Notice what's happened to the emotions. They will have amplified and may even be more intense than when you first started or even had the experience.

This exercise is call Out of Sight, Out of Mind.

Use this with a client who keeps dwelling on an event and you think it would be useful for her to put it to the back of her mind and get on with things. Before doing this exercise, check with the client that she wants to change the way she remembers an event. Some people will want to leave things just as they are, and that's their choice. If she agrees to do the exercise, before changing any submodalities, ask her to consider what positive things she can learn from the event. Even negative experiences teach us something. Start by using the door example earlier so she is familiar with what you mean by mind pictures.

If working with a client to diminish overwhelm, stress or upset, only work with issues up to a scale of 8 out of 10 until you get more experience. Do not work with trauma or therapy issues unless you have received formal training. See the section on 'Identifying when therapy is the answer'.

1. **Instruct her to remember the event and grade it on a scale of 0 to 10.**

   See what she saw, hear what she heard and notice how she felt, then notice the predominant emotion and on a scale of 0 to 10 give it a number.

2. **Tell her to point to where the image is and notice its location, its distance from her and its size.**

   Is she associated or dissociated? Is it still or moving? Is it colour or black and white? Is it 2D or 3D?

3. **Instruct her to reduce the size and move it farther away, to step out and see the past event as an observer, and to freeze the image to a tiny still picture and drain the image so it becomes translucent.**

   It will have already changed to a 2D image.

4. **Quickly ask her to close and open her eyes, making the picture black then white, black then white. Tell her to do this rapidly for a minute.**

5. **When she has followed the instructions, use these exact words 'Try to recall that past experience but notice what's different now'.**

Clients find it virtually impossible to retrieve the old memory in the same negative way. They report that it's now farther away and looks irrelevant and has no emotions. Clients have, with their own thinking, given the brain instructions to literally 'get some distance from the event'. Note though that on some occasions, you may need to do this exercise twice with a client.

Consider the applications for this technique with business clients, which can include:

✔ Getting over a bad presentation

✔ Dealing with bullying in the workplace

✔ Moving on from a mistake

Focusing not on that but this

Great leaders focus not on the problems but on the solutions. They keep the bigger picture in mind, have clarity of vision and make good decisions based on the information to hand. All these phrases tell us about the inner world of excellence and what they focus on. The following exercise reorganises the brain to keep on a positive track and to focus on the desired outcome of any situation.

This exercise is called Swish Pattern. Ask the client to think of an event that didn't go the way she wished it had. If she had the chance to do it again, with hindsight would she want to behave or act differently?

1. **Tell her to point to where the image is and notice its location, its distance from her and its size.**

   Is she associated or dissociated? Is it still or moving? Is it colour or black and white? Is it 2D or 3D? We call this the 'past image'.

2. **Do a break state: Have her stand up and shake herself out before doing the next part.**

3. **Instruct her to imagine a large screen called her 'success screen'.**

   On this, ask her to see herself disassociated, in colour and in a movie, handling the situation the way she wished it had gone. She should create a short movie of success and edit the movie until she is happy with the outcome. We call this the 'success movie'.

4. **When she is satisfied the 'success movie' is the best it can be, tell her to shrink it down to the size of a postage stamp.**

5. **Tell her to bring back up the 'past image' and position the postage stamp-sized 'success movie' in the bottom right-hand corner.**

   Ask her to do this step quickly. Tell her to push the 'past image' off into the distance over the horizon, have it get smaller, so tiny it becomes a speck and flicker it on and off, on and off and then quickly pull open the postage stamp 'success movie' so it becomes big, bright and colourful.

   Do this a few times, ending with the 'success movie'.

   Each time, it gets more difficult to recollect the original 'past image', which is exactly what you want to happen.

6. **Instruct her to 'now think about the event'.**

   The brain automatically retrieves the version of 'success movie'. Effectively, you have now installed a new way to think in relation to the event.

Go there first – practise on yourself before using these techniques with clients. Some of the techniques may seem silly, but they're not stupid. They retrain and imprint the mind to think in resourceful ways.

Changing the Internal World by External Means

The environmental part of the State Behavioural Model is the path of least resistance for many people. Rather than learning how to change state by managing physiology and thinking, they simply reach out for external chemistry in the form of food, drink and drugs to change internal chemistry.

Self-medication does not deal with the presenting problems that are the causes of dysfunctional behaviours. Self-medication is simply a coping mechanism. Being able to manage the inner world, the way clients think and feel, empowers them to cope better with the external world.

When an exorcise is the best exercise

Margaret was the director of a graphic design company who was experiencing difficulty getting her business out of the early growing stages of simply surviving. She had three staff members and struggled with confidence whenever seeing clients or attending network events.

Steve asked Margaret to point to her head and tell him where the criticising internal dialogue was coming from. She pointed to the top and front of her head.

'What do you say to yourself and what is the tonality you use when you think about attending client meetings or networking events?' Steve asked.

'I don't say anything. He says it to me and says I'm worthless and useless and have nothing worthy to offer,' Margaret replied.

At this point, Steve had a voice inside his head saying, 'Ah oh!'

'Who is he?' Steve asked.

'It's the devil,' Margaret said.

Steve paused the coaching session and asked Margaret if she wanted to deal with this issue of the devil criticising her. With years of therapy

experience, including working with clients with schizophrenia, Steve was in a position to assist Margaret. Although Margaret had not seen the doctor, had she revealed this internal self-talk to her GP, she would no doubt have been diagnosed as schizophrenic and put on a course of medication.

Now, some coaches reading this may suddenly acquire an internal voice saying, 'If clients think they talk to the devil, then coaching's not for me'. Rest assured, after 15 years of coaching thousands of people, this has only ever happened twice.

Since the age of eight, Margaret had talked to herself in a harsh, self-critical voice that, over time, she had begun to associate with the devil and not her own internal dialogue.

With Margaret's permission, the work took a few hours of coaching (therapy) to pull apart and scramble the negative dialogue. Over a few days she learned to talk to herself in a nicer, kinder, more loving and supportive tonality. She was now free to show up at meetings with confidence and to be the business leader she was always capable of being.

Identifying when therapy is the answer

The techniques and concepts covered in this chapter deal with self-awareness and self-management, empowering all individuals to acquire the qualities and characteristics of self-leadership. While coaching clients to manage their thinking and emotions, you may encounter extremes that are beyond your training and experience. As tempting as it may be to offer respite and relief, you must learn to recognise where the limit of your skill set is as well as the limit of your brief time with the client.

Recognise whether you're out of your depth and, if need be, call a halt to a coaching session. You're always best to be honest with clients. As you build trust with them, they often reveal personal habits, behaviours or characteristics that go beyond your remit and abilities. Don't feel disgrace in admitting that you aren't trained or able to assist with an issue. Find experienced, competent people who can deal with therapy issues so you can always refer clients on to the right people.

Presenting problems to be aware of and to refer on include:

- ✔ Clients who hallucinate auditory or visually and find it difficult to distinguish between hallucination and reality
- ✔ People addicted to substances – food, drink and drugs
- ✔ Clients suffering from post-traumatic stress disorder
- ✔ Clients diagnosed with bipolar or who haven't been diagnosed, yet demonstrate large mood swings between euphoria and depression
- ✔ Suicidal clients
- ✔ Clients who exhibit violent or aggressive behaviour

You must always be of service to your clients. However, always put your own physical well-being first. If you're ever at risk or feel intimidated, bring a halt to a coaching session. We also recommend that in your trading terms and conditions, you include a clause for terminating a coaching arrangement if you receive any form of abuse from a client, whether physical or verbal.

Using mindfulness, meditation and the mysterious to support business

Any interventions that help with stress, depression and addiction are impressive. Introspection promotes psychological flexibility, awareness, resilience, job performance, better decision-making, reduced absence rates and the ability to learn new tasks. No wonder businesses are interested in developing leadership programmes that actively promote these skills.

Mindfulness is defined by the National Health Service as an 'evidence-based step' for better mental health – paying more attention to the present moment, to your own thoughts and feelings and to the world around you.

Until recently it was a term confined to Buddhist texts and meditation retreats, part of a spiritual path to awakening. The practice is no longer seen as simply spiritual or a New Age, tree-hugging fad and is rapidly being welcomed into executive boardrooms. The list of blue-chip businesses that have adopted mindfulness programmes continues to grow and includes well-known companies such as Apple, Google, Ikea and Sony. Apps and web courses on mindfulness proliferate, as do reports on new ways in which the practice can do good and benefit the individual and the organisation.

The basis of mindfulness and meditation in its many forms is to enable individuals to achieve a greater self-awareness and to quieten down the hectic mind and allow themselves to be more present and in the moment.

Many similarities exist between the mindfulness approach and that of 'flow', a term coined in 1975 by Hungarian psychologist Mihaly Csikszentmihalyi, one of the founders of positive psychology. He noted that the act of creating seemed at times more important than the finished work itself. He was fascinated by what he called the *flow state*, in which the person is completely immersed in an activity with intense focus and creative engagement.

Csikszentmihalyi identified five factors of flow:

✔ Intense and focused concentration on the present moment

✔ Merging of action and awareness

✔ A loss of reflective self-consciousness

✔ A sense of personal control over the situation or activity

✔ A distortion of temporal experience

Flow is the fourth choice in the flight and fight patterns. If you look at the factors identified by Csikszentmihalyi, you see why the flow state is such a useful state to practise entering on demand, not just in stressful situations but whenever you and clients want to perform at optimal bests.

Follow these instructions and experience mindfulness, being present, in the now and in the state of flow all in one simple exercise.

1. **Stand up, feet shoulder width apart, facing forwards.**

2. **Quieten down the internal dialogue by saying out loud in a soft whispering voice, 'shh, shh, shh, shh, shh, shh' (six short) and then 'shhhhh, shhhhh, shhhhh, shhhhh, shhhhh, shhhhh' (six long).**

   The mind quietens down. Let it stay quiet and allow any thoughts that might drift in to simply drift off.

3. **Do the 7/11 stress reset exercise described in the earlier section 'If things aren't looking up, looking up helps'.**

   You are now standing perfectly physically relaxed with a quiet mind.

4. **Imagine extending in front of you at chest height from left to right a line that represents time.**

   The past is to the left, and the future is to the right. Immediately in front of you at heart level is the present moment, the now.

5. **Reach out with your arms at shoulder width and imagine taking hold of the timeline and quickly bending it by pulling back with your hands to create a point in front, with the past going behind you to the left at 45 degrees and the future behind you to the right at 45 degrees.**

6. **Slowly pull this line inside of you so the present moment is now in the middle of your body.**

7. **Let your hands drop to your side and relax in the present for a moment.**

This technique uses timelines (see Chapter 9) and visualisation to reorganise how you process a quiet mind and being present. Many people experience a sense of quiet stillness, of time slowing down, of being aware yet detached, all of the characteristics of flow. Use this and coach your clients to use it whenever they want to access the state of flow.

Chapter 11

Helping Leaders Recognise 'I Did It My Way' Isn't the Best Epitaph

In This Chapter

▶ Building credibility by acting authentically

▶ Embracing adaptation

▶ Thinking purposefully to get results

▶ Managing ambiguity

How a business is perceived is a reflection of how it is led and managed. Leaders who are incapable of taking the views of others into account can literally run their business into the ground. Those who bring great people into their leadership teams and who are receptive to new ideas create sustainable organisations. In a fast-changing world, businesses need to be able to adapt and quickly. Leaders need to be self-aware, able to manage in a range of conditions and good at recognising when their own ego may be getting in the way of making the right choices for the business.

This chapter highlights some of the ways you can avoid the curse of blind faith in 'my way' thinking if you're a business leader and how coaches can help leaders create a healthy legacy in business.

Recognising that Inflexibility Sometimes Leads to Extinction

Adaptable organisations embrace flexibility, and the bigger they are, the more decentralised they need to be to remain successful. Adaptable organisations are comfortable with chaos, trial and error. They're comfortable with making mistakes and risk-taking.

The desire to succeed isn't the same as ruthless ambition

Bernard Arnault, the CEO and chairman of Louis Vuitton who created the group through acquisitions in 1987, is known for his desire to win. He's not a celebrity businessman and seemingly never described as a ruthless person, even though his acquisition strategies may be. In a recent interview for the *Telegraph*, he denied that his drivers were money and power, saying, 'What feels good is choice. Having the freedom of choice. The only thing that is imposed on me professionally speaking is my own long-term vision of things'. When asked for the single professional moment he would like to relive, he replied, 'The moment I knew that I would be able to buy Dior. . . Right then, I knew that I was going to build the biggest luxury company in the world'.

Arnault has a good 'My way' story that he created by seeing products through the eyes of the customer, bringing in new creative talent, creating a strong board, dominating the market and presumably taking good advice. He's created an enviable business legacy.

Not many of us will be coaching a CEO with Arnault's net worth, but the principles of creating successful business and legacy are in Arnault's story. Clear about what drives him (choice and desire to succeed), he's created a group that reflects his drivers (a variety of business holdings and enough variety in the range of businesses to handle poor results and ride out economic downturns). He's taken in new talent and created new products to attract new customers in new markets without compromising the look and feel of the brands under the group's umbrella.

If you watch a game show, you'll see human behaviour in relation to risk appetite writ large. Any game involving risk and money normally sees participants willing to gamble a decent amount of money in the hope that they will gain a larger amount, even though they take the risk of losing what they already have. Others adopt a more utility-based approach, which sees them keeping the banker's offer because the amount is more than they could ever hope to have and they fear losing that rather than doubling their money. It's no different in business or the stock market. A business without any risk appetite is a static business.

Knowing that process and product innovation requires adaptive leadership

CEOs and senior leaders hold the big picture. They can see how the mosaic of their organisation and their industry fits together. For an organisation to function, the processes, systems, structure and flow of ideas need to work, but it's the ability of leaders to articulate what they want and why that creates the glue and avoids the bits breaking off. Leaders who don't explain why well begin to look like 'because I said so' leaders. Popping a copy of *How to Win Friends and Influence People* in their Christmas stocking is unlikely to change them. Personal insight comes through personal reflection and application of learning.

The degree of adaptation at the organisational level depends on the type of organisation, economic conditions and the demands of their stakeholders. The arts offer great examples of this. Museums and art galleries have had to adapt to survive due to changes in arts funding and changes in customer demand.

Adaptation requires that leaders are confident in both identifying and taking opportunities, in trial and error and in mistake making. Obviously, the cost of risk taking has to be at a level the business can tolerate. It also requires that people be given freedom to act and be trusted to act in the best interests of the organisation. Leaders need to be able to trust people to deliver and acknowledge contributions. An overly controlling leader can get into difficulty and become more of a hindrance than an enabler if he doesn't learn to step back a little.

How even the most traditional organisations adapt

The Victoria and Albert Museum, while having an amazing traditional art and design collection, has increased its range of ticketed contemporary exhibitions. The recent Alexander McQueen exhibition saw nearly half a million visitors.

Another iconic London attraction, Westminster Abbey, now has a head of customer experience. With its 1.2 million visitors each year and a relatively smaller proportion at 70,000 coming to worship each year, you can see why. The Abbey receives no government funding and relies on public entry fees and commercial hire of its various premises. It's learned to adapt. In its 2014 report, its receiver general stated, 'We have for the first time established a marketing function, with its initial responsibility to even out the pattern of visiting to the Abbey between the quieter and busier months and to increase the proportion of visitors who come to us from the UK rather than overseas. Over nine-tenths of our income comes from tourism. That will always be an uncomfortable proportion, and we continue to look for ways to diversify'.

Checking risk appetite to temper or grow ambition

Loads of risk-related management tools are out there: from Porter's five forces, which help you look at the impact of various external factors on the business, through to risk matrix analysis to help you consider the relative impact of different risks and how to manage, mitigate or tolerate them. Equally, using simple SWOT (strengths, weaknesses, opportunities and threats), PEST (political, economic, social and technical), force field analysis and scenario planning exercises can help organisations identify the risks that may impact. These planning tools are designed to help a business explore its position and in particular the impact of various risks and opportunities:

- **Porters five forces:** Any industry is influenced by the power of suppliers and buyers, the threat of new entrants and of substitute products, and the degree of competitive rivalry in the market.

- **SWOT:** Examines the relative strengths, weaknesses, opportunities and threats in a business, a product or new idea.

- **PEST:** Explores the political, economic, social and technical factors that impact or may impact a business.

- **Force field analysis:** Considers the pros and cons of a specific change in the business or an idea.

- **Scenario planning:** Looks at a range of possible futures based on known driving forces, conditions and risks. Once these are articulated, the scenarios can be explored and draft plans developed to assess their viability.

Imagine that you were coaching a senior leader or business owner. Depending on the size of the organisation, he needs to be heavily involved in developing a risk matrix or he has a team of leaders who would feed that information upward for consideration. Assume the organisation has undertaken a risk analysis where likelihood and consequence have been identified using a red, orange, green light system (see Figure 11-1).

Senior leaders are mostly concerned with red risks, with knowing that risks are being handled and that reporting up the line is robust.

Helping a leader critically examine his own ideas using a risk matrix can help him see his idea more objectively before acting on it. Using the matrix, he sees how much risk his 'my way' thinking might create and whether the business can actually tolerate it. Take whatever matrix your client has or work with the matrix shown in Figure 11-1. If he believes he is the only one whose opinion counts, help him see the contribution of others. Use the simple risk matrix overview and ask him to look at all the red risk areas. Then ask him to transfer those areas to the overview sheet and walk you through who is leading on what. Help him to imagine how he could handle these risk areas on his own if the person who holds the lead overview or the operational responsibility weren't there. Would he know what had to be done? Would he know what the processes are in his organisation that support the handling of that risk and how to handle the situation presented by the risk?

Figure 11-1:
A risk matrix helps leaders determine the likelihood of a risk occurring and possible consequences of unwanted outcomes.

			Consequence				
			How severe could the outcomes be if the risk event occurred? →				
			1 Insignificant	2 Minor	3 Significant	4 Major	5 Severe
Likelihood	What's the chance of the risk occurring? ↑	5 Almost certain	5 Medium	10 High	15 Very high	20 Extreme	25 Extreme
		4 Likely	4 Medium	8 Medium	12 High	16 Very high	20 Extreme
		3 Moderate	3 Low	6 Medium	9 Medium	12 High	15 Very high
		2 Unlikely	2 Very low	4 Low	6 Medium	8 Medium	10 High
		1 Rare	1 Very low	2 Very low	3 Low	4 Medium	5 Medium

Illustration by John Wiley & Sons, Ltd.

We've given an extreme example in Table 11-1 to illustrate the point. You want the leader to take a reality check on his relative power and to see the value in the contribution of others.

Ask him to consider how he can acknowledge the role of his direct reports and their teams for managing the red risks. You want to help him get some perspective on the role he plays in leading through other people. Help him see that adaptable, agile organisations need the senior leadership to take the overview rather than take decisions down in the detail.

Table 11-1		Simple Risk Diagnostic				
Risk Identified (describe it)	**Likelihood of Risk Occurring (definite, likely, 50-50, unlikely)**	**Consequence if It Does Occur (critical, moderate, negligible)**	**Handling Strategy (mitigate, manage, ignore)**	**Who Maintains Overview? (initials)**	**Who Handles Operationally? (initials)**	**Reporting Timeframe (update and review dates)**
Possible civil war in xxx market	Likely	Critical	Mitigate – repatriate staff in next two months, move office to India, close operation, retain local agents	PB – lead on planning and finance ST – lead on repatriation AY – lead on office move	IW – finance AS – staff issues TY – agent issues ER/TD – office moves	Weekly – overall plan Daily – local situation

Being Willing to Ask for Help When Out of Your Depth

Everyone hits a little wall of conscious incompetence in life – that space where the realisation dawns that we don't know something we need to know or aren't as competent as we thought. Mentors with more experience of business or a specific area of expertise can really support people here. A good mentor may be able to help a coach identify what he doesn't know about developing his practice and help him plug the gaps. A mentor may be able to identify a learning plan and set up an accountability check-in to keep the coach on track. It's advisable to have a framework and to have the business owner/coach record his progress and challenges because this framework helps the mentee to recognise patterns and consolidates learning.

A learning plan may look something like Figure 11-2.

To keep a mentee on track and maintain momentum, you may want to introduce a weekly self-review. You can use an 'accountability check-in' document like this. Marie uses this document when mentoring coaches in her own practice. It's adapted with permission from a format used by Steve Chandler, author and coach. To use this format for yourself, simply use the numbered paragraphs; the Mentee/Mentor paragraphs illustrate how the questions may be answered.

Mentoring Plan

Mentor	Mathew Green	Mentee	Robbie Burns
Date	July 2015–December 2015		

Mentee Learning Goal

To learn how to develop a training strategy for the leadership team

How will the mentoring be delivered?

4 x 1-hour mentoring sessions face to face during the next 6 months with email check-ins and mentor email support.

Proposed Mentoring Outline

Learning mini goals	Resources e.g. books, podcasts, individuals, meetings, training	Target date
RB will understand the elements involved in developing a comprehensive training plan for senior staff.	MG to share experience of developing plans in OT Inc. and the Chocolate Factory. To outline the process of developing a training-needs analysis and the elements required. RB to establish the outline and prepare a presentation to the team on the proposed way forward.	July-Sept
Consider key stakeholders and strategies for gaining support from key individuals.	Identify internal stakeholders and anticipate objections and supporters. Discuss appropriate strategies for gaining sufficient support and keep the CEO and VP of HR advised.	Aug-December
Direct learning and reading on training-needs analysis and training design.	MG to recommend books, podcasts and a training course on training-needs analysis and training design.	July-November

Illustration by John Wiley & Sons, Ltd.

Figure 11-2: A sample mentoring plan.

Mentoring Accountability: Nadine Shaw, Shaw Coaching

Date: 22 February 2016

1. **Inspired actions I have taken/experienced in my coaching and business since our last discussion.** (Inspired *actions* are actions that fill me with energy or make me feel alive.)

   Mentee: Called six people in my coaching pipeline, had four conversations and converted one into a paying client.

   Mentor: *Wooo hooooooooooo!!!* What are you going to do to celebrate this achievement? How will you acknowledge it?

   Mentee: Invoiced FR and chasing up for feedback and testimonial.

   Mentor: Yes, and notice how much time these processes take from invoice to payment as this is good noticing for you to consider in terms of the balance of your cash flow and the balance of the work you take on. (I am suggesting you think about this a little bit rather than make it a huge focus. This is about working on the structure of your business.)

Mentee: I've been drafting my value add. I think the purpose is for me to be comfortable with my offering and able to say it confidently.

Mentor: *Yes!* We can practice this when we meet next time if you wish.

2. **Breakthroughs or learnings: What have I realised about myself, others, my situation that is important for me going forward?**

Mentee: Feeling a bit underwhelmed with my training offering to lawyers in the first 30 days and want to review it. I just don't enjoy doing it.

Mentor: This is great noticing. What would make that a more exciting offering for you and for them? How could you use that material in a different way or adapt it for a different group?

3. **Check-in: What's irritating and grating, and what's going great guns?**

Mentee: Booked to see Matthew Jones this week, also seeing MD of Agile Learning and looking forward to both.

Mentor: Look at how brilliantly you are doing at getting into conversations with people to talk about possible work. You are doing great.

4. **Explore: What's happening in my business, and what is working? Where am I with the outcome goals and the process goals I defined for myself?**

Outcome	*Update*
1. A larger network to increase my opportunities for coaching and consultancy work.	**Mentee:** No new progress this week. **Mentor:** Notice that you are arranging meetings and this is the first very important step towards this outcome.
2. Three new paying coaching clients within the next two months.	**Mentee:** Flyer out to design, will use on web page and organise delivery in locality. **Mentor:** Brilliant and you have already secured one!
3. Three consultancy clients within the next four months.	**Mentee:** Planned work secured with Every Work and Consultancy Inc. Will ask both for feedback once completed. **Mentor:** Great! Keep going, and as you said, build these two relationships even more as we discussed to secure further contracts.
4. Increase skill in winning and delivering consultancy assignments and coaching clients.	**Mentee:** Not sure if I've progressed here. **Mentor:** You are doing this. Everything we've discussed supports this.

5. **Challenge: What's next and where's the stretch? How does business/ life feel right now?**

Mentee: Sort out flyer to get coaching clients. Carry on looking for paying coaching clients.

Mentor: What would happen if you stopped looking for clients and simply put the flyer out there and had some more conversations?

6. **Articulating desired intention: What would make the week ahead wonderful for me and my practice/business is . . .**

Mentee: WA will sign up for a coaching programme. I receive some calls from the flyer drop.

Mentor: Try to make your intentions more specific – for example, by the end of the week, I want a minimum six-month coaching commitment with WA and seven calls from the flyer drop.

Deploying the Right Thinking to the Right Problem

Busy, busy, busy . . . sometimes we're too busy in business to think in a straight line or to think in wiggly ways when the need arises. We go off-track, and in doing that we can forget that other people have thoughts and ideas to contribute too. The majority of our thinking has a purpose and yet may not be focused in the right way.

Thinking purposefully

Purposeful thinking is about creating thinking awareness. It's about understanding the quality of our thinking and what gets our attention. It asks questions such as: Where do we need to focus our thinking in this situation? What are we assuming? How can we look at this differently? What beliefs do we have in this team in relation to this issue? What values do we hold dear? What are we not asking ourselves? What isn't present here? How can we look at this idea without judging it in this moment?

People make judgements every day based on assumed information. They do so because working on false assumption costs in business. We've known businesses (more than one or two) that have been in discussions about mergers or joint developments that have had several exploratory meetings before they realise that they're having different conversations. One thinks they're proposing a takeover, the other thinks they're looking to create a partnership. Alternatively, perhaps the figures they've been discussing have been in different currencies. Much has been written on thinking in recent years, and it can be useful when coaching to help clients understand the difference in fast and slow thinking, which is described in Table 11-2. This table can help you invite a client to approach a specific problem using a different thinking strategy.

Table 11-2	Fast Thinking versus Slow Thinking
Fast Thinking	**Slow Thinking**
Low awareness level	High awareness level
Instinctive and intuitive	Deliberate and reasoning
Automatic and immediate	Planned and requires time allocation
Less than conscious mind processing	Conscious mind processing
No sense of control	Sense of control
Memory and perception plus familiar pattern retrieval	Memory and generative ideas plus identification of a new sequence
Effortless	Requires effort
Sometimes answers an easier question than the question asked	Mostly knows the logical process by which the question was answered
Body sensations respond quickly and unnoticed by self	Body sensations often noticeable to self
Cannot always see that mistakes are about to be made	Can more readily spot potential errors
Can appear in control when the body or mind is not	Can appear in control when the body or mind is not
Cannot be switched off – is always ready for action	Is switched on by the thinker at will for considered thinking
Is in the background waiting in case it needs to answer a quick question, solve a quick problem or react to a situation	Is in the background having seemingly random thoughts and connections most of the time
Responds to triggers that provoke a response of thoughts and behaviours	Monitors and controls thoughts and behaviours
Can get caught up in creating generalisations and responding only to external stimuli to generate thoughts	Can create intense focus and become unaware of stimuli that normally attract attention

Source: Marie Taylor 2012 based on the work of Kahneman and Mihaly Csikszentmihalyi

Take a look at Table 11-2 and notice where you hang out most of the time. In coaching, you're mostly encouraging people to engage in slow thinking – to allow room for their own thoughts and wisdom to show up. Leaders are paid to think, and yet if you look at the average executive team agenda, is there room for both slow and fast thinking? Are you giving your people and yourself time for considered thinking and time to create? Dare we suggest that too much fast thinking in organisations creates 'my way' thinking where people simply agree because they haven't got time to do anything else. You need both.

Exercising your thinking

You can begin to notice how you experience your thinking by practising the following at the individual level and the team level. You can easily share all these exercises with a client if you're working with him on thinking flexibility.

Fast thinking, individual level: Judge nothing and notice everything

Adopt a non-exploratory, non-reasoning approach for a full day and notice what happens. Decide to judge nothing and analyse nothing. Respond to everything instinctively. Be sensible and recognise that, although you may think or feel something, it may not be politic or life enhancing to say it! Simply notice what you notice.

Fast thinking, team level: Review and respond from the gut

In any regular meeting, pause the meeting after 15-20 minutes and ask everyone to take a piece of paper. Ask attendees to quickly write down three assessments of what just happened during the meeting. For example: 'Are things going well?' 'Do you understand what we are being asked to consider here?' 'What is your gut reaction to what has been presented in the last 15-20 minutes?' Tally the yes and no responses and adjectives used to describe the gut reactions. Decide how to carry the meeting forward from there, making any necessary adjustments.

Slow thinking, individual level: The three-minute reflection

Slowing down thinking in order to reflect and absorb can be really useful. Set a nice, gentle alarm for three minutes. Sit comfortably with your feet flat on the floor, keeping you grounded. Let your hands lie loosely in your lap and, if you want, turn your palms so they're facing upwards. When you're ready, close your eyes. Gently bring your attention to your breathing. Notice the in-breath, bringing energy into your whole body. Observe the way your diaphragm fills and expands. Notice the out-breath and feel that sense of releasing all that you no longer need. Ask yourself the following question internally. Rather than forcing the answer, just notice what comes to mind.

What have I learned today?

Slowly open your eyes and come back into the room when the alarm rings.

If you need to learn diaphragm breathing, watch a baby or put your hand on your belly. As you breathe in, the belly extends, as you breath out it contracts. It is the opposite of breathing at the top of your chest.

Slow thinking, team level: Reducing mental ping-pong

Set up an ideas sharing meeting. The purpose is to listen to ideas and ask questions about the idea rather than judge or evaluate the detail of the idea at this point.

The person with an idea speaks completely uninterrupted for five to ten minutes. The chair asks what ideas or input that person would like from the group. When this input is clear, each person speaks in turn to address the issue for three or four minutes each. No one critiques or interrupts. At the end of the dialogue, the ideas person makes a request or suggests if and how he would like to take his idea forward. Assuming that the chair determines the outcomes of the meeting and resource allocation, the chair then agrees or disagrees, explaining her rationale.

Seeking certainty when ambiguity may create something wonderful

Sometimes, 'I don't know' translates into 'I am incompetent and I don't care who knows it'. Our craving for certainty can result in a ridiculous human habit, namely that we seek out certainty where none exists. Leaders will give a knee-jerk response rather than look uncertain or without clear opinion. Hanging out in the land of ambiguity, however, can be creative for clients in helping them think differently and create new solutions.

Encouraging your client to sit in ambiguity with an idea, to go for a walk with it, sleep on it or just leave it for 24 hours and not think of it actively at all can create new ways of thinking and adapting. Encourage clients to play with these simple strategies.

Developing Alternative Perspectives

Coaching is often about helping clients test their reality – to explore a perspective and see whether that lens is helpful to them and their organisation. Opening a leader's thinking can pull him out of the delusion that everyone truly shares his view. The enneagram is a great map to help you consider your orientation (how we show up).

What follows is an invitation to consider your own leadership paradigm using the enneagram as your lens. Each enneagram type in this context is simply a predominant orientation. Consider each of the descriptions in worldview. Then take a look at the orientation in the seek-and-avoid behaviours. Then look at the overarching gift that each of the nine types brings into a business. Finally, consider the questions at the end of the section.

Considering leadership styles

The enneagram can really help leaders to get out of the rut of their own thinking. Working with the nine types on the enneagram can help leaders understand the other eight types and the interplay between them.

The worldview of each enneagram type (adapted with permission from the work of Ginger Lapid Bogda):

- ✔ **Type 1:** A leader's job is to set clear goals and direction. To feed back to others what is right or wrong and inspire the team to achieve high standards.

- ✔ **Type 2:** A leader's job is to assess the strengths and weaknesses of team members. To harness those in others. To motivate the team to deliver organisational goals while developing themselves.

- ✔ **Type 3:** A leader's job is to create a results-oriented environment. To be part of a winning team where people understand the organisation's goals and structure and where they fit in.

- ✔ **Type 4:** A leader's job is to create organisations that align with individual's sense of meaning and purpose. To create teams that are inspired to do excellent, meaningful work.

- ✔ **Type 5:** A leader's job is to develop an effective organisation through research, deliberation and planning. To help the team experience the organisation as one system with a common mission.

- ✔ **Type 6:** A leader's job is to solve organisational problems and work with their team and others to enable them to play their part in creating the solution.

- ✔ **Type 7:** A leader's job is to get people excited and to create innovative ventures. To help the team work in line with the vision and support the whole to identify a number of opportunities and run with them.

- ✔ **Type 8:** A leader's job is to move the organisation forward by being direct, decisive and clear about expectations. To create a successful team by empowering capable and reliable people and directing them into the right jobs to get things done.

- ✔ **Type 9:** A leader's job is to help achieve the collective mission by creating a harmonious work environment. To enable a team to work together, play to strengths, and achieve and celebrate collective results regularly.

It can be useful in coaching to help clients explore how their worldview informs what they tend to innately seek and avoid in leadership. This can give leaders valuable insights into their own behaviour and identify areas where they may need to develop behavioural flexibility to become an even better leader or handle a particular situation. Table 11-3 shows what each type of leader seeks out and avoids.

Table 11-3   What Leaders Seek and Avoid by Enneagram Type

Enneagram Type	Seek	Avoid
1	Perfection, accuracy, clear accountability	Mistake making in areas of own/team responsibility
2	Appreciation for effort and being needed by others	Feeling unworthy or team being unrecognized
3	Admiration and respect for their efforts	Personal failure or having a failing team
4	To create connection with others and have deeper feelings acknowledged	A sense of rejection personally or having a team whose contributions are discounted
5	Knowledge, a breadth of information and wisdom	Personal intrusion and loss of energy
6	Meaning, a level of certainty and trust in others	Negative scenarios and acting to prevent them
7	Stimulation through new ideas and experiences that are pleasurable	Loss of freedom to act or discomfort in the team
8	Control of self, others and situations and justice in unfairness	Feeling vulnerable or weak or team being viewed as inadequate
9	Harmony and comfort with others and environment	Conflict with others, conflict or competition within the team

Source: Used with permission of Ginger Lapid Bogda

Applying leadership gifts in business

Each of the nine enneagrams brings particular gifts that can be accessed easily. Helping a client identify his type and notice what he can deliver almost effortlessly can be useful. Sometimes a client finds an aspect of leadership comes so naturally that he isn't aware of the gift he brings to the business and those around him. A great coach can hold up the mirror and show him his gift and how to harness it.

1. **The King/Queen of Quality:** Expecting and striving for excellence in all areas

2. **The Magic Mobiliser:** Enabling others by aligning service to their people with organisational outcomes

3. **The Results Raconteur:** Achieving ever bigger and better results year on year

4. **The Passion Connector:** Aligning pursuit of meaningful goals and the desire to engage others in interesting ways

5. **The Seeker Sage:** Using the evidential approach to create success and measure outputs

6. **The Reliable Aromachologist:** Encouraging insight to find acceptable solutions to business problems and increase loyal followership

7. **The Ideas Gymnast:** Envisioning new products and ways of delivering to create agile business

8. **The Determined Herdsman:** Harnessing talent and setting clear expectations to drive delivery

9. **The Patient Warrior:** Engaging across the business to develop agreed workable outputs with minimum disagreement

If you take the various descriptors of each of the nine types, which most closely describes your leadership paradigm? You'll orientate predominantly from one type across all four dimensions, although you will probably recognise aspects of your orientation in other types. Don't worry if you find it hard to identify your type; it can take time. We have provided free access to Marie's short book on the types. Go to `marietayloronline.com/dummies` for a free copy of *What's My Type* by Marie Taylor and Jenny Williams. If you were to identify your own originating enneagram type and draw your own paradigm, what would it look like?

Table 11-3 shows how you can use the enneagram descriptors as they relate to leadership style and behaviour. (Figure 11-3 shows Marie's leadership paradigm as someone oriented to type 7.) You can create a personal leadership paradigm based on an individual's personal identification of his type. You could work with a group and coach them to identify their own paradigm based on the enneagram. Help them consider their potential individual impact and the potential impact of the group as a team given the balance of their self-identified types in the team.

Some questions to consider when you have described your own leadership paradigm include:

- What does your paradigm indicate about how you lead? How does this translate in practice?

- Think about the leaders in your own team. Which paradigm most closely describes their worldview in your opinion? (Remember it's just your opinion and may not be accurate.)

- When you put this information all together, what do you notice about your team?

- How do think they may see you as a group? Would they see you as you see yourself or differently?

- If you were to imagine yourself coming from the map of one of the possible types in your team, how do you imagine that person would experience you?

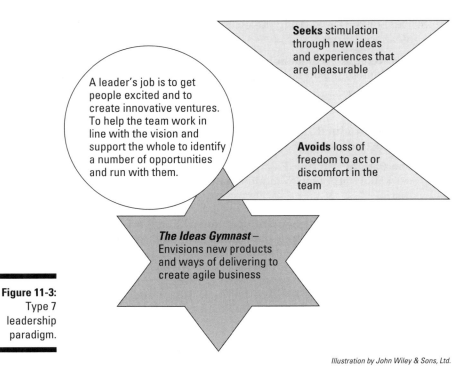

Seeks stimulation through new ideas and experiences that are pleasurable

A leader's job is to get people excited and to create innovative ventures. To help the team work in line with the vision and support the whole to identify a number of opportunities and run with them.

Avoids loss of freedom to act or discomfort in the team

The Ideas Gymnast – Envisions new products and ways of delivering to create agile business

Figure 11-3: Type 7 leadership paradigm.

Illustration by John Wiley & Sons, Ltd.

✔ What can you learn as a leader from this wider leadership map?

✔ What insights can you gain about the potential of your leadership team?

✔ What can you do differently (if anything) in aligning your team to your vision and business strategy?

✔ Are there any developmental considerations or adjustments you can make to lead your business or organisation to create the greatest impact?

Use probing questions to help your clients see themselves as others may see them. Open them up to the possibility that how they present may not be enabling and motivational for all members of their team, particularly if the client has a low level of behavioural flexibility.

Chapter 12

Mentoring for Personal Success and Empowering Leadership

In This Chapter

▶ Getting clear on success

▶ Developing leadership flexibility

▶ Understanding the role of mentors in providing leadership stretch

*L*eading an organisation in a functional area can be rewarding and personally fulfilling. It can also be tough. The guidance and wisdom of a mentor can be invaluable. The wisdom imparted by someone who has 'been there, seen it and done it' can save a leader oceans of time. Mentoring support provides reassurance and can prevent mistake making or unnecessary risk taking in a leader. Ultimately, this intervention benefits the business.

This chapter takes a look at mentoring in the context of success and leadership. We consider how to help a client define success and handle thoughts of limitation when they show up. Many of the tools can be used in other leadership areas. We invite you to consider the exercises from your perspective as a leadership mentor and as yourself, in whatever capacity you lead – as an organisational leader or as the leader in your life.

Being a Great Leadership Mentor

Chapter 1 has an explanatory grid setting out the different helping disciplines. Think of coaching as the use of a professional skill set where the well-trained coach doesn't need to have experience of a particular type of business, specific leadership role or experience in the same functional area as the person being coached.

   ✔ The coach is using a set of skills and experiences to help the client find solutions and make sense of things from the client's own resources.

- ✔ The mentor, sometimes called the trusted adviser, uses coaching skills to help a mentee explore situations. The mentor draws on her experience, knowhow and wisdom to help someone plan or manage similar situations.

- ✔ Both coach and mentor enable their clients.

You might be asking yourself if it's possible to be both. The answer is yes. We both coach executives on aspects of business and mentor coaches looking to establish their coaching and training practice.

If you're a mentor who has fallen into mentoring because your experience, skills and knowledge are in demand, get some coaching skills. From our experience, this training is the difference that makes the difference.

Some leaders have a number of mentors or a mentor-and-coach combination. This situation can be helpful in specific short-term circumstances. We have seen a few leaders over the years who are overdoing it on the coaching and mentoring support. This overload can have the opposite effect. It can create an indecisive client who is lost in an advisory muddle. The responsibility for avoiding this situation lies with everyone: the leader, mentors and coaches.

To avoid any confusion about who's giving your prospective client advice, make sure your contracting includes a check about what formal and informal mentoring and coaching the person already has in place. The boundaries of these relationships should be discussed upfront at the contracting stage. This ensures you're aware of who else is giving the person advice and guidance; they may take a different view or approach to you. Knowing this can help you decide if you want to work with the client; it also helps you manage your own boundaries if and when your client says, 'Ah, well, my mentor, Jim, disagrees with your approach because. . .' Remember, enabling others to be more authentically who they are and increase their capacity to lead isn't a competitive sport.

Challenging the Delusions of What It Means to Be Successful

What does success mean to you?

- ✔ Is it stuff? Stuff is the property you have, the car you drive, the brand of clothes you wear, the watch on your wrist, the credit cards you have in your wallet.

- ✔ Is it symbols? Symbols include the school your children go to, the university you attended, the postcode where you live, the clubs you can get into.

✔ Is it experiences? Experiences include where you take holidays, the kind of sport you're involved in, the restaurants you go to, the amount of personal grooming you can afford.

✔ What is *your* measure of personal success?

We have both asked this question hundreds of times. Nothing you say can shock us. A guy Marie coached in financial services – let's call him Ben – described his measure of success as always staying ahead of Joe, a colleague who was also exceptionally good at gaining high-value clients and therefore bonuses. He was quite proud of the fact that he had just been invited by one of the senior partners to join a crowd on Friday afternoons once a month at a VIP 'gentlemen's' club. He considered that a sign of acceptance and a signal that he was on the way to being promoted and even more successful. In Ben's world, this signal made him more successful than Joe.

Before you go all moral on us, it's a fact of life in some areas of business that men and women do things their parents may not like in order to further their careers. As a coach or mentor, you need to find ways to get beyond this. Your job as a coach is to help your clients observe their experience and change it if they choose to, not judge them. You may want to challenge someone to consider her definitions of success and happiness or what any risky behaviour might mean for her. Passing judgement on her lifestyle, however, isn't your role. This issue is a boundary issue. If someone's measure of success doesn't map to your own expectation, what are you going to do? Work only with clients who share your values, measures of success and worldview? Good luck with that one.

What is your personal definition of success? Write it down in two or three sentences.

Success and culture

What people value as a measure of success in a culture often becomes part of the measure of success for the individuals in it. This statement is particularly true when an individual is working within that same cultural context. Cultural overlays exist in defining success, and if you mentor internationally, understanding the drivers of success in a particular culture is important. While your client's definition may not reflect those drivers, it can be useful to get a sense of what determines success in someone's country of origin and/or in her country of heritage. If we asked you to give us three quick keywords to describe success in different cultures, some or all of those would be different. Jot down three words for: Singapore, New York, Sweden and Sydney. See what we mean?

It can be an interesting area to mentor and coach around, particularly in working with foreign nationals who are spending an extended period outside of their country of origin or for those leading across several cultures.

It may be important for some people to work with a mentor who has a specific cultural background. If you're responsible for identifying mentors, this selection consideration may be an important one also.

If you're working with a client who is from a different culture to your own, spend time getting to understand her world and what has formed her cultural worldview. Doing so is particularly important if your client is expected to lead across different cultures or if she's leading within an organisation that has its roots firmly grounded in an alternative culture. If you were working with someone from Japan who takes her first leadership role in a US company, it would be useful to help your client explore her experience of the differences to help her anticipate and navigate difference.

Mentoring questions along these lines can be helpful:

- ✔ What is valued most in your country of origin, and how do professionals define success?

- ✔ What do you take from that?

- ✔ How did/do your parents define success for you?

- ✔ How do you experience (the organisation) and the overall values of the country you're now working in?

- ✔ How do you think the definition of what success means in this business and this culture differs from your previous experience? What is the same?

- ✔ What about the other territories you're responsible for? How do you think colleagues there might define success overall?

- ✔ What is your own personal definition of success – for you?

- ✔ What is it for those who are important in your life?

Success isn't a destination

We live in an increasingly fast world. We are the VUCA generations, living and leading in Volatile, Uncertain, Complex and Ambiguous times. The flow of information, increased globalisation and our ability to travel with relative ease in business is creating destination addiction. If you listen long enough in any organisation, you'll hear people competing with each other about being busy as though that is a measure of effective business. Most leaders we know are always busy 'going' somewhere.

Robert Holden, an international coach, author and speaker, writes about destination addiction in his brilliant book, *Success Intelligence* (Hay House). He says, 'Being busy looks damned impressive and necessary. It looks like purpose, focus, drive and huge productivity . . . Busyness is often just noise. It has no real substance to it'. We agree. Society has invented a cause-and-effect relationship between busyness and effectiveness, between effectiveness and success. This perception is in our work-based DNA and increasing globalisation; the 24-hour work culture compounds it. The assumption is, 'If I look busy, I must be effective, and if I am effective, I must be successful'.

The risk is that society so often associates success with being busy. We rarely question it because we're in it and can't see the rapid elevator we're travelling in because everyone else is travelling at the same speed for the most part. Coaching and mentoring are powerful. Having a trained supporter to help people see what they can't yet see helps them make active choices based on their own exploration of success and what it means for them. So many people never even ask the question – they're too busy running on the treadmill of someone else's life.

Exploring the True Nature of Success

If this book were on life coaching, we'd explore the nature of whole life success. Mentors mostly leave that to transformational coaches. Mentors come into their own when helping leaders to create or sustain success in particular areas of business. More recently, those mentors who have led organisations during periods of recession and growth have been in demand. They can help leaders see how to manage issues of risk, volatility and new market entry; how to handle efficiency measures resulting in mergers, joint ventures and the like. If a leader has gained most of her experience in an organisation during growth, mentoring can help her gain the alternate perspective.

A mentor may share her experience in the session like this:

> **Mentor:** So today you wanted to focus on how to handle the people and budgetary aspects surrounding the acquisition of Company A in two months' time given that you will inherit two new teams in Sweden and Germany? Anything else?

> **Mentee:** Yes, that's what I need to focus on. I am particularly concerned as I have handled a merger previously, but it was very harmonious. It was a joining together of two companies with different product lines and skill sets that were complimentary. I'd value your insights into handling the people aspects post-downsizing. I think people are very scared, and I need them to get on board and assess opportunities quickly.

> **Mentor:** What do you expect will be different in this situation?

> **Mentee:** Well, Company A is being acquired by us. Like us, they've been through significant change and downsizing during the recession. They're still reeling from the sale and the changes in-house. There are four or five key managers whom I really can't afford to lose, and I want to get the team off to a good, productive start. I'll need to start looking at two new markets and have been tasked with leading our entry into the Indian

market with one of our microprocessors. I need a plan in place within four weeks of the merger, and I need someone out in Bombay to recruit a new team by week 6 post-merger.

Mentor: So, in a minute I will tell you about my experience of doing something similar at Eskimo Inc. when we acquired Ice Ice Baby, and I want you to pay attention to the process I was following and how I got people on board. Then we can look at the risks and opportunities you're facing and how you might mitigate and manage some of those. We also need to look at what might distract you – the stuff that really isn't important in this three-and-a-half-month period. We can look at how you might develop a plan for the new-market entry but also how you'll motivate specific individuals to get on board and stay. We can discuss how to keep an eye on potential opportunities and the level of risk appetite in the business in entering the Indian market. The idea being that you leave here today with some ideas for the strategies and tactics you need to put in place to get ready to deliver this. Is that what you want?

The process of mentoring here is as follows:

1. **Identify the overall issue the mentee would like support with and what she is looking to you for.**

2. **Identify specifically what she would like your help with (preferably no more than two or three issues).**

3. **Identify what the mentee considers might be outside of her current experience and the concerns/learning needs she has around the issue.**

4. **Outline what you propose and outline the process you propose for the session.**

5. **Tell her what to listen for and get her agreement that this process is what she would find useful.**

6. **Run the session by sharing your experience and then help the mentee apply it to her own circumstances. Help the mentee determine what her next action steps are, whom she will discuss her plan with and check whether she needs anything else from you.**

Your client can't always achieve success if she hasn't explored it fully, so help her do that. Ask her the success question in a few areas, such as

✔ How will you know that this transfer of staff has gone well?

✔ What will success look like and feel like to you in three months' time? In six months' time?

✔ How will your CEO/Chairperson measure your success?

✔ How will you know that they've noticed you have been successful?

✔ How will you ensure that you succeed in meeting this goal?

You'll want to do the above within the boundaries of a mentoring agreement and process, which is explained in Chapter 1.

Dealing with the 'I Should' or 'I Ought to' Traps of Success

Most of us experience self-doubt. The truth is, in leadership, self-doubt can create restriction and limitation in a business. If we asked you to imagine a library full of books where the titles describe your life up to now, what would the titles be? Would any of them say things such as

- ✔ I ought to have grown up by now.
- ✔ I really ought to work harder.
- ✔ I should have a bigger bonus and a better car.
- ✔ I ought to see my friends more.
- ✔ I should be happier.
- ✔ I should grow this business.

You get our point. When we ask people these questions, they invariably come up with a mix of positive and wistful book titles. Try it with your clients.

When the list is complete, Marie gets her client to take every one of the 'shoulds, oughts and musts' and consign them to a new library. You can help your clients do this activity by taking all the should, ought and must statements and, for each one, ask

- ✔ What's stopping you from having this now? and/or
- ✔ Is it something you desire/want in your life now?

Work through the list of should, ought and must statements, and if the answer to any of them is 'I don't actually desire or want that anymore', it goes in the should, oughts and musts library. Marie has her clients imagine the statement floating away into another dusty library with a notice on the door that says 'Deposits only – no retrievals'. Then she asks them to take the piece of paper they wrote the title on, tear that title off, rip it up and place it in the waste bin. In this way, they metaphorically consign it to history.

When we come to a title that is something she wants, but she doesn't have it yet, Marie asks, 'What is getting in the way?' or 'What do you believe about getting this?'

Invariably a limiting belief emerges. A *limiting belief* is something we think we can't have or can't achieve, a constraint or limitation that stops us from even questioning whether we can have it or achieve it. Limiting beliefs aren't always about getting more or achieving more. They can be about having, achieving or doing less too. Sometimes clients have a clear view about limitation such as 'I'm not confident enough' or 'I don't have time'. Often clients don't know what limits them. You may need to help your client surface the limiting belief and challenge it. The next sections explain how to do that.

Removing limiting beliefs before implementing change processes is crucial; otherwise the client tends to get in her own way.

Why look at limiting beliefs in mentoring?

If you think about what you're doing in mentoring, you're imparting your wisdom to help clients examine what they might do the same, adapt or discard. Sometimes their response can be a head-level response such as, 'Yes, I understand how you did that and why you handled the issue that way'. Then comes the 'but'. It sounds like this: 'But I'm not sure I could do a similar thing in this context. I can see that it would work. I just don't think I could deliver it'. Alternatively, you'll hear in the client's language that she keeps talking in the abstract or in the third person, as though this situation she is looking to resolve belongs to you or someone else. 'I can see how you would do that . . .'

As a mentor, you need to challenge this issue head-on as you want to help the client take action. A challenge might be, 'Now that you can see how I did that, walk me through how you'll apply this learning in your particular context'.

This point is when the limiting beliefs may emerge. The beliefs are born out of fear. This fear normally is of not succeeding; not being good enough, confident enough, capable enough; of looking stupid, looking arrogant, looking some way that the client doesn't want to be perceived. We all do this. Your job is to help the client remember that we are all making it up. Such thoughts are just beliefs – they're not real.

Be kind when you help the client remember this because she hasn't realised yet that she has built some of this wall of self-limitation herself. She may not have put the foundations in; she may have inherited that from someone else's story.

The next section offers a process for helping your client manage the fears that are holding her back from getting what she desires – wherever the fears came from.

Your client may have formed a limiting belief so long ago that she can't recall where and how she became fearful. She, and you, as the mentor, don't need to understand it. You just need to question it, and then get rid of it so your client can move forward.

The good news, brilliant news even, is that people hold the controls of this complex system of thinking, and with a bit of magic dialogue you can empower clients to examine those and check whether they're true. To do that, you need to help your client slow her fast thinking down.

Finding a strategy for examining and eliminating limiting beliefs

This option dialogue is taken from Mandy Evans's book, *Emotional Options* (Yes You Can Press). It produces amazing shifts by encouraging slow thinking using simple, powerful questions. Try this activity yourself with something you believe you can't do or can't have – something that you want. This process isn't a wish fest – don't make it 'I'd like to win the lottery and I don't think I can'. Choose something that is real for you.

Work your way through the questions and write down your answers. Identify the feeling you're feeling – for example, unhappiness, anger, guilt or worry – and work through the dialogue step by step in the order of the questions. No skipping ahead!

- ✔ What are you (unhappy/angry/guilty/worried) about?
- ✔ Why are you unhappy/angry/guilty/worried about that?
- ✔ What are you concerned would happen if you were not unhappy/angry/guilty/worried about that?
- ✔ Do you believe that?
- ✔ Why do you believe that?
- ✔ What are you concerned would happen if you did not believe that?
- ✔ What are your concerns?
- ✔ Do they still seem real to you?

As soon as you get practiced working with the structure of this dialogue, you can obviously ask different questions and make it relate to the issue in hand more elegantly. Work with it first and get comfortable with the process.

> **CASE:** This is a real situation that Marie had with a client, but the name has been changed to protect the emerging self-believer.
>
> **M:** So how can I help you with your project today?

C: I can't seem to get this project off the ground. I know we've been through what makes a project presentation successful, but I won't get buy-in from the Executive Board. They won't commit the full 750K, and I can't do it for less than that. I'm not going to meet my quarter 4 objectives on this project.

M: What would you like to have happen?

C: Well obviously, I'd like them to agree to my proposal and commit the full amount of spend in quarters 2 and 3.

M: When did you ask the Exec team, and what response did you get?

C: Well, I haven't asked them yet – they'll say no.

M: Say no to what? The proposal or the funding?

C: I think they will like the proposal. I've worked hard to get external stakeholders on side, but the Exec will want to cut corners. If we do that, we won't deliver the best service to customers. The team will get disheartened, and I think a couple of them might leave.

M: What makes you think they'll say no to the funding even though they sound as though they'll like the proposal and it's something they'll want?

C: Because they've reduced budgets on the last three projects Bill and Sally put forward.

M: Why?

C: I don't really know, but I do know that it's not good for your reputation with the Exec team to have a project bid reduced. I think having them reject something can mean a level of mistrust and scrutiny. I'm afraid the proposal won't be agreed.

M: What are you really afraid of?

Long pause.

C: I suppose having my proposal rejected and found wanting and, if that happens, I will feel rejected. That my reputation will not be good if this proposal is rejected.

M: And when you say that, how do you feel about it?

C: Angry.

M: Why are you angry about that?

C: Because they might rubbish my ideas, make me feel small, expect too much of me and I'll feel like a kid who got it wrong and is sent back to do her homework and come up with a different answer.

M: What are you concerned would happen if you were not angry about that?

C: Well, I'd be a pushover. If I wasn't angry about them rejecting my ideas and expecting too much of me, then I might agree to something unworkable.

I might come away and find another way of doing it, and the customers wouldn't get what the focus groups tell us they want.

M: And what are you concerned would happen if you were not angry about that?

C: Well, we say that we are customer-led. How can I sell that to my staff if I come out of that Exec meeting with a budget that doesn't allow us to deliver what customers want?

M: Do you believe that? That the Exec team will think you're a pushover, that you would be okay with not meeting the company value of being customer-led and would roll over and agree to do something that your research tells you that customers wouldn't want?

C: I'm not sure. I do think the Exec team want to give customers great service and be customer-led, and they like to see the research and the research supports the level of spend.

Pause (because the client is thinking)

M: What are your concerns?

C: I'm not really sure because as I think about it, my idea that they will reject it and me in the process doesn't seem true. I can see how they may just go for it.

M: Do your concerns about what might happen still seem real to you?

C: No. I think I have a well-thought-out, workable project plan, and I can see how to influence them to say yes. I just need to stick to my guns really.

M: And how do you feel about it now?

C: I think they will go with it. I feel confident they will. I think the Exec team know that I'm straight down the line on costs – I don't put lots of cushion in and I relate it to the customer well.

M: And how do you feel now?

C: Quite determined actually. I can't see a reason why they would want to challenge the costs I'm proposing. They're right and reasonable given what we're doing. I can't believe I've made such a big thing of this . . .

Did you spot where and why Marie started to address the limiting belief?

It was with the 'What are you afraid of?' question. In using this dialogue, you patiently wait for the opportunity to allow the fear to surface. Doing so is like waiting for a fish to swim by before you hook it to stop it getting caught in a twisted fishing line. Then be patient and wait to allow the client time to think.

This process works because of the way the questions are asked. You're encouraging the client to slow down her thinking long enough to recognise that certain powerful thoughts may need questioning.

In the case example, Marie's next question was, 'So what will make this presentation really successful? Visualise it – what will you see, hear and feel when this is going really well?'

She had the client walk through seeing himself achieve his successful outcome, and he all but skipped out of the room. He seemed a foot taller. Most important for the client, the Executive team simply nodded it through in 15 minutes.

Identifying the Common Qualities of Great Leaders

What makes a great leader? We've been working with leaders for 30 years, and the answer is more complex than a simple list of attributes. Certain things make standout leaders, and yet it depends where you're looking from and whose perspective you're taking. Looking at a leader from an investor perspective is different to that of a staff member, a chairperson, a business owner or a supplier. This fact may explain in part why we keep studying it. We're looking for the magic formula as though we can bottle it and sprinkle it on others if only we can identify it. Leadership isn't a science. We can't isolate the variables long enough to take a look at what's really going on. Leaders deploy a complex skill set to create a vision and harness multiple strategies and resources. Leaders need institutional and/or specific industry knowledge and the ability to manage complexity and change.

When mentoring around leadership, it might be tempting to think that a mentee is looking to play the leadership game like you. She may well not be, particularly if she's under 30 and you're over 30. She's interested in some of your qualities plus the opportunity to discuss some of the new leadership qualities that she may feel are increasingly important. What she values is your wisdom and support about how you do or did leadership so she can decide how she might do it for herself. Helping her discover what qualities are important to her personally and within her area of work is the work of a mentor working with leadership.

Looking and behaving like a leader

What does a leader look like? Churchill, Steve Jobs, Karan Bilimoria, Deborah Meaden, Karen Brady, Tom Singh, J. K. Rowling, Oprah Winfrey, Mark Zuckerburg, Tony Hseih? Tick all the above.

Until the 1990s, leaders mostly wore suits and carried briefcases. Not wearing a tie or a suit and heels meant it was dress-down Friday, the day when we could walk around thinking 'Really? You wear *that* at the weekends', has all but gone. We've gone casual every day in many organisations. Even the Institute of Directors, a British institution established in 1903, has recently created a dress-down feel at one of its London premises.

So what does a leader look like? The simple answer is that she looks like the image that her industry expects her to look like, and she behaves and wears what reflects her. She presents with the skin she's comfortable doing business in – mostly.

If you're mentoring a leader or a prospective leader, consider both your own image and how your client may need to think about her look and behaviours depending on the business you are both working in, the culture of that business and any cross-cultural norms. For mentors, this topic can be tricky as your assumptions of what a client ought to look like in a leadership role and what behaviours you believe she ought to display are often skewed by your own experience of leaders. Mentors may have a set of assumptions about what it takes to be taken seriously in business because when your average business mentor was a leader in her 20s, 30s, 40s, 50s and 60s, the suit was an important part of being taken seriously. It still is in some areas. You might want to examine your own assumptions on how a client might dress or need to come across as a leader.

A mentoring conversation around look and behaviour can focus on personal brand and how your client wants to show up and be perceived by the range of stakeholders she interacts with. You can read more on personal brand in Chapter 13. Alternatively, you might want to help her look deeper.

You can find literally hundreds of ways to describe effective leadership, and in mentoring you want to help clients learn from your experience of leading and encourage a degree of focus on aspects of leading: self-awareness, appropriate use of resources, change-management skills, self-presentation, industry knowledge, network development, understanding of governance, social responsibility, an overview of marketing, finance and people management. The list goes on. To help you focus, we have created Table 12-1, which is our own matrix of leadership qualities, drawing on a range of leadership models and our own experience.

Adapting your style to create followers

No matter how senior leaders are, paying attention to how you can make it easy for people to follow can be a useful exercise. You can't expect people to follow if you don't consider what they might want from you in making that decision.

Table 12-1	Leadership Qualities Matrix: CEO and Executive Level Leaders	
Stakeholder Wants/Needs	**Leading the Business**	**Self-mastery**
What people want to experience to feel confident in the business	Clear vision and strategic 'holding' of the business through strategies, and expectation of alignment down through goals and tactical operational plans	Self-development and continual learner focus
	Values articulated and demonstrated	High breadth and depth communication skills
	Knowledge of the industry/professional area	
		Values driven
	Clear ethics and governance, including sustainability measures	Ethically responsible
		Global mind-set
	Understanding key strategic aspects of finance, HR, marketing, sales and product range	Cultural intelligence
		Emotional and social intelligence
	Expects results and motivates for delivery	Desire to impact beyond profit
	Monitors key activity proactively	
	Takes decisive action even if unpopular	
	Leads change proactively	
	Strategic industry and peer networks	
What people want to feel and see to feel confident in the leader as a person	Confidence	Inspiration
	Honesty	Gut instinct
	Commitment	Trust in self and others
	Creativity	

You need the matrix, at least three sheets of A4 or a flip pad, coloured pens or a single pen depending on whether you mind map or write narrative. When you do this exercise, resist the temptation to read ahead. That way, you'll get a closer experience to the one your client will have if you use this exercise with her.

Use the matrix shown earlier in Table 12-1 in relation to yourself.

1. **Pick four elements: two from the 'What people want to experience to feel confidence in the business' section (one from 'Leading the Business' and one from 'Self-mastery') and take any two from 'What people want to feel and see to feel confident in the leader as a person' section.**

2. **Take a sheet of paper and draw a mind map or write a narrative on 'When I do (the 'Leading the Business' element), how do I deploy the ('Self-mastery' element)?'**

3. **Ask yourself what others would see in you or experience from you that gives them confidence that you have these qualities? Write it down.**

4. **Think of two specific stakeholders you relate to.**

   Change seats and get into the first person's orientation. Imagine that you're the other person, seeing you from her perspective. Look at your answer from this person's perspective.

5. **Write down any feedback she may give you and additional notes she might write.**

6. **When you have finished being in the position of the first stakeholder, change to a third seat and do the same from the perspective of the second stakeholder.**

   Again, really get into her orientation. Put her coat on, imagining that you're her seeing you from her perspective.

7. **Now look at your answer from this person's perspective and again note any feedback.**

8. **Stay in that seat and imagine that these two stakeholders were asked to suggest specific stretch activities or learning for you that would help you develop more flexibility in the way you lead the organisation and how you show up.**

9. **Go back to the original seat (your seat) and review what you have.**

   What do you notice? Do the stretch activities (there may be just one) feel appropriate? Can you gain some insight into how others may see you at this time?

10. **Agree one stretch activity with yourself and give it a timeline for completion.**

When you do this exercise with a client, the room set-up is all-important. If you can, put the three chairs around a round table and sit away from the table space completely yourself. If you don't have much room, an alternative is to ask your client to walk around three positions with markers on the floor and articulate her stakeholder one and stakeholder two dialogue out loud.

You can take the preceding exercise a step further. If you can record yourself speaking this dialogue beforehand, do so and give yourself the experience your client will have.

1. **Take the two 'Confidence in the leader as a person' elements.**

   You will have just two words.

2. **Stand with your feet slightly apart in a relaxed but strong pose.**

   Really ground your feet into the ground and relax your shoulders and knees.

3. **Notice any tension and take your attention there and breathe into it until you feel strong in the body and a strength between your body and the floor beneath your feet.**

4. **Close your eyes, or look at a point ahead of you on the wall and keep your gaze relaxed. Now allow those two words to just float around inside your head.**

5. **Ask yourself the following questions:**

   • If I were demonstrating this more often, what would other people notice?

   • How would I feel? Notice those feelings.

   • If I were empowering others in my team to do more of these two elements, what might I notice in them?

   • How can I increase followership by simply paying more attention?

6. **Open your eyes and take a few seconds to re-orient and then write yourself a note.**

7. **Develop a stretch activity or two in this area.**

   If you can, integrate the stretch identified in the preceding exercise and do that if you want.

You don't have to use our matrix. If you're working in organisations with a set of leadership competencies or a leadership model they use, you can overlay these two exercises onto their framework tools.

Allowing Others to Lead While You Follow

The more senior a leader becomes, the more she will need to delegate and enable her own reports to lead the organisation on her behalf. The more senior a person becomes, the role is one of a steward – one who holds the organisation in trust for future generations and leads by being in service to her people.

Allowing others to lead requires a willingness to give up power. Leaders need to be confident and emotionally intelligent to do this; to be able to trust others to deliver and do the right thing; to trust themselves not to interfere in the detail or keep taking power back once given. Helping leaders to get out of the detail and to relinquish power is a great area for mentoring.

If you're working with a client on this, you can use the exercise on adapting your style and focus on the following three qualities in the leadership matrix (Table 12-1): expects results and motivates for delivery; desire to impact beyond profit; and trust in self and others.

Enabling leadership across generations

Leaders are always impacting potential leaders by how they model leadership. However, some active ways stand out that leaders can use to help to grow next-generation leaders in the business. These ways provide opportunities for mentors to support the senior leader to delegate and understand the next generation and also mentor the leader in how to be a mentor.

Generational difference can be a key issue for mentoring. This difference is particularly so in family businesses where older leaders may be concerned that younger members are too inexperienced to lead what they've built. Passing the leadership baton in a family business is more complex than in most organisations because it shifts personal relationships, which may impact the family. No such separation exists in a family business. Any Friday feuds may well linger over into the family Sunday brunch. Mentoring can extend into private considerations of juggling identity issues about the family and the business. This situation requires an exceptionally high degree of trust in the mentor.

Whether a family business or not, a leadership handover will normally happen when established strategic goals and tactics are in place. If you were born before 1981, you will probably value this type of handover as you can see an agreed strategic direction for you to perform within and deliver. For a younger, millennial leader, the world moves fast and this notion may seem less attractive.

Mentoring may also need to be sold to different generations in different ways. The needs of generation X are different to generation Y (millennials). The latter tend to place less value on wisdom and experience than generation X. Their sense of being given a direction to follow is less attractive. In their worldview, information is readily available, so the value in gaining understanding from a more experienced, wiser person may need some explaining. They like immediacy too.

Mentoring millennial leaders

Some consideration of how emerging leaders perceive you as a coach or mentor in contributing to their success can be useful. Often, If a millennial leader can't see the value of the experience you bring, initial engagement might be difficult. In general, their preference from their own managers is for a more mentoring style; an individualised learning experience with less hierarchy. How you position mentoring will be important. In particular, you may want to create more ways for a millennial to have quicker, bite-sized access to you. They've grown up with social media as a key communication tool. They like short questions and bite-sized answers. They've grown up having ready access to digital information and to receiving lots of ongoing feedback and more praise than their own leaders.

The issues for mentoring new millennial leaders can show up in anyone, but for this group in particular, the issues are likely to be in areas such as

- The 'how' of delivering
- Making the transition from a more junior role to a leadership role
- Managing relationships and seeing the value of contribution and quality over speed
- Slowing down thinking and finding ways to engage a range of stakeholders
- Selling ideas and more efficient ways of delivering
- Aligning the organisation's values with social contribution and ethical principles while making a profit

The tools throughout this book enable you to support millennials in business. The most important thing to remember is that their expectations in business and of their careers may be very different to your own. In mentoring in particular, your wisdom is a key asset to help them develop and succeed. Helping them receive that wisdom and use it may require a lot of behavioural flexibility on your part.

You may want to consider email mentoring or telephone mentoring if you don't do that already. Although debate is common about whether this kind of activity really is mentoring or simply advice giving, fast methods increasingly have a place, particularly for emerging leaders under 30. In terms of structure, your mentoring model may need adjusting to provide a mix of short (5–15 minutes) and longer (45–90 minutes) sessions. If you're mentoring across time zones, be particularly clear in the contracting about your availability.

Part IV
Creating a Successful Business Identity with the Support of a Coach

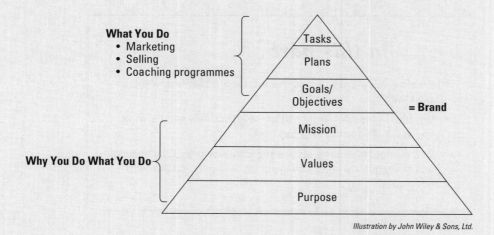

What You Do
- Marketing
- Selling
- Coaching programmes

Tasks

Plans

Goals/ Objectives

= Brand

Mission

Why You Do What You Do

Values

Purpose

Illustration by John Wiley & Sons, Ltd.

Individuals must answer the question 'Who am I?' when they take on a new role in a company. Discover how you can help clients navigate this transition with the free article at www.dummies.com/extras/businesscoachingmentoring.

In this part . . .

- ✔ Create a value-driven brand that will inspire clients to want to work with you.

- ✔ Develop successful relationships, collaborations and networks that will build a successful business.

- ✔ Find out how to engage, inspire and influence clients, customers and colleagues to join you on your own magnificent business adventure.

Chapter 13

Developing the Brand of You

In This Chapter
▶ Defining a valuable brand
▶ Coaching with authenticity
▶ Realising your true worth

*I*n this chapter, we explore the characteristics and mind-sets that enabled individuals, such as Victoria Beckham and her equally successful husband David Beckham, to build a personal brand worth millions.

In Chapter 8, we explore how to define your values and purpose. In this chapter, we explore these subjects at a deeper level.

Enter Personal Branding

A *brand* is a 'promise to deliver'. It's like a bank note that promises to pay the bearer the value on the note; it's only worth the face value if people trust that it will be honoured.

Business brands have generated considerable significance and interest in the 21st century. Who could have guessed 100 years ago that today one of the top 20 brands in the world, ranked number 7 with an estimated brand value of just under £5.6 billion, would be a luxury clothing and leather goods retailer? Burberry sells luxury goods, and although it may be one of the most counterfeited brands in the world, its story of exclusivity and quality keeps it in the top-20-brand list. However, although its work to challenge the counterfeiting through legislative change is successful and ongoing, it's background noise. The really interesting brand news is Burberry's ability to sell its craftsmanship and its ability to customise goods as a result. In a world where the Burberry brand is potentially seriously compromised, Burberry has developed a niche within a niche.

Advisors to Burberry no doubt developed grey hair thinking about the counterfeit issue and the associated risks to brand. Yet the key strategies seem to have been to focus on dominating the highest-end luxury goods market and developing an online market that still offers customers exclusivity, quality and service. It is bizarre and brilliant that in a world where the sale of quality counterfeits is on the increase in the mass market, Burberry is selling a luxury handbag at £20,000. This is a clear example of an organisation retaining a positive business outlook in challenging circumstances, taking a decision to stay with the brand values to maximise quality, craftsmanship and exclusivity.

Another exciting 21st-century development is that of the *personal brand*, the individual who is able to exploit and showcase his talents and package them in multiple ways. Victoria Beckham rose to fame in the 1990s with the all-female pop group Spice Girls and was dubbed Posh Spice. When she announced that her ambition was to be a brand as globally recognised as Kellogg's, a lot of people sniggered. How she has proven them wrong!

In the past decade, Victoria has become an internationally recognised fashion designer, style icon and businesswoman named top entrepreneur of 2014 by British business magazine *Management Today*. The Victoria Beckham label was named designer brand of the year in the UK in 2011. The brand was built with the assistance of music impresario Simon Fuller, famous for first discovering the Spice Girls and for creating the *Pop Idol* television franchise. Fuller's XIX Management owns one-third of the Victoria Beckham business, which is reportedly worth more than £300 million. First launched in 2008, her fashion business now includes dresses, luxury handbags, makeup and fragrances with annual sales of almost £50 million with an exclusive store in Mayfair, London and her range of products available in high-end retailers around the world.

The only apparent difference between corporate branding and personal branding is that instead of marketing a product or service, a person is being promoted. The common denominators that define all stand-out successful brands whether corporate or personal are

- ✔ Quality
- ✔ Distinctiveness
- ✔ Consistency
- ✔ Relevance

Developing your own personal coaching brand ensures that in the modern business landscape where few have expectations of jobs for life any longer, and it's more important to be employable than to be employed, you can showcase your own unique brand of coaching and mentoring so you're counterfeit proof and have a thriving coaching practice.

Defining How Brands Work When They Work Well

Branding, marketing and selling are not synonymous. Three distinctions are apparent:

- **Branding** is a promise to deliver an experience.
- **Marketing** is building a relationship with your target audience, finding out their needs and communicating that you offer a solution to these needs.
- **Selling** is helping potential customers to make a decision.

A brand defines:

- Who you are
- Why you do what you do
- What you do
- Who you serve
- What you give
- What you get

Your personal brand guarantees a client a particular experience that is only of value if you deliver. The promise to deliver is made up of many component parts, including your own name, your history, your talents, how you present yourself, your logo, your coaching style and your after-coaching support. In addition, the better you know yourself and how you operate and are perceived by customers, the better you can define your brand and realise your true value as a coach.

Your brand is your reputation and your promise to deliver. This brand is valuable and can open doors and keep them open when it's built upon solid foundations of trust.

Protecting brand reputations

Brand reputations are among the most prized assets major corporations have. Surveys show that brand valuations are often so high that they compare to the market values of the public companies that own them.

The US Silicon Valley firm Apple has become so well known as a brand that its name and image is worth £75 billion. At the time of writing, Apple is the world's biggest company with a stock market valuation of £385 billion. Its brand value alone has increased by 21 per cent over the past 12 months. A particularly strong correlation exists between branding and profitability; profitability is a key performance indicator that a business is delivering its promises.

However, brands can fall as fast and as hard as they have climbed. In 1982, the DeLorean DMC-12 was released after much hype and expectation to poor reviews. Famous for being the car in the movie series *Back to the Future*, its performance off-screen was not so well received – it quickly became known for its poor production quality and uncompetitive pricing. The company's break-even point was estimated to be 12,000 units, and its first year sales failed to exceed 6,000.

The company brand, already undermined by poor performance, was further damaged when in 1982 founder John DeLorean was arrested for smuggling cocaine worth $24 million into the US. It was alleged to be an effort to salvage his struggling brand. John DeLorean 'the man' was inextricably linked to DeLorean 'the car' by reputation. So although he was ultimately acquitted, the DeLorean Motor Company was not so lucky. The company went bust that year.

On the TV show *The Apprentice*, an unfortunate contestant who in his CV claimed to be an 'amazing team leader' and a 'super salesman' was called into the boardroom after his team failed to sell under his project management and were beaten by the other team. He came under much criticism from his colleagues for his management style and poor performance in selling. After listening to his explanations, Lord Alan Sugar pointed to him and said: 'Personality opens doors, character keeps them open, but your reputation follows you wherever you go – you're fired'.

Brand reputation changes over time and is a reflection of how the organisation operates and is perceived. Even the biggest and best of brands such as Amazon sometimes come under fire for seemingly failing to walk the walk and talk the talk. In recent years, it has been criticised for allegedly not paying taxes and treating its workforce poorly. The best way to protect a brand value is to deliver your promises.

'Your brand is what people say about you when you're not in the room'.

–Jeff Bezos, founder of Amazon

Building a Brand on Purpose

Consider your personal brand as a project that never ends. It evolves over time, adapting as you more clearly define who you are, what you do, whom you serve, what you give and what you get in return. Corporations are always redefining themselves as market conditions change and customer needs alter, but underlying the redefining, their core values and purposes for being in business remain constant and give the business a sense of direction.

Anything that's going to be exceptional is worth spending at least a day working on. Some coaches spend more time designing their business cards than examining who they are, what they do and who they serve. Invest time in building your business on the solid foundations of purpose and you will reap the rewards.

Defining your purpose

Use this guided visualisation to ask a powerful question. Do this exercise when you have 5–10 minutes of uninterrupted time. You may want to play relaxing instrumental music in the background; Vaughn Williams 'The Lark Ascending' or Ennio Morricone's 'The Missions' are excellent choices.

As with all visualisation exercises, do them only when you have a clear mind and are relaxed. See Chapter 10 for techniques that get you into a calm, relaxed creative state.

1. **Take a moment to sit back comfortably and close your eyes, allowing your breathing to relax. Imagine breathing in through your heart, breathing in comfort and ease and exhaling any stress or tensions.**

   With each outward breath, allow your jaw to relax and your mind to quieten a little bit more.

2. **After a few minutes, imagine shining down upon the crown of your head a beautiful white light and give the light a liquid texture that is soft and gentle.**

   Imagine the liquid light flowing in through the crown and down through your mind as you continue to breathe comfortably and easy. Allow the white liquid light to flow down through your head, down your neck and spine, one vertebrae at a time. As you breathe in, see the light fill the part of the body you're focusing on, feel the texture move through your bones, muscles, skin and blood supply. As you breathe out, release any tensions from that part of the body. Imagine the light flowing through your arms down to the tips of your fingers. Take a few minutes to imagine it flowing through your body, past your waist down to the very soles of your feet and tips of your toes progressively, relaxing each part.

3. **When you're as relaxed as you can be from the top of your head down to the tips of your toes, imagine the future extends ahead like a pathway cutting across a large open field.**

   Imagine floating above the pathway so you're looking down at your future. Then, travel off above the future. There's no need to pay attention to the details of the future; just imagine it to be full of fun, success, good health, happiness and all the qualities that for you define a successful fulfilling life.

4. **After a few minutes of travelling off above the future, imagine the pathway ending. Give no time frame to this, just get a sense that it's a long, long way off into the future.**

   This step represents the end of your life.

5. **Imagine that below you is a group of people standing around a headstone. It's all your friends and family, work colleagues and clients attending your memorial service.**

   Beyond them, you can see the field ends and beyond that is a horizon full of stars. Allow yourself to float off into the star-lit sky. Take a moment to enjoy flying among the stars and experiencing a sense of peace, joy and tranquillity.

6. **Then in this space, ask the question, 'What is my purpose?'**

   Simply ask the question and allow whatever comes to mind to present itself without questioning it or examining it. (Some people get an insight; they may hear an answer or see an image or series of images defining their purpose; some get an answer immediately, others may get it days, weeks or even months afterwards in the form of an inspired thought.)

7. **Float back to the edge of the field and the memorial service, bringing back with you the sense of peace, joy and tranquillity and any insights you have from asking the question 'What is my purpose?'**

   Listen to the group of people talking about you; someone is giving a eulogy and talking about your work. Maybe you know him, maybe he is a stranger, someone you haven't yet met. Listen to what they have to say about the difference you made to their lives.

8. **When you have listened to the eulogy, float back above time, returning once again fully to the present and drop down into where you're sitting and slowly bring your attention back to the here and now.**

9. **Take a few minutes to reflect upon the answer to the question and the kind words that were said about you.**

10. **Write them down. This answer is your purpose, why you do what you do.**

This powerful exercise can have a huge impact on the life direction of anyone. We have witnessed people suddenly get insights into how their life should be; some realise just how off-track they are, which means they now know what to change, and others are reassured to find they're already on track.

When you do the 'defining your purpose' exercise, if you come up with a simple purpose, that's okay. You aren't comparing your purpose to others' to see if its grandiose enough. If you didn't get an answer straight away, you can repeat this exercise or simply sit in quiet reflection asking the question 'What is my purpose?' and it will come to you. An indicator that the answer is right is that it feels right. It can inspire you and may even seem a little daunting, which is a good sign because all exceptional things can seem challenging at the start.

The quality of the questions you ask determines the quality of the answers you get. This is one of those big, powerful life questions that is worth reflecting on. If you aren't sure that your purpose is your right purpose, consider it to be the right one for now. It evolves as you evolve as a person.

Keeping the business intact and your values on track

With a defined purpose, take time out to consider your values: 'What's important to you'. Keep the list of values together with your purpose. (See Chapter 8.)

Think of purpose as the Northern Star giving you a sense of direction and values as the inner compass system that lets you know whether you're on track or veering off course.

When all business decisions and your actions align with purpose and values, you're said to be *congruent.* A good indicator that you're congruent is that what you do and say feels right and often seems easy. When incongruent, it feels wrong and can seem like an uphill struggle.

This exercise is called the 'Tell it to the lamp post' exercise, where you get to practise saying out loud your purpose and values until they feel and sound natural and congruent. Follow these steps:

1. **Take your written purpose and list of values and write a short paragraph that defines these.**

   When you have a paragraph that sums up for you why you do what you do, go tell it to the lamp post. The lamp post will not question or critique you.

2. **Keep practising saying the mission statement out loud until it feels natural and right.**

3. **Write your mission statement down and put it in places to remind you of who you are and why you do what you do.**

Here is an example of how congruent purpose, values and mission should look when written down. When said out loud, after some practice, it will sound and feel authentic and natural:

- ✔ **Purpose:** My purpose is to be an inspirational teacher and trainer to others so they can live fulfilling, happy lives.

- ✔ **Values:** Love, fun, honesty, variety.

- ✔ **Mission:** My mission is to inspire business professionals to enjoy their working lives, learning to love what they do and do what they love, and challenge them to be true and authentic to themselves.

Figure 13-1 shows the levels that combine to make up a brand. 'Why you do what you do' is built up from first defining purpose, values and mission. The 'what you do' is built from the marketing, selling and defining of your products and services. This is represented by first defining goals and objectives, putting plans into place and then allocating and doing the tasks to achieve the goals and objectives. (The 'what you do' is covered in Chapter 8 where we explore developing visions. In Chapter 9, we look at turning visions into workable plans.)

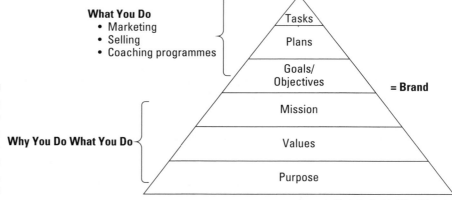

Figure 13-1:
Visually building a representation of a brand.

Illustration by John Wiley & Sons, Ltd.

All the actions you take, what you do, whom you serve, what you give and what you get in return are defined with purpose, values and mission in mind. With this approach, you create a brand that can inspire you every day and distinguish you from those who are simply doing a job.

Making sure you're the real thing

While travelling through India, Steve stopped at a street vendor in the sweltering heat to buy a bottle of chilled Coca-Cola. Coca-Cola was established in 1886 and has a globally recognised brand identity. In 2013, the Coca-Cola company name slipped from being the world's most valuable brand for 13 years; it was knocked down to third place by Apple and Google. In 2013, it had a brand valued at $79.2 billion.

The Coca-Cola company mission is to

✔ Refresh the world

✔ Inspire moments of optimism and happiness

✔ Create value and make a difference

After taking one sip, Steve spat out the drink and poured the rest away. What appeared to be Coca-Cola was upon proper inspection a poor imitation, a fake. On the outside, it appeared to be the same but the experience failed to match to one of Coca-Cola's famous tag lines 'It's the real thing'. Coca-Cola has a distinctive recipe that aligns with the four qualities that define a brand: quality, distinctiveness, consistency and relevance.

Align all your actions to your purpose, values and mission and customers know that you're the real thing by the way you show up and conduct yourself. You can truly stand out from those who aren't being true to themselves.

Looking in the Mirror of Self-Critique

> 'For the past 33 years, I have looked in the mirror every morning and asked myself: 'if today was the last day of my life, would I want to do what I am about to do today?' And whenever the answer has been 'No' for too many days in a row, I know I need to change something. Almost everything – all external expectations, all pride, all fear of embarrassment or failure – these things just fall away in the face of death, leaving only what is truly important. Remembering that you are going to die is the best way I know to avoid the trap of thinking you have something to lose'.
>
> *–Steve Jobs*

There are two common insights that clients get when they do the exercises in the previous section:

✔ We are already aware of purpose, vision and mission, and our actions are all in alignment with them. (This is rarely the case.)

✔ What we do isn't in alignment with purpose, vision and mission, so we must change what we do (which brings up the opportunity to do some valuable coaching).

The next two sections contain exercises to practise first with yourself and then with your clients. They can assist you to define and change 'What you do' in order to be the brand. Begin by asking the question, 'What quality (or qualities) would I need to cultivate in order to conduct myself (or corporation) if I were fully aligned with purpose, values and missions?' What you're looking for is what's missing, what's not there, what can be done better. Both techniques are designed to give clear messages to your unconscious mind that 'this is the way I am and this is the way I want to be'. They're hypnotic by design.

When you do these exercises and make comparisons with others, you don't do it so you can criticise yourself and feel bad; that's called having a 'pity party'. Rather the purpose is to honestly reflect on what can be better and set an intention to change. The only person to measure against is yourself and how you have improved.

Cultivating the qualities of brand excellence

The following exercise uses a technique known as a 'visual squash'. Allow the process to happen naturally.

1. **Having assessed the qualities that need developing, sit comfortably and hold both hands out in front of you, palms up, ensuring that your elbows are not resting on any arm rests.**

2. **In the left palm, imagine how you show up now, doing what you currently do.**

3. **Take a moment to reflect on what is working and then shift your attention to what is missing.**

4. **Look directly at the palm of the right hand and imagine yourself having had developed the missing qualities (use the 'having had' language given); see yourself walking the walk, talking the talk, with all your actions and behaviours being consistent with your purpose, mission and values.**

   Present yourself acting and behaving consistently the way you aspire to be.

5. **Keeping both hands up, stare through the gap in the middle. As you do this, allow your hands to naturally move together.**

   This action happens of its own accord, and the movements may seem jerky. For some people, the hands move together quite quickly; for others, it may take a minute or two. Keep staring through the gap into the distance and imagine the two images blending together with the one on the left hand being absorbed into the image on the right hand.

6. **As the hands begin to move closer together naturally, bring them together and focus on the desired outcome, the image that was on the right hand and then pull your hands towards your heart, and imagine pulling the image inside of you. Then close your eyes.**

7. **Allow yourself to just sit for a minute and imagine having absorbed the missing qualities (or the ones that needed developing) and imagine presenting yourself with these qualities of brand excellence as habits and behaviours that you naturally do.**

The first time you do this exercise, it may seem weird. It even shocks some people as they experience the technique. When trying this technique with clients, simply reassure them throughout by saying 'That's right . . . allow this process to happen naturally'.

Stepping into a brand-new you

This exercise is best done immediately after the exercise in the preceding section because the intention to behave in a particular way has already been set. However, you can also do it at a later time.

1. **Stand up and in your imagination see yourself standing in front of yourself with your back towards you. Run through in your mind all the behaviours, qualities, skills and talents that define you and your brand at present.**

2. **Imagine the representation in front of you having practised all the qualities you want to cultivate and enhance until they're natural habits.**

   If, for example, these qualities are enthusiasm, professionalism, a calm demeanour under pressure and relentless perseverance, add each quality one at a time into the image. See yourself as you want to be. Build up the representation of the 'best version of you'. Do so by giving each quality a colour and then see the colour pouring into the image.

   As they add each colour, some people see one colour replace the previous one; others see them blend or mix. Whichever way you represent the colours is okay and right for you.

3. **When the representation looks as good as you can get it, close your eyes and take a step forward into the image.**

   Step into the best version of you. Stand how you would stand, breathe how you would breathe. Get into the physiology. (In Chapter 10, we cover the importance of physiology.) Take a moment or two to imagine walking around in the shoes of this you.

4. **Open your eyes and imagine looking through the eyes of the best version of you, for now.**

   We say for now because room for improvement is always there. Notice what you believe, what you no longer believe, what's important to you, what is no longer of importance. See the world the way it would be looking through the eyes of this version of you.

Doing this technique is setting an intention for you at a conscious and unconscious level, and you're conditioning yourself to present yourself with all these qualities enhanced. Get into the good practice of repeating this exercise a few times and especially whenever you want to demonstrate the qualities you want to cultivate.

Presenting Yourself with Style and Substance

The purpose of developing your personal brand or the brand of your clients is so you get noticed and get on the shortlist. Then, when customers make a decision, they choose you. It's important to get noticed for the right reasons because every communication you make gets processed; you can easily make the wrong impression and find it not so easy to change it. In Chapter 15, we cover how to engage, inform and influence people to say yes. How you're perceived is a complex process, but your brand stands out from the crowd for the right reasons if you commit to always

- ✔ Doing your best
- ✔ Raising your standards
- ✔ Being authentic

Remember that phrase 'fake it till you make it'? Consider what this phrase really means. It's about pretending to be what or who you're not. Nobody likes a fake so, instead of faking it, use the 'stepping into a brand-new you' exercise as a reminder to practise how you would like it to be until the practice becomes habitual.

Recognising When Incongruence Strikes

Four thousand years ago, the Toltec nation of southern Mexico had a group in its society known as Naguals. They were spiritual masters who developed a set of principles designed to help people be 'better people'. These principles have been handed down through the millennia and offer an ancient way to achieve modern-day results. They provide an effective way to check whether you're presenting yourself as the best you in alignment with purpose, values and mission.

The Toltec four agreements are:

- ✓ **Be impeccable with your word:** A great brand delivers its promises.

- ✓ **Don't take anything personally:** When you get feedback, listen to it, learn from it, don't take it personally. It's a gift from the person who gave it, so use it to improve.

- ✓ **Don't make assumptions:** Ask people what they really think about you and what's needed to improve. Be willing to ask and hear the perceptions of others, and don't be blinded by your own point of view.

- ✓ **Always do your best:** Set the intention to be excellent, and if you fall short, see the second agreement.

When a brand doesn't work, it has violated one or more of these agreements. It has failed to deliver, failed to listen to feedback, made assumptions about customers' needs and wants and failed to do its best.

This exercise, 'Practising daily ancient wisdom for a lifetime of modern excellence', can help you put into practice the agreements for creating your brand.

Choose an agreement for the day. Commit to demonstrating and practising this quality throughout the day and notice how useful it can be for guiding you to present yourself with style and substance. Commit and make a promise to do the exercise (see agreement 1). If you make a mistake, don't make it about you (see agreement 2). When you do the exercise, don't assume you know what you will experience (see agreement 3) and do your best (see agreement 4).

Valuing What You Have to Offer

The department store John Lewis has a tag line 'Never knowingly undersold'. Its website (www.johnlewispartnership.co.uk) explains that this tag line means:

- ✓ **Quality:** 'We have the very highest standards when it comes to product quality, plus we regularly benchmark John Lewis-branded products against the competition to ensure that we're not just market-leading in quality, but also on price'.

- ✓ **Price:** 'We set highly competitive prices for all our products, with a dedicated team regularly checking them against other high street competitors'.

✔ **Service:** 'John Lewis staff are partners in the business, and are highly trained to offer helpful, impartial advice on all products. Our service doesn't end with your purchase – we provide excellent after-sales and a great choice of expert services to help you, from delivery to installation'.

They provide a valuable service and deliver to standards of excellence, and they value what they do and charge appropriately for it. When you operate your coaching business to similar standards of excellence, you can rightly and congruently charge for it as John Lewis does.

Many coaches, especially those new to the profession, often struggle with valuing what they do and charging for it, often underselling or discounting to get work. The strength of your brand and how it's perceived affect your price. Also, the price you charge can affect your brand in a negative way. A low price suggests that you're not in demand and are therefore not good at what you do.

Charging what you're worth

John LaValle, the president of the Society of NLP, shares a wonderful coaching story to demonstrate the importance of valuing what you do and never knowingly underselling yourself. When he first began consulting (read coaching), he was heading off to his first meeting with a client when his wife asked him what he was going to charge. 'Three hundred dollars for the day. That's what Charlie charges, and he's been consulting for a few years'.

As he closed the door, he heard his wife say, 'Of course, you're a lot better than Charlie'. 'Yes, I am better than Charlie!' he thought to himself. By the time he got to his car, he was up to £400. On the drive to the client's, he thought about his rates and how much better he was than Charlie, and by the time he arrived, he had talked himself into charging £500. When he arrived, the client was held up in a meeting and asked him to wait. John decided his time was valuable and he had been kept waiting a long time, so he would charge £750.

The meeting went well, and they got to the point where the client asked his day rate for the three days' consulting. 'It's £1,000 a day', John said confidently. The client looked up and said, 'Wow, that cheap. Why so low?' John answered, 'Well, that's my introductory rate. It's a discounted first job. I normally charge £1,500 a day'. 'That's what we normally pay our consultants', replied the client.

Too many people value what they are not and undervalue what they are.

–Malcolm Forbes

John's metaphor demonstrates two lessons about valuing your brand worth:

✔ Never underprice what you do.

✔ Never assume you know what someone is willing to pay.

Value your brand, and price based on the difference you make and not the time you spend, and you will earn well.

Realising your value

The perceived value of your brand equals the sum of the difference you make to your clients and the uniqueness of your products and services. This approach to appreciating and realising your value is shown in Figure 13-2.

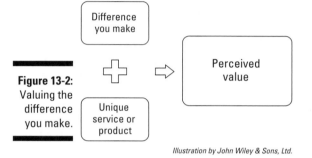

Figure 13-2: Valuing the difference you make.

Illustration by John Wiley & Sons, Ltd.

There are three principles to consider when deciding your value:

- ✔ **Principle 1:** Value is determined by the difference of what you do makes to the customer and the uniqueness of what you have to offer, compared to the competition. The more difference you make and the more unique you are, the more valuable you are.

- ✔ **Principle 2:** People buy solutions to their needs. The more desperate the needs, the more value your solutions have. Make your business solutions focused.

- ✔ **Principle 3:** People value specialists and experts. Position yourself and your brand as a subject specialist and you add value.

Following a six-step model

Here is a six-step model for having a six-figure coaching practice:

1. **Identify the desperate needs of your potential clients.**

   Research your market, listen to forums and chat rooms to identify problems, ask business people what their greatest problems are.

2. **Identify your needs.**

   Define your purpose, values and mission so you're clear about what type of work best suits you.

3. **Create a coaching solution to the desperate needs of your clients that satisfies both your and their needs.**

   This approach guarantees a win-win for both you and client. Think about who the customer is, what pain they experience, how you can alleviate that pain.

4. **Position yourself as a niche specialist in providing the solution.**

   Use social media, articles and books to position yourself as an industry expert.

5. **Market and sell your services.**

   Find the most cost-effective way to inform people about what you do and discover how to get them to say yes when you ask for the order. See Chapter 15 on engaging, informing and influencing.

6. **Charge appropriately for your services.**

   If you underprice, it is a win for the client and a lose for you. That's not a good recipe for a sustainable business.

This six-step model works not just for coaching but for any business. It's possible to have two or three niches to specialise in or more if you or your clients operate a business. However, if you're self-employed and have too many, it's often perceived as you being a 'jack of all trades, master of none', which dilutes your brand value.

Positioning your brand

In the restaurant trade, two extremes are evident – Michelin star restaurants and burger stands – and a whole range of choices can be made in between. Each caters to a distinctively different market and prices accordingly. They both meet the desperate needs of the hungry, and there is a place in the market for both of them.

When deciding where to position your brand, ask yourself the following questions:

✔ Who are my ideal clients?

✔ Are they looking for the coaching equivalent of the Michelin star restaurant or burger bar experience?

Use Figure 13-3 to determine where your brand fits best and ensure that you price according to the sector you fit into.

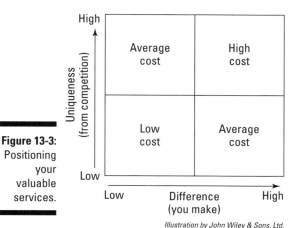

Figure 13-3:
Positioning
your
valuable
services.

If you choose to offer the burger bar experience, aim to offer the best burger bar experience possible. Some amazing street food vendors are out there who offer outstanding quality of food and service, run respectable businesses and have queues of customers who keep coming back for more and refer the business to their friends.

Adjusting your financial thermostat

The main reason coaches fail to charge appropriately is that they have a poor relationship with money. This exercise helps you to readjust and break through any financial fears you may have. Even if you suspect that you have no money issues, still do this exercise. We have worked with fabulously wealthy clients who after doing this exercise have had breakthroughs in earnings and wealth creation.

This exercise is called 'Busting through financial thresholds'.

We all have unconscious thresholds, limits that we often aren't consciously aware exist. With money and wealth, these thresholds affect what we believe we are worth and affect earnings potentials.

1. **Sit down comfortably and review your purpose, values and mission.**

   This step primes your mind to consider earning with all actions being aligned to them. (If you don't have a purpose, values or mission, hurry to Chapter 8!)

2. **Think about how money comes your way and notice how you represent this idea in your mind.**

   It may be in cheques, direct to the bank, by cash or a combination of all. Consider the quantities and frequency in which money comes your way. Do you see a bank statement, a graph, money flowing in from above or from the side? Someone once described seeing a digital readout that changed as money came in. You can represent this idea of money in multiple ways, so go with whatever works for you.

3. **When you have a representation of how money comes in, consider how you represent it going out.**

   This representation includes money spent on household bills, business outgoings, overheads, holidays, entertainment and so on. Some people see the bank statement reducing, others actually see notes and coins diminishing from a pile or disappearing down, above or to the sides. The client who imagined the digital readout saw the figure reducing and turning red when in deficit.

4. **When you have a representation for money flowing in and flowing out, double the income.**

   That's right. Whatever you generate, imagine it was to double and notice what happens. Common reactions to this idea are 'Wow, that would be nice' or 'Ugh, that feels uncomfortable'. If you experience a feeling of discomfort, you have reached an unconscious threshold. Slightly reduce the amount until it feels comfortable and sit with that for a moment and then raise it in increments until the amount is doubled.

5. **When doubling the income, most people see more coming in and more going out, which is understandable as this increased spending is what most people do.**

   As they earn more, they spend more.

6. **Double the amount again.**

7. **If you're uncomfortable with the amount, repeat the instructions in Step 4.**

8. **Double it again.**

   As you see money flowing in and flowing out, there comes a point where you see yourself earning more than enough for all the costs of living and the stuff of life, so imagine any excess money going off into investments and projects that align with your purpose and values.

9. **Double it again and keep doubling it until the amounts seem ludicrous, even unrealistic.**

   It can get to the millions and even billions, and you feel comfortable with it.

When you have completed the exercise, simply sit with the experience for a few minutes, allowing your mind to reorganise the clear messages you have given it. Those messages are to remove any limitations and thresholds you may have had around wealth generation and to align all you do with purpose, values and mission, leaving you free to accept your true value.

Promoting Yourself with Shameless Humility

Our deepest fear is not that we are inadequate. Our deepest fear is that we are powerful beyond measure. It is our light, not our darkness, that most frightens us. We ask ourselves, Who am I to be brilliant, gorgeous, talented, fabulous? Actually, who are you not to be? You are a child of God. Your playing small does not serve the world.

–Marianne Williamson

This partial quote from Marianne Williamson's book *A Return to Love* sums up the approach of far too many great coaches. They play small out of fear. They undervalue what they do and the difference it makes. During the recent recessionary years, a commonly used word was 'austerity'. The theme for governments and businesses was to cut back and save. Money stopped flowing, and business began to grind to a halt. Only so much can be cut back whereas what can be created and generated by business is limitless. As a coach, you have the privilege to assist businesses to create and generate wealth and to flourish and thrive. Think of it as irresponsible for you not to shamelessly promote your services when it serves the greater good.

When a business is service-orientated, its focus is 'How may I be of service?', it provides the solutions to the desperate needs of others and when no fear is evident around charging, the business will flourish financially.

Follow these simple rules and flourish and thrive:

- ✔ Be service-orientated and ask 'How may I be of service?'
- ✔ Know your mission by heart and welcome any opportunity to get into a conversation about it.
- ✔ Have your business cards to hand and make sure yours is the one people remember because of the way you present yourself.
- ✔ Always answer your phone when it rings. It's someone waiting for you to take his order.
- ✔ When people enquire about your services, don't tell them about what you do; give them an experience that demonstrates the difference your coaching makes. Give them a 'Wow' experience.

✔ Never assume that a client can afford you or not afford you. They all can or will find a way when you demonstrate that you have the solution to their needs.

✔ Ask for the business. It's been said that a 'yes' lives in the land of 'no'. Even of a client says 'no', turn the 'no' into a 'know' by asking why and learning to get better at engaging, informing and influencing clients to make the good decision to coach with you.

✔ If the business isn't right for you or the client lets it go, always work from a win-win perspective. Enough clients are around to keep all coaches busy. When you work with clients who are a good fit for your business and inspire you, you're being true to your brand; you're no longer just doing a job – you're doing inspired work.

Lighting Up the Room When You Walk In, Not When You Walk Out

Have you ever walked into a room and picked up the tension in the air? No one needed to say anything; you just naturally knew something was up. A principle comes into play here called *harmonic resonance*. Harmonic resonance is an extraordinary phenomena observed throughout physics where two seemingly separate systems (in this case, two people in a room) interact and exchange energy, and both take on some of the qualities of the other. They are said to resonate in harmony. Humans experience this phenomena at a physiological level. Imagine two pianos in a room. A note is played on one piano and the same note vibrates on the second. Physiologically, we do the same. If an extreme state such as fear or anger is evident, the neurology picks up the signal through 'mirror neurones' and resonates.

Consider two scenarios, one where a coach walks into a networking event. He has done all his branding work, is competent and capable but is worried about how he is perceived. Then think about the same coach with the same competencies but not thinking about himself and instead thinking about how he may best be of service to this group of strangers. Here you have two different thinking styles, two different states and two rather different harmonic resonances.

Before entering into any situations where you get to present your brand, set the intention to be 'the best you'. Your state of mind then affects others in a positive way, and when the business cards get swapped, yours is the one that people recall as making them feel good. Because you're in a good state, you are in a better psychological frame of mind to see and hear the opportunities to get into conversations that can lead to business. See Chapter 10 on state management.

Leaving a Legacy Footprint

Experts have estimated that the average person spends 90,000 hours of his life at work; that's an average of 11,250 working days or 2,250 working weeks, and what is there to show for it? Perhaps the mortgage is paid off, the children are put through school and university, some holidays and all the other things that make up the sum total of the average human life. In terms of leaving a legacy and making an impact on the world, deciding how you spend your valuable time is important. Doing the exercise in the 'Defining your purpose' section earlier in this chapter, where you got to hear your epitaph, will help you reflect on the difference you made with your time on planet Earth. What if the epitaph you heard was that you worked really hard? Maybe it would get you to reconsider what you are currently doing and whether it makes a difference in the world.

On a coaching seminar, the trainer asked the group a question: 'How many people have had a near-death experience and how did this experience affect how you treated the rest of your life?' The purpose of the question was to get people to 'wake up' and enjoy life. Perhaps there was a different question to ask: 'How many people have had a near-life experience? That's when you get to the last day on planet Earth and look back and go, 'damn I wished I'd done it differently'.'

Bronnie Ware is a nurse turned author who spent several years in palliative care working with people in the last 12 weeks of their lives. In her book *The Top Five Regrets of the Dying*, she lists the common regrets people have when they think about how they spent their valuable lives. In order of biggest regret first:

1. I wish I'd had the courage to live a life true to myself, not the life others expected of me.

2. I wish I hadn't worked so hard.

3. I wish I'd had the courage to express my feelings.

4. I wish I had stayed in touch with my friends.

5. I wish I had let myself be happier.

When you define your personal brand built on purpose, aligned with your values and only choosing to do work that inspires you, you'll spend those precious moments being true to yourself. You'll be well on the way to becoming one of the few people who can put a line through the first most common regret.

As a coach, you get to make a dent in the universe and to impact people's lives in powerful ways, the full consequences of which often show up in time and in ways you can never predict and often don't share. Your purpose-driven brand leaves behind a legacy footprint of empowered individuals, teams and organisations that in their own way make a positive difference.

Making a difference one at a time

A man is walking along a beach after a storm out at sea. Ahead of him he sees a line of starfish washed up by the tide. As he walks closer, he sees a small bent-up old lady with a walking stick crouching down to pick up one starfish. She turns and hobbles down the sand to the water's edge and throws it back into the sea. She turns back and slowly makes her way up the sand to collect another starfish. The beach is littered with thousands and thousands of dying starfish. As he reaches the old lady, he asks her what she's doing. 'I'm saving the starfish', she replies as she casts another out into the water. 'But there are thousands. You're not going to make a difference', he says. She stops and looks out towards the starfish she just threw. 'Well, it made a difference to that one', she says as she turns to collect another.

You are not in the business of rescuing people. Coaching is about making a positive difference. Keep this idea in mind and remember the value you add by what you do.

Remembering that You Have No Sell-By Date

Branding demands commitment to continual reinvention; striking chords with people to stir emotions; and commitment to imagination. It is easy to be cynical about such things, much harder to be successful.

–Richard Branson

Retired footballer David Beckham recently announced he is taking up acting. Beckham's business interests include a large stake in his wife's successful clothing company, Haig Club (Whiskey) and Miami FC with a range of Beckham-branded products to his name. He provides a great example of a brand known for delivering results. With a great work ethic and a commitment to excellence, his brand has evolved over time and will undoubtedly continue to evolve even beyond his acting career.

The uniqueness and worth of each individual changes over time. As you develop as a coach, you gain more experience and have more to offer. With a solid personal brand underpinning what you do, you get the chance to repackage throughout your career.

Chapter 14

Developing Relationships at All Levels

In This Chapter

▶ Developing a healthy relationship with yourself to increase personal flexibility

▶ Establishing relationships with others that develop and sustain the business

▶ Handling potentially unhealthy relationships

*B*usiness coaching needs to be business and leader led. It's impossible to do one without the other. This chapter looks at how business leaders choose to relate to themselves and others. Coaches and mentors have a role to play in supporting leaders to consider how they show up, how they manage relationships with others and what that means for their reputation, their business and themselves personally.

Establishing a Successful Relationship with Yourself

Relational leadership is a style where leaders encourage positive relationships and working context among those they manage. It's often synonymous with behavioural flexibility and emotional intelligence. Business leaders need both, and coaches can add value in helping leaders explore what these mean in their day-to-day management of themselves and others.

Emotional intelligence (EI) relates to interpersonal and intrapersonal intelligence. The ability to know, accept and manage yourself (self-awareness, self-regulation, empathy, motivation, social skills) and an ability to work effectively with others. Self-awareness is about understanding personal strengths and your impact on others, your weaknesses, what you value and what drives you.

Business leaders aren't always shy when the stakes are high

Successful business usually has synergy between the identity of the business and the public persona of the business leader. Take UK fashion and retail, and think of Sir Philip Green. He's known for his taunting phone calls to the chairman of Marks and Spencer during an attempted takeover bid and an alleged lapel-grabbing incident when he taunted Sir Stuart Rose with the comment 'the only jet you will ever know is EasyJet'. Now, nothing is wrong with EasyJet. EasyJet is a highly successful business and beloved by many across Europe and beyond. Green's reference was to his own commute to work between his home in Monaco and his office in London on his private jet. Like many areas of business, retail is highly competitive and markets can be ruthless. His taunts were characteristic of someone who is known for his ruthless pursuit of wealth creation for the thrill of winning.

Through the coaching process, you can help clients bring their strengths and areas of development into awareness. It can be useful to both the coach and the leader to start from an agreed baseline. You can establish the baseline in various ways. You can buy an off-the-shelf EI product and give it to a cross-section of your client's team, then feed back to her, or you can help her explore the level of her own awareness through a combination of personal data gathering and getting to know the client, her motivations, setbacks and known development 'wants'.

Whether as a leader or a coach, you may want to complete the exercises in the next section.

Establishing the Baseline

You have a number of ways to help a client see herself and become aware of the impact of her experience and how that may manifest in behaviour and habits. The following is just one three-step process you can use in a two- to three-hour session.

Step 1: Gathering the personal map

Ask your client to bring every bit of objective and subjective data she has about herself to the session. This data may include psychometrics (MBTI, DISC, OPQ and the like, reasoning tests, talent assessment data), personal appraisals, career review documents, CV and prior training record.

Wherever your client sits, notice where she is facing. Use a table to the left of her if you can or the left side of a large table. Ask her to use the data to write 20 or 30 sticky notes that summarise the information about herself that is indicated in that data. Ask her to position them on the table and organise them as she wants. Use prompt questions to help, but let her describe her data in her own words.

Step 2: Identifying high points and low points

Stand where you have enough room for both of you to walk and create a timeline by putting A4 pieces of evenly spaced paper on the floor from left to right that represent each decade from 0 to the client's current decade (0, 10, 20, 30, 40 and so on). Get your client to stand on the 10, to look back to the 0 and consider her first 10 years of life. Ask her to just talk you through her key informative experiences as she recalls them – the high points and low points.

TIP

Let your client decide what to include. Some will want to highlight significant life events at each decade; others will want to highlight only those from working age. Work with what your client gives you. There's no need to dig around in the recesses of her childhood. Remember this isn't therapy; you are simply encouraging the client to reflect and identify the indicators that have informed her experience to date. You may want to write them down for her as you go along.

When she has arrived at 10 and is complete, ask her to walk to 20, to look back to the 10 and consider the decade 10–20. Go through the process for each decade, noting the high points and low points as you go. If the client isn't currently of an age ending with 0, end by asking the client to consider the period from now back to her last decade marker. When you have elicited the timeline, ask your client to look back along the timeline while you read through the notes at a storytelling pace so the client hears her story retold. She may want to add other things.

Ask your client to combine the two sets of information (the sticky notes and the timeline), and ask her what she notices about her strengths and high points. What made them high points, and what is the client noticing about her own abilities? Really help the client see and feel her strengths and wisdom.

Coach her at a slow enough pace for your client to hear the volume and weight of her success. Coach and encourage her to breathe it all in by saying things such as, 'Notice how you were good at x from a very early age. You must have been unconsciously competent at that for a very long time. Some people spend years trying to acquire that skill. Can you see how valuable that is in you and for other people?' . . . and so on. Your job in this part is to help her really get a sense of the value she brings. You may sometimes see a client stand a little taller and straighter when you do this. Just notice it for yourself – no need to comment on it.

Ask what she notices about the low points when the feedback indicated she wasn't operating at her best. Really help your client see her whole self and understand the learning she needs to do. If she is struggling to see her contribution to the low points, ask her things such as, 'So when you consider that low point, what can you take from it that may help you now and in the future?', 'What is there for you to learn here?', 'What would others say if you asked them?'

By now, your client is really becoming aware of patterns in her past behaviours and possibly gaining some new insight into how others experience her. You want to keep her there a little longer. Just give her plenty of space to notice her whole self.

Step 3: Discovering desired improvement

The next step is to help your client determine what she may need to do more of, try out or change. Where does she want to direct her strengths to increase her own behavioural flexibility? What would she like to create in her relationships? What may she need to work at and with whom? Encourage her to begin to create specific outcomes and to articulate how she will know that the improvement she wants is on track or has been made.

Ask her to create a visual map that shows what she wants to improve and what can create more success. Help her recap what she has learned about herself; where things have worked out and where they haven't. Suggest that she considers how she can use the insights she has noted. Encourage her to share her self-discovery with others beyond the coaching to garner their support in managing her own areas of development as she tries new ways of delivering and makes small or major adjustments.

This subject also relates to you. This isn't just information. Self-awareness is a cornerstone to help you deliver flexibly and enable others to succeed. You need to be able to catch yourself when you have patterns of behaviour that don't support you and to notice what you do that works so you can do more of it. Do the work if you want results.

Working on Yourself

Self-awareness and self-development are ongoing for leaders and coaches, particularly senior leaders. Technical and professional skills are obviously important, but if these skills are your focus as a senior leader, think again. Research shows that as leaders become more senior, the importance of technical skill diminishes and the need to manage self and relationships with others increases. The focus on self-awareness and relationships creates business and career opportunities. The same is true for coaches. Clients want to know that a coach has technical coaching skills and a broad toolkit. In business coaching, this factor isn't usually the distinguishing one. The relationship a coach creates with a business owner/leader is often more important. Coaches are in the impactful conversation business. The way you relate as a coach and how your prospective client experiences you is critically important.

If you ever thought that clients must 'run out' of issues to coach on, or that there just aren't enough clients out there with issues that require coaching support, you may well not be doing enough work on yourself. (Ouch, that hurt a little didn't it?). Coaches who struggle to find clients often have work to do on their own beliefs to get them beyond their 40 days and 40 nights in the coaching client desert.

Being authentic

If you're a coach, expect any business leader you coach to ask you what work you've done on yourself and what your ongoing development entails. They're trusting you with their history, their fears, hopes and desires. To them, it's personal, and you need to create and maintain rapport by sharing something of yourself.

It seems reasonable for a client to expect a coach to have a coach – to be working with a coaching supervisor, coach or mentor. This person keeps you on track, helps you with the inner work and stretches you to develop your practice and work on your own self-awareness. Both of your humble book authors have experienced mentors and coaches that we draw on for our ongoing self-reflection and development. We have failings, foibles and frustrations like most of the adult population. Our clients bring things to coaching that press our buttons, touch our emotions and make us question our thinking.

Observing yourself and increasing your self-awareness is key for a coach. Like your clients, you need a sounding board to discuss your practice and your business, someone who holds up the mirror and says, 'Take a look, it isn't pretty' or 'You're fabulous, you just can't see it at the moment'. Ask yourself, 'If I am going to be the best leader in my business or coaching practice that I can be, what do I need to have in place to ensure that I remain on top of my game?' Do you need a coach, a mentor or both to help you keep it real?

Practise what you preach and be what you teach. If you're a practising coach, get a coach who pushes you beyond where you think you can reach, no matter how experienced you are. Do the work and then, sometime later, be prepared to do it again.

Staying in the game

Leaders and coaches need to have fresh ideas and insights. Ongoing professional development and your understanding of business are important. You need to stay connected to the world of business and your profession or industry area. For some, this may mean reading the business and economic outlook pages in a newspaper regularly, listening to business programmes and meeting up with colleagues in a network. For others, regular training and maintaining professional hours and accreditation are important. Keep the thinking and the skill set moving. A stale leader is like stale bread, and you know what happens to that – it becomes toast.

A great coach can spot a fellow professional who is coasting around the toaster from 50 paces. They're delivering the same talk that they delivered three years ago, using the same stories and the same slide deck. They're coaching and leading people using 'their way' or riding out their role by attaching themselves to a client for far too long. This situation is like self-service at a supermarket checkout where the cashier has left the keys in the cash register. They're primarily serving their own needs and interests, and expecting others to fall in as they sing, 'I did it my way' down the aisle marked 'I'm the only game in town'. They're not, and unfortunately their complacency takes them out of the game. You can read about working with a 'my way' attitude in Chapter 11.

Starting strong and avoiding needy

Ted was an entrepreneur who had been seeing his business mentor for two years since he supported him with a pitch to a bank. The mentor was an ex-banker who retired about 25 years ago at 55. He had never trained in using the coaching skill set or carried out any mentorship development. He was a self-styled mentor who had adopted the title on his business card and was trading on his many years of successful experience in finance and investment banking, which he was exceptionally good at. Ted came to see Marie to discuss the possibility of her coaching him. He was selling his company and creating a new venture. He wanted to create an organisation fast to take an existing but enhanced testing solution into the biotech market within 15 months and had secured significant capital funding for start-up and first-phase development.

Marie asked what he had worked on with his mentor so far. She wanted to understand how Ted's mentor had helped him get to this stage and where she might add value going forward. Ted told her that his mentor hadn't really been involved in supporting him on developing his thinking or the process of creating the spin-out idea. He'd worked that through with a friend and business owner who had created several businesses. He also said that he saw his mentor four to six times a year for a 'chat and accountability catch up'.

You've probably guessed that the mentor was acting as Ted's financial conscience. He was an accountability partner who was holding Ted to account on the detail of the finances that the mentor had helped him secure. This isn't mentoring! If Ted were learning from the exchange and getting value, then maybe what they called it would be irrelevant. Marie asked Ted what he found helpful about the meetings and what was it about the way they worked together that supported him in moving forward. She wanted to tease out any nuggets that had worked for Ted that could be taken into the coaching relationship.

 If something has worked well for a client, you'll find that useful to know. Understanding how a prospective client has worked well with another coach or mentor can give you valuable data to help you design a coaching programme for her.

Ted took quite a long time to answer and eventually said, 'Help me? Well, he has made sure that the business has delivered what we said we would to investors. He's checked the contractual agreements regularly and made sure that the business stayed within the lines on those financial agreements. He's spoken with our investors when we've had cash flow issues and helped to draw down additional temporary capital'.

Can you guess what Marie's next question was? 'Have you got a finance director and/or a chief operating officer (COO)?' Answer: 'Yes'. Next question? 'Is he/she coming with you into the new company?' Answer: 'No. I need someone more robust who can handle some of the complexity and relationships with these new investors more proactively'. At this point, Marie breathed a sigh of relief. She established that the financial 'mentor' wasn't going to be involved in the new company either as the investment had been secured through a group of business angels who didn't want him on board. They were putting one of their people with financial skills on the Board. Thankfully, someone in that investment group was paying attention. This example is a classic one of an advisor serving his own needs and creating foggy boundaries with the COO role. The COO role is where the duties the 'mentor' was performing should have been located.

Marie didn't coach Ted. When they discussed his requirements, he really wanted short-term consultancy support to look at how to design the organisation, to know what elements to put in place and how to set up a senior structure and attract talent quickly. She did a piece of consultancy with him and, as he brought his senior people on board, facilitated some planning and leadership away days with his C suite of COO, chief accountant and chief information officer. Ted's experience of 'being mentored' had clouded his understanding of the difference between coaching and mentoring and consultancy.

Don't assume that leaders know the distinction between coaching, mentoring and consultancy, or that the support relationships they've enjoyed or endured with previous coaches, mentors and consultants meet with your own understanding. The important thing is for coaches to be clear about the offering and the business that they're in and for leaders to be clear on what service they're looking for before investing in a relationship. If you're unclear, the distinctions are set out in Chapter 1.

When meeting leaders to discuss coaching, don't assume that it's necessarily the right solution. It may not be what the business really needs. Check assumptions and be prepared to explore other possibilities. Keep the needs of your client's business uppermost and leave any egotistic desire to be needed and to get a coaching contract at all costs at the door. It will pay off in the end. Your reputation is only as good as your last coaching assignment and your ability to help people get what they need to move forward.

Maintaining Client Relationships

When you have established a coach-client relationship (see Chapter 4 and Chapter 1 for ideas on creating great client relationships), it needs your ongoing attention. Nurturing relationships requires planning, commitment and contact. Sounds easy, doesn't it? In fact, this is an area where coaches and leaders can come unstuck. You can both get so engaged in the coaching that the coach forgets that they're in the relationship business or the leader forgets to review the relationship and what she wants from it. This slide can lead to disenchantment and, before you know it, the client starts cancelling because she's not seeing the value in turning up. This problem translates across all aspects of business, not just coaching. Checking that you're delivering what the customers want to the standard they expect is important and can make the difference between losing or retaining a key piece of business.

A great deal of business gets created through relationships more generally. This business may be collaborating with others on products and joint marketing or even creating a merger or spin-out company. It could be a decision to partner in a new market under a different name or with new products, or simply creating new customers and distribution channels because of a conversation you have at a networking event. Learning how to relate to others and actively managing relationships creates leverage in business. This skill isn't optional.

Creating a sustainable business requires a degree of focus on nurturing the business, not just the delivery of the product. Set time aside in the diary to actively work on the business. Call a client you haven't spoken to in a while and meet just to catch up and explore opportunities. Suggest to existing clients that you spend time reviewing how things are going and what they think of your offering. Get to grips with what's working or not working for the client and whether you're meeting her expectations. Remember to check that the client is actually getting what she wants.

Checking commitment and desire

Neuro-Linguistic Programming (NLP) includes a technique that relates to getting specific about desire and checking commitment towards that desire by creating well-formed outcomes. This consideration can be useful when working with any customer/client. Most organisations define their outcomes using SMART goals – checking whether an outcome is specific, measureable, achievable, relevant and that it has a definitive time scale. The theory is that if it's not SMART, it's too loose and is at risk of not being delivered.

Those of you who have been around organisations for many years will have seen many beautifully drafted outcomes, objectives or goals. Call them what you like, they're gradations of an intention to deliver something for some-one with a set of resources within a certain timeframe. Intentions that have been poured over by leadership teams, reworked, redefined and planned out meticulously, leaping through approval hoops and back again to land in some form in a performance plan somewhere. Sometimes they're not realised because of economic circumstances, movements in personnel, changes in markets, the unexpected curve ball or a lack of required expertise. Most times, delivery isn't achieved because of human factors: simply, a lack of commitment and desire to achieving the articulated result. This area is great for coaching.

One of the things you may want to do with your beautifully crafted SMART goals is check the level of commitment and desire that those responsible have towards delivering them (see the following section). Help them get as specific as possible. Getting specific creates a commitment and stops a goal from being merely aspirational. In business terms, it's the difference between planning what to do and actually delivering and measuring what you said you would do.

Case example of how to check for commitment to goals

The following coaching example shows you how to check for commitment and desire to established SMART goals. You can ask individuals to do this exercise on their own or do it with them.

Business outcome: By the end of December the customer services team in the meat packing unit will have improved the time for acknowledging and answering initial complaints from five days to three days and have improved customer satisfaction with our complaints process while reducing packing and delivery errors.

On the face of it, this situation looks specific, measurable, achievable, realistic and timed. You have enough here for someone to go away and work out a delivery plan but it has no 'juice'. If you were coaching the customer services team or the managers in that team, you would want to help them create a really rich picture. You want to help them flush out any concerns they're aware of and any unconscious factors that may block them.

You can use a structured dialogue and ask them:

- ✔ 'Given this is a goal you're expected to deliver, what specifically do you want to deliver?'

  Keep asking, what else, specifically what? Get the team to be really specific and to articulate it out loud. Get it onto flip charts or an electronic whiteboard. This meat company example is a real case. Steve helped the group to make it real. They came up with things such as 'I want to hear Geoff in the freezer section say, "Well, you have stopped Marston's Meats from complaining every week. I'll make the coffee for a week for your team."'

- ✔ 'How will you know without doubt that you have achieved your outcome?'

  You want really concrete measures here. You want them to position themselves in absolute faith that this has been delivered and they know it because . . . This team knew their figures and could say readily what that reduction in complaints would mean in terms of the volume of paperwork in the next ten months. They could calculate in their heads what it would mean for their customers and that it would mean a strong possibility that they would keep a key customer without whom the jobs of some butchery colleagues could be at risk. They all knew exactly what it would mean for their Christmas bonus, one of them to the penny. This involvement is what you want. You want rich, meaningful, personal feel-good indicators that will motivate people to deliver. The fact that the bonus could be higher isn't enough by itself.

- ✔ 'What evidence will you show to others that the goal has been achieved?'

  Building on the last question, you're asking the group to really imagine what and where is the proof that lets others know that they've delivered as they said they would. Steve worked with this group to elicit how they would celebrate, how they would go down to the local pub on Friday night after work and spend the kitty that their manager was going to give them from their Christmas fund. They agreed to hold some of it back until the end of the month to have their 'three days three beers three teams fest'. Through facilitating the group, Steve was getting them to imagine it happening and how wonderful it would feel to drink that first celebration drink together.

✔ 'How will they know?'

Here you're looking for whether the team can put themselves in the shoes of others who have an interest in them succeeding (or not) and how they will know that others have noticed their achievements. This team came up with things such as, 'Mr Drew will see the movement in the weekly figures and he will know if we are going to hit our average by the end of November from the complaint logs. He will see the electronic chart shift red to amber'.

✔ 'What specifically will they experience/see/hear/feel?'

Help the team think about what people around them may experience as well as themselves. You're helping them to attach emotions and visual images to their developing story. The more they can create that, the more likely they are to be motivated to do it and to notice the simple specific indicators that let them know they're on track.

✔ 'What colour is it?'

This part is where some of them say, 'Huh?' Stick with it and push them for the detail. They've a colour in mind. They may feel weird to admit it. They have one. By sharing something that makes them go, 'Huh?' and creating a dialogue about it, you're making connections to the outcome and creating dialogue at a different level of abstraction, in this case quite an amusing one about, 'How could an outcome delivered be green and a complaint be pink – surely they were all red'.

✔ 'What shape is it?'

Again a question designed to get them talking about how they saw the outcome so they have a common picture. This team created a set of circles with a fountain sprouting money in the middle. So now they had a green-and-white outcome, which had moved from red and pink over a ten-month period, and it was a set of interlinked circles with a fountain of money in the middle.

✔ 'What does it sound like?'

By now, the team will be rolling with it or will be cajoled into playing along. This team were clear – it sounded like a cascade of coins coming out of a slot machine at high speed. (Some of them even attempted to sound it out.)

✔ 'What does it smell like?'

So now their successful outcome has a clear picture with sound attached, and they agree that the smell is of cold frosty morning – clean and fresh.

You now take all the information they've given you and play it back to them while they simply listen and imagine themselves achieving it between now and the deadline. Encourage the client to close their eyes and make the picture – to feel the sensations they've described and hear it all internally.

Just notice what fun you can have with a seemingly bland outcome or goal. It can really fire people up and get them motivated. It makes a fairly boring sentence on a page come alive into something with possibility behind it.

Although we have described this process as a group one here, you can walk through this with individuals or you can work with a group and ask them to work through their own process individually as you guide them through it.

 If you're thinking of using a structured process such as this one with clients, you can record it on a phone or laptop for them. That way, their own dialogue is there to play back. They have the process available to access anytime they choose. Small things such as a recording can really add value for clients. It places them in control. Empowering clients builds the relationship.

Managing Stakeholder and Sponsor Relationships

All businesses have stakeholders and all have sponsors of some kind. A *stakeholder* is anyone who has an interest in the success of a business, such as staff, suppliers and investors. A sponsor is someone who supports an individual, a project or activity and who normally has influence because she gives time or allocate money and resources for specific activities.

Being clear about who your stakeholders are and how to manage those relationships can be business critical. Sponsors are important because they can have significant influence over what gets done and how it is delivered. Both types of relationships need to be nurtured over time.

Managing stakeholder relationships

Think about the business objectives you're responsible for. Who is involved in delivering those? Who stands to gain or lose if those objectives aren't delivered? Think broadly in terms of internal and external people and groups.

1. Make a list of stakeholders.

2. Consider the list and have in mind one of your broad objectives.

   • Whom do you need support from to deliver it?

   • Who on the list can help you do that?

   • Who may try to get in your way or hinder your delivery?

   Revisit that list and circle those stakeholders.

3. Which stakeholders are **highly committed** and invested in your outcome (an advocate)? What level of influence do they have on your outcome?

   • **High influence:** They can make things happen or put a stop to things directly.

   • **Medium influence:** They can have an impact through influencing others.

   • **Low influence:** They cannot change or influence others even though they personally may be supportive.

   Put their names in the appropriate box on the grid in Figure 14-1.

4. Which stakeholders are fairly neutral? They have **medium-level commitment** towards your outcome and may be persuaded either way to support it or not. What level of influence do they have on your outcome?

   • **High influence:** They can make things happen or put a stop to things directly.

   • **Medium influence:** They can have an impact through influencing others.

   • **Low influence:** They cannot change or influence others even though they personally may be supportive.

   Put their names in the appropriate box on the grid in Figure 14-1.

5. Which stakeholders have a **low commitment** towards your outcome and are a potential naysayer or adversary? What level of influence do they have on your outcome?

   • **High influence:** They can make things happen or put a stop to things directly.

   • **Medium influence:** They can have an impact through influencing others.

   • **Low influence:** They cannot change or influence others even though they personally may be supportive.

   Put their names in the appropriate box on the grid in Figure 14-1.

The simple grid shown in Figure 14-1 can be used to help leaders decide where to maintain or increase effort to gain commitment and where the influence of others impacts success favourably or less favourably.

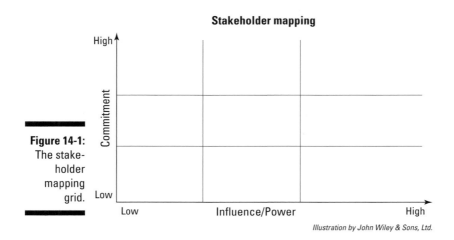

Figure 14-1: The stakeholder mapping grid.

Illustration by John Wiley & Sons, Ltd.

You have a map of stakeholder influence and if you overlay that with the four quadrants of keep informed, manage closely, minimal effort and keep satisfied (as shown in Figure 14-2), you can see where your efforts need to be directed to get your outcome delivered. These four strategies can be utilised depending on the pattern of stakeholder relationships.

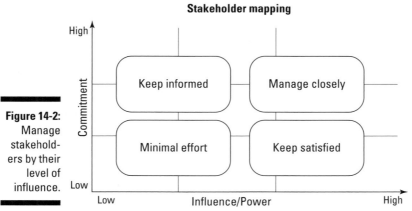

Figure 14-2: Manage stakeholders by their level of influence.

Illustration by John Wiley & Sons, Ltd.

Leaders can make the mistake of thinking that if they hang out with supportive stakeholders, they will be able to deliver, which may not necessarily be the case. The level of influence that a stakeholder or group of stakeholders have on an outcome is more important than whether they like you. The relationship management effort needs to be with the high-influence people to keep them engaged and to persuade them to influence others, particularly those in the neutral commitment area. This process is how you get the neutral and high-commitment stakeholders to actively support. You also need to minimise the impact of those with high influence but low commitment by winning them over or garnering support elsewhere.

When you think about this outcome now, what relationships do you need to cultivate? Where can you place your efforts? Where can you collaborate with others to get things accepted by the high-influence, low-commitment people? Where can you anticipate conflict? What relationships may you need to actively monitor? Where may you need to build trust? What networks may support you and whom may you need to network with for support?

Can you see how you can work through your key deliverables one by one or as a whole to look at how you manage and develop relationships?

If you combine the checking commitment and desire exercise and the stakeholder mapping exercise, you begin to develop a level of detail to inform you where to place your relationship management efforts and emphasis to create success.

Communicating in triangular situations

Three-way relationships can be tricky if the roles aren't clear and distinct. Sponsors usually play a third-party role in relationships where they commit resources and have a degree of responsibility for the outcome. Normally, you also have the project manager and the manager that the project manager is accountable to. These tri-partite managerial relationships overlap and can be complex to navigate for everyone involved.

In organisational project management, the sponsor is often the project chair with high influence and high commitment to the project. Such a person exerts power and needs to be kept actively informed. In terms of influencing a sponsor, the Project Management Institute describes the need for the project manager to establish a relationship of trust with the sponsors to understand their motivations, expectations and the constraints they operate under. The PMI sets out the conditions for developing and managing the relationship with the project sponsor if you're the project manager:

✔ Work out what's important to them and focus on helping them be successful.

- Connect your project objectives to their objectives.

- Remind them gently if they don't fulfil the team's expectations of support.

- Deliver any negative news in person.

- When you present a problem, have a proposed solution.

- Tailor your communication style according to how they like to receive information.

- Stay connected and keep them proactively updated.

As the line manager supporting your member of staff taking a project management role, coaching her around these factors may be useful. You want to empower your staff member to manage expectations and complexity.

Complex relationships are a fact of life, and many leaders now find themselves managing across matrix teams and multiple project groups. Learning how to trust, motivate and set stretch goals, how to give feedback, manage expectations and handle difficult conversations when they arise are all part of the 21st-century skill set.

Sponsoring a coaching intervention

The sponsor relationship in a coaching situation is different. The sponsor can be the person who commissions the coaching for her member of staff or may be the HR director or a senior manager offline. Although the coach normally relates to the sponsor initially, the boundary in this triangle between the sponsor, the coachee and the coach needs to be explicit. The paymaster may be the sponsor holding the resources but the client you're serving is the coachee. A coach needs to be clear on this relationship at the contracting stage and throughout. The coach may want to keep the sponsor informed of the coachee's attendance at sessions but not the detail of them. The coachee may be encouraged to have conversations with her line manager to keep her informed of the impact of her coaching.

The coach may well report back in broad terms on the process of coaching towards the agreed coaching outcomes but not the content of the coaching itself. This can sometimes present a concern if a sponsor hasn't understood her role in the coaching context, particularly if she acts as sponsor in projects and expects to be more involved and informed. If leaders in organisations don't understand the role of a coach and the nature of the triangular relationship (or sometimes four-way relationship if the sponsor isn't the line manager), don't be shy about making it explicit before the potential for mistrust creeps in.

Manage expectations proactively. Be clear about confidentiality and reporting throughout. If not, these things may be a source of confusion and even conflict.

Building Synergistic Collaboration

Developing collaborative relationships within and outside of a business can help to leverage ideas, investment, innovation and the like. Many high-growth businesses have been spawned through collaborative working and the development of specific industry networks. The hi-tech sector in particular has actively identified synergies in new products or joint working and collaborated to create spin-outs and new joint ventures. This situation is particularly evident in hi-tech business clusters in Silicon Valley and Cambridge. A study undertaken by Myint et al published in 2005 demonstrates the importance of networks and collaboration. Their mapping of the development of the Cambridge Silicon Fen shows how *social capital*, an investment in key relationships over time, has created economic capital in the Cambridge area.

Creating synergy and serial entrepreneurship

Serial entrepreneurship has encouraged and supported new ventures and encouraged businesses to establish themselves in the Cambridge area and take advantage of localised social ties. This situation has helped firms access funding more readily and shows the power of a network to create and leverage innovation and synergy fast. The region has become expert at creating spin-out ventures in both biotech and hi-tech areas. The highly successful ARM and Conexant Systems are both spin-outs from Acorn computers, which were established in the 1970s.

Serial entrepreneurs have similarly established many of the companies with staff moving between organisations regularly over time like a synergistic collective. These synergies have supported inward investment. Investors have found it easier to invest within the cluster over a long period of time due to proximity and the high-level social networks created there. The relationships between people have been instrumental and have created entry routes for many new entrepreneurs. You can find some complex stakeholder maps that show the complexity of the relationships and the connections that have created this infrastructure.

Growing wiser and creating value

You can find hidden business mentors supporting business growth in many locations. In the Cambridge technology region, for example, they may not call themselves mentors, but their specific wisdom and experience on investment, technology transfer, business development, growth, organisational development and new market entry has been instrumental in growing the region. This positive improvement demonstrates the power and value creation in effective business relationships. This has been achieved through formal means such as angel investors sitting on Boards through to informal social networking. Proximity to the university obviously helps with ready access to new research, innovative biotechnology, engineering and microtechnology. Still, the network map of relationships developed over a 40-year period in hi-tech is impressive. Figure 14-3 shows the business creation generated through the network of related business owners and investors.

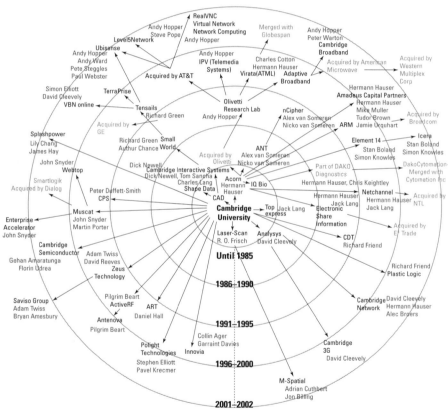

Figure 14-3:
A network map of hi-tech start-ups associated with Cambridge University.

If you were to create your own cluster map for your social and business network, where could you create or expand your own mini-cluster in your industry? What would it take for you to develop enough trust in yourself and others to collaborate more and co-create rather than compete? Now there's a thought – creating social capital and cash flow by collaboration. Obviously, you would want measures such as nondisclosure agreements in place at the appropriate time to mitigate risk, but that's a sidebar if the idea of creating synergy excites you.

Serial entrepreneurs tend to be highly networked and sit on the Boards of more than one company. Learning to be a Board director can take many forms. If you want to create multiple businesses during your leadership career, do you have a plan for that? Are you being coached towards that goal?

Networking Is a Deposit in the Karmic Bank

Networking is reciprocal. You can develop your network in different ways, and traditionally face-to-face relationship creation has been the norm. This method often consists of getting together at evening network meetings with like-minded business professionals over canapés and a glass of wine or at a business breakfast with a speaker and mingling while you chew on a croissant and drink average coffee. The organised network of small businesses or professional associations such as BNI, the Institute of Directors, the Small Business Federation and the like where business cards are swapped and elevator pitches are honed to perfection have sprung up during the last 30 years too.

A new wave of networking is happening in small and medium-sized business where the social aspect of doing business by having membership of shared office space is becoming popular. Clever, opportunity-spotting entrepreneurs are making a business out of this. Wework, a company established in 2010, has grown to $6.4 billion in five years by developing high specification serviced office spaces in the US and, more recently, the UK. Wework is more than a serviced office; it's more of a networking and business-building concept. Wework is funded on a rolling subscription based on usage. Members are encouraged to network, share ideas and create community. The system is a vibrant model and a great way for young businesses to make connections, get recommendations and get things done business to business.

Equally, online networking has taken off and enjoyed massive growth in the last decade. We don't mean spending time on Facebook sharing the latest photos of your birthday-type networking. Rather, using social media such as Facebook, Twitter, Instagram and LinkedIn to make business contacts and network easily. The power of online networking is huge and has created large revenues for business too.

The answer to 'Do you network and how?' has become more complex. We're doing it at multiple levels. What are you doing to create new relationships and developing existing ones actively?

The concept of business networking started with the Industrial Revolution according to historians, but what about the marketplaces of Ancient Greece and Rome? Whole civilisations were built in trade and transaction. The principle of networking is the same today: a deposit-and-withdrawal game. The investment may be worth its weight in gold if you get clear on two things:

✔ **What are you networking for?** Identify networking groups that meet your interests. Some networks are all about making contacts and pitching to each other for business. Others are based on learning and making social contacts for future projects.

Are you looking to mentor a new business owner, for example, or are you networking to swap contacts and increase sales? Get really clear on what your aims are as doing so helps you focus your attention and determines where you want to network, whom you want to meet and why.

✔ **What are you prepared to share, and what is your boundary?** How trusting are you of others, and what are you willing to share with them? Networking involves the development of trusting relationships for mutual benefit. It's reciprocal, and when it works well, lifelong relationships are built. If you think of networking as transactional, you're really missing the point. Think about what your boundaries are around the relationships you intend to create.

Networking is business creation, and it gets richer as an experience when you focus your attention in the right places. Develop your skills if you need to. Discover how to engage with others, to actively listen and take a genuine interest in them. Ask good questions that create a dialogue rather than leaving the other person feeling she's been interviewed. Be clear about if and how you may be able to help someone, and follow through on your commitments. Get clear on what you would like from each networking relationship. Become confident in talking about yourself, your business and your aspirations.

Relationship management is a great area for coaching. This area isn't like step-by-step coaching to get a date (which is popular, by the way), more like coaching a client to develop strategies to meet their networking goals. Some of this coaching may be about helping a client get clear on answering those two questions: 'What are you networking for?' and 'What is your boundary?' Alternatively, it may be a specific skills area that a client wants to develop.

Starting small creates memorable network results

Ben, a newly appointed assistant director and rather shy, had an objective to increase his network of contacts within the insurance industry during a 12-month period. He would be taking over the insurance division of a legal firm at the end of the year. When his coach explored this problem with him, it was clear that he wanted to build his confidence in talking to new people. One of his concerns was that he would meet someone in person and forget her name during the conversation. When the time came to move on, he handled the 'goodbye and keep in touch' badly because he couldn't recall the person's name and would be so focused on the business card he would look rude and disinterested. This issue seems a small thing, but it was really getting in Ben's way.

Remembering a name creates rapport and makes people feel good. His coach demonstrated a simple tried-and-tested method to help him with recall. You can try it for yourself. When people tell you their name, attach it to a memorable thing about them, such as Rory red tie or Sharon works for Guinness and comes from Canada. Obviously, you don't then introduce them to others at the networking event like this! You could attend a networking 'mingle' with a colleague or your coach and make the learning fun. See how many of the same people you both meet, what you used as your recall tag and what you can remember, and discuss follow-up commitments.

If you find networking a challenge, you may be shy, lacking confidence or just need to practise it. Break down the skill set of approaching and introducing, active listening, recall, describing yourself and your work, making a request, closing and agreeing on follow-up. Focus on getting just one element right. Then build on that and work on the next. Remember, networking is a skill, and skills require practise.

Building Trust and Rebuilding Broken Trust

Relationships are built and broken on the basis of trust, and we need to place our trust in others in our businesses every day: in external stakeholders (bankers, accountants, lawyers, insurers, contractors, investors, suppliers) and internal stakeholders (staff, associates, virtual assistants, board members). You know you have healthy trusting relationships when people do what they say they will, when you share a secret and it remains a secret, when you feel you're travelling in the same direction and creating wins that look like a win-win from all angles.

Truth is, things do go wrong. Sometimes people let us down and we let them down too. You find a lot in this chapter about how to build relationships, but how do you build organisational trust and what do you do when things go wrong?

Developing trust at the level of the organisation

People want to trust the organisations that they work in and relate to. We all have psychological contracts with organisations, a tacit set of promises that we expect to govern our dealings with each other. The most important contract for staff isn't their employment contract that sets out the agreements to pay, when, where and how. Their implied contract is most important, the expectations they have of being treated fairly. These are evident in most of our business dealings. In general we're looking for fairness in how we relate, in terms of process and in terms of outcome. This aim is true of any business arrangement including coaching arrangements.

We want to experience organisations as places where the processes apply fairly and evenly throughout. We want to see that those HR practices are applied consistently and, if not, that someone can justify why not; that if something goes wrong with a contract, the supplier and the organisation will come to some accommodation to create an outcome that is fair and reasonable.

Organisations spend millions creating policies, operating procedures, compliance documents and the like. The written and unwritten rules contribute to trust-building for stakeholders. If you're a new entrepreneur and don't like rules, ask someone who has pitched for second- or third-round funding or sold a business what it was that made or broke the deal. Often, the due diligence is the factor, and this process is looking for the rules, breaches of rules and the risk in the absence of rules. You may find it all fine and wonderful to create and develop business with your best buddy whom you love and trust, but you wouldn't invest your life savings without an agreement and some rules, would you?

Here are a few starter questions for a session that a coach can use if she is working on trust with a client:

- ✔ If you think about your own business, whom do you trust and why?
- ✔ Do you trust until your trust is broken, or do you expect people to earn it?

✔ Where are the weaknesses in your system? Where are the risks, and who is holding those areas? How do you know you can trust them to do that well? How can you check?

✔ Are there any areas of your business that would benefit from your efforts in engendering trust in the direction the business is taking?

✔ Which stakeholders like you? Which trust you?

✔ Who on your Board would replace you tomorrow? Why?

✔ Where are you contributing to potential mistrust as a leader?

✔ How can you create more open and trusting coaching conversations?

✔ How do the people you're responsible for coaching know they're trusted and can trust you?

Food for thought, eh?

The model shown in Figure 14-4 was developed by Marie when working with a group of leaders around coaching and trust. It summarises the elements that create a trusting relationship with yourself and with others. Over time, these elements increase self-awareness and active relationship building. You can use it in self-coaching or in coaching leaders in developing self-awareness and trusting others.

Resolving conflict and avoiding mutually assured destruction

Oh, if we could only get by in business with no conflict. The corporate law-yers would be penniless, and the civil courts would be empty for most of the week. Conflict is a fact of life, and you need to find out how to handle it as constructively as possible. If you don't, it can get expensive and time-consuming. We've seen good small businesses go under because of the costs of handling litigation that could have been avoided and de-escalated with a bit of proactive dialogue, honest brokerage and common sense. Business partners fall out of love, with their originating business or with each other. Partnerships are dissolved weekly, and it can be painful. This area is one that coaches sometimes find themselves on the edge of, and you need to help cli-ents see how their behaviour and the behaviour of others can escalate when things start to go wrong. So how can you avoid the fires and put them out when they flare up?

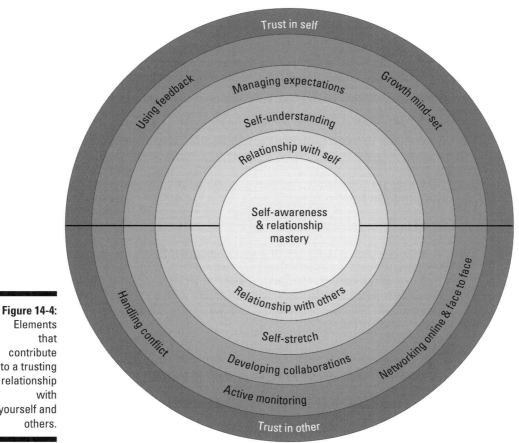

Figure 14-4:
Elements
that
contribute
to a trusting
relationship
with
yourself and
others.

© Marie Taylor

In simple terms, business agreements need to allow for processes of conflict resolution. You may want to check to see whether yours take you straight to law if a dispute occurs or whether a mediation clause exists. Think about how you want to deal with conflict if it arises before it even becomes a possibility. Some business owners think 'It will never happen here. We're like a family'. Float that notion by the employees and directors at that former investment giant Lehman Brothers. In their 2007 annual report, their employee statement said 'Our people are our most valuable asset'. Ten months later, when the firm declared bankruptcy, those people were walking out of the door carrying the contents of their desk in a cardboard box and scrawling less than complimentary messages on the walls about their Board as they exited. They thought they were part of a family that would look after them. The CEO had been there 42 years, longer than many marriages last; an indicator of commitment to family for some staff. Because it looks like a happy, protective family-oriented business doesn't mean the business is protected from human failings and market conditions. Protect your assets with clear agreements and processes.

If you find yourself in dispute at the level of the individual or group, keep talking; keep the door open for dialogue. When people stop talking, you have a problem. So be open to conversation, be as honest as you possibly can, be fair, be reasonable and look to create solutions even when you can't give people everything they want before you close the door.

Coaching people around a dispute can be helpful. A leader may find it hard when criticised by her people, her Board, the press or at the AGM. Being the sounding board and giving space for people to vent their frustrations is an invaluable part of the coaching relationship. The job of the coach isn't to resolve the coachee's problem or to make her feel better with platitudes or joint meditation and chanting. The job is to help her regain perspective, to remind her of her successes, of the times when she has handled things like this before and to help her see the whole of her reality. That said, a bit of mindfulness meditation can sometimes be a well-placed suggestion.

Having the Courage to Let Go

Sometimes things are just not working, and leaders need to bail out employees or encourage or require people to move on. Coaches can help leaders prepare for these conversations by helping clients anticipate the reactions they may get and work through those. Courage involves speaking with a level of candour. Some leaders need help with framing those honest conversations, particularly if they're direct in their approach or find it hard to relay bad news. When you're ending a relationship, the way you say things is often as important as what you say.

Practising a dialogue can be helpful when you need to have a difficult conversation. You can use this empty chair technique as a self-coaching tool or with a coach guiding and supporting you. It can feel a bit weird at first, but stick with it. To use the three chairs and 14–16 feet technique:

1. **Take three chairs and arrange two opposite each other and one slightly away in a kind of triangle configuration.**

   The 14–16 feet for those of you who don't like maths – 3 chairs with 4 feet equals 12 plus your 2 and sometimes plus 2 belonging to the coach.

2. **Sit in the first chair and speak to the empty chair.**

   (If you have an office with open blinds or a lock on the door, draw down and lock up first; otherwise your people may be sending for those nice people in white coats.)

   Imagine the person you need to have the difficult conversation sitting there. Really imagine him. See how he would sit, what he would wear, how he would act if he were in front of you. Imagine him just listening to what you have to say.

3. **Go to the other person's chair and sit in it. Imagine that you're that person, hearing what you just heard.**

4. **Wait a minute until you have taken it in and respond as you anticipate that person would.**

5. **Come back to the original chair and go backwards and forwards in both positions again.**

6. **Sit in the third chair and imagine you aren't part of this dialogue but are watching it.**

   What do you notice? What is helping? What's not? If you were advising the person sitting in the first chair to do something differently or do more of something, what would it be?

7. **Think about how you're going to handle that conversation now, and then either do it or schedule it.**

This technique is useful in many contexts – when you're trying to work out what the objections may be to a proposal you're making, for example. Physically moving chairs makes a difference. Don't be tempted to leave that detail out.

Chapter 15

Coaching to Help Business Engage, Inform and Influence

. . . .

In This Chapter

▶ Communicating at multiple levels of awareness

▶ Understanding how people make decisions

▶ Influencing decisions by changing your communication

. . . .

*H*umans are the chatty, social species. We are masters of communication, and even during our brief moments of silence, we speak volumes. Over generations, we have developed the ability to communicate across the boundaries of gender, age, race and culture, enabling us to create alliances for the greater good as well as evil.

In this chapter, we focus on the underlying patterns of communication. You discover how to inform, engage and influence ethically, as well as be better able to recognise when someone else is attempting to influence you.

Understanding the Importance of Effective Communication

Underlying communications are common patterns, concepts and principles that influence social behaviour. Understanding and being able to use these concepts and principles in your coaching enable you and your clients to become better communicators and masters of persuasion and influence in multiple business contexts. Effective communication is increasingly recognised as a key determinant of business success.

This recognition has resulted in a proliferation of training and coaching programmes, all of which a coach can specialise in: copy writing, media presentations, presenting to audiences, sales, customer service, negotiation and arbitration. These specialisations all influence human behaviour, and what is common to all these programmes is:

- How people internally process communication
- How people are influenced by communication to make decisions

These concepts of communication are used in many business contexts, such as the following:

- Marketing:
  - Capturing customer attention and engaging people in conversations that lead to business
  - Influencing behaviours and the resultant actions and decisions that people make
  - Creating powerful brand associations
- Selling:
  - Getting people to say yes and to mean it
  - Overcoming objections to propositions
- Negotiating and conflict resolutions:
  - Bridging seemingly insurmountable differences of opinion
  - Creating situations where differences don't matter
- Gaining compliance:
  - Ensuring that people listen to learn
  - Getting people to follow up on declarations
- Striving for greater understanding:
  - Imparting information to ensure that people understand your communications
  - Informing people so they take specifically desired actions

Communicating Quicker Than the Speed of Conscious Thought

Here are two concepts about how the mind processes communication received by the listener (or receiver), which ultimately affects and influences behaviour:

- **Communication is verbal and nonverbal.** The mind processes millions of bits of data per second, way beyond the conscious ability to process all the incoming information; yet it's all being processed at some unconscious level. Everything you see, hear, feel, smell and taste is being processed, even if you aren't consciously aware of it. Whether you or your clients like it or not, the external is influencing how you perceive, think, feel and act.

Research shows that while processing verbal communications, we are aware of and influenced 7 per cent by the spoken word (what's said), 38 per cent by voice and tonality (how those words are said) and 55 per cent by body language (what's not said). Nonverbal communication, which includes the 55 per cent body language, also includes other forms such as visual aids (graphs, charts and models) as well as information conveyed through the senses of touch, taste and smell.

✓ **You cannot not process the communication.** As soon as the verbal or nonverbal communication is made, the listener processes it regardless of whether he is consciously aware of it. The package of information has been delivered. (See the sidebar "Every communication counts" for an example of this concept.)

For example, think of a situation where you have said to a client 'Just imagine how successful this venture will be'. In order to make sense of the sentence, clients have to first make a picture in their minds of how they imagine a successful venture would look. (In Chapter 10, we explore how visual mind pictures affect behaviours.) You influence your clients by everything you say and do, whether they (or you) are consciously aware of the degree of influence or not. With your communication, you're getting them to create pictures in their minds and are therefore influencing their behaviours. They're also doing the same with their customers, suppliers and colleagues with every communication in all formats and media.

If clients want to engage, inform and influence, they have to first get the attention of the listener (receivers). A simple way to get this attention is to ask a question that forces listeners to become engaged in the communication so they're now in a state of curiosity. Get their attention first, then build up interest (curiosity), then desire, then instruct them what action to take. This sequential chaining of states moving towards a desired action is known as AIDA – Attention, Interest, Desire, Action.

Whenever given the opportunity to demonstrate your coaching and its effectiveness, take it as a gift. Give clients the experience of coaching rather than the theory; this is an opportunity to convince them of the benefits of what you do. These benefits are a powerful influencer for both clients and their customers when it comes to making decisions to buy any product or service.

Understanding the power of these two concepts – whereby communication both verbal and nonverbal is processed unconsciously and that the communication goes in regardless of whether the receiver is aware of it or not – opens up a whole toolbox of communication tools and concepts available to you and your clients.

Every communication counts

On UK TV, Derren Brown gives a powerful demonstration of the power of unconscious communication to influence people. In one episode, he gave two designers a brief – they had half an hour to create a logo for a pet cemetery.

When they had created their logo, Derren unveiled one he had prepared earlier, which was a mirror image of theirs using all the design elements they had used. The designers were dumbfounded at the uncanny similarities.

On the cab journey to the studio, images had been strategically placed throughout the journey to influence their decisions. There were stickers of teddy bears, posters of angel wings, they drove past iron gates – all of which later appeared in their design proposal. Although the designers were not consciously aware of the images, they had processed them nonetheless and been influenced to use them.

Understanding Why People Say Yes

Imagine an open fridge door and inside is celery and cheesecake. Which do you choose? Behind the decision to choose the obvious answer, which is undoubtedly cheesecake, is a lot of internal processing of information.

What people say yes to and what they also say no to (two sides of the same coin) is influenced by a number of key questions the mind asks itself:

- What is it I value, or what's important to me?

- What do I move away from to avoid? (Also known as pain, which can be in the forms of physical, sexual, social, financial and emotional)

- What do I move towards to gain? (Also known as pleasure, whether physical, sexual, social, financial or emotional)

The mind processes the above variables and presents the answer. The processing happens in fractions of a second, and the answer is given in the form of mind pictures. In the above scenario, if the answer is celery (as unlikely as that may be), the mind picture of celery and what it means to the individual will seem more appealing compared to the way cheesecake is represented. In Chapter 10, we discuss 'submodalities', which are the qualities and details of the visual images we all make in our heads. Two aspects to submodalities are critical to understanding how they influence what people say yes to. These aspects are:

- **Comparative analysis:** When presented with choices, people unconsciously process the options, and the comparative analysis of the submodalities of the choices (the differences between the choices) determines their decisions. One choice will appeal more than the other: it may be bigger, brighter, more colourful, in 3D or a movie compared to small, dull, monochrome, 2D and a still image. If clear distinctions exist between the choices, then the decision literally 'appears obvious'. If the distinctions are similar, people often find it difficult to make a choice.

✔ **Seeing a desired outcome:** People say 'yes' when they see the outcome of the decision and it makes them feel good. The submodalities of the mind pictures can be static or moving but will generally be associated and create feelings of desire, comfort or a sense of certainty.

These two unconscious decision-making processes are exploited in negotiation, advertising and selling, although most people in these professions have no awareness that what they do and say influences and changes the submodalities in people's minds. For example:

✔ The negotiator may point out the pain and costs of someone sticking to a position and build up a picture of desire by discussing the benefits of agreeing to a new position.

✔ The salesperson often describes the financial pain of missing out on an offer and the pleasure and benefits of buying the product, often getting people to hold the product or try out the service so they effectively experience the desired outcome.

✔ The advertisers create lifestyle images so the viewer literally imagines living the dream or owning the product – stepping into the pictures painted and becoming associated with the product.

 These processes are just two ways to influence people's actions and decisions and to get them to say yes. Firstly, if they have choices, use your communication to diminish the mind pictures of the choice or choices you would prefer them not to take and then enhance the desired choice. Secondly, use verbal and nonverbal communication to create mind pictures in people's heads where they see a desired outcome that makes them feel good.

If You Have the Need to Influence, You Get to Do All the Work

Have you ever been communicating with people and had the sense that you were talking to yourself and they weren't hearing the communication? Anyone with teenage children will be familiar with this notion. If you or your clients are the communicators and you want the listener (receiver) to be engaged, informed and influenced, start by taking total responsibility for doing all the work. Don't expect listeners to adjust what they're doing; they have no need to. The person with the need gets to do the work.

If someone is unwilling to listen or receive the communication, then you need to adjust what you're doing and do something else to engage him (for more on this, see the 'If You Aren't Getting the Desired Results, Change Your Communication' section at the end of the chapter). In Chapter 5, we cover the concept of 'identifying the enemies of learning' and how important it is to get attention and engage the client. This concept applies to all forms of communication where the intention is to influence.

Navigating the Political Landscape

The political landscape of every business you coach is totally unique and idiosyncratic and changes over time. No two businesses are alike. When preparing any communications with the intentions to engage, inform and influence, remember that communication is more than simply one person talking and another listening. Instead, the communication happens within the context of the political landscape of the listener. The listener is operating in a complex world that affects how he perceives the communication, what it means to him and ultimately the actions he takes.

The elegant and effective communicator takes the landscape into consideration before crafting his communications. In Chapter 9, we introduce the Information Grid, a diagnostic tool that can be used to transform great visions into workable plans. Parts of the Information Grid can also be used to bring order into the complex political landscape within which communication happens.

 When creating communications – whether a newsletter, speech, sales pitch, website or report – coach clients to consider the listener's perspective and political landscape before crafting the message or messages. Ask the questions:

- ✔ What's important to the listener, what does he value?
- ✔ What may the listener object to? (Move away from)
- ✔ What may appeal to the listener? (Moving towards)
- ✔ What would the listener need to see, hear and feel in order to say yes?

Then use parts of the Information Grid (listed as follows) to consider the wider context within which the listener operates and ask this question for each grid square: 'What may affect the listener and prevent him from agreeing or saying yes?' Could it be:

- ✔ Time
- ✔ Money
- ✔ Effort

✔ People

✔ Beliefs and values

✔ Skills

✔ Capabilities

✔ Environment

✔ Ecology

✔ Legal

Revealing hidden resistance to being influenced

Colin was MD for a property development group. During a coaching session, he raised a problem that he and his team were struggling with. They had negotiated an 'in principle' deal with Stuart, a farmer, to redevelop a parcel of agricultural land for mixed light-industrial and part residential units. Over an 18-month period, they had finally obtained planning consent, yet Stuart was unwilling to sign the contract so work could commence. Colin and his team had a good relationship with Stuart, who was unable to explain his reluctance to sign.

It was suggested to Colin that Stuart's resistance was caused by an unconscious factor. After reviewing the Information Grid by imagining seeing things from Stuart's perspective and asking the question 'What may be affecting Stuart and preventing him from agreeing and saying yes?', Colin was instructed to further examine two categories with Stuart to find out what unknown influences were causing the resistance. These influences were:

✔ Beliefs and Values – What would selling the land mean to Stuart?

✔ Ecology – What else and who else in Stuart's world would be affected by the sale of the land?

Colin arranged a meeting with Stuart and returned to his next coaching session to announce that they had gotten to the bottom of his reluctance and the project was now off the table. Colin discussed with Stuart what selling the land would mean to him and what and who else would be affected by the sale. After a moment's reflection, Stuart had a 'light bulb' moment of insight. Stuart was the descendant of a long line of landowners, and although he needed the money from the sale of the land, he realised that he didn't want to be known as the first in his family for generations to have to sell land. He would see himself as a failure and was sure that others would see him that way too. Had this resistance, hidden deep within the political landscape of Stuart's life, been identified earlier, it would have been easier to address at the start of the negotiations or, if found to be an insurmountable obstacle from the start, Colin would have let the project go and saved the business considerable time, money and effort.

With the knowledge of what the resistance was, a meeting was arranged with Stuart to offer him a restructured deal giving him a small percentage part ownership of the project for less money. Stuart was able to release valuable equity from the sale and still be the landowner for future generations to come.

Clients are wise to spend time researching and finding out from prospective listeners what they would have to hear in order to be influenced. Market research, surveys and think tanks give valuable information enabling communications to be crafted specifically to meet the needs of the listener.

Ethically Influencing and Persuading for Results

When looking to influence and persuade, always keep the end goal in mind and consider what could be an obstacle or resistance to reaching it.

Always think, what does my language do to the submodalities of the listener or receiver?

The word *manipulation* is an emotionally charged one, especially in the context of influencing and persuasion. For many, it implies being underhand. The word manipulation means 'to use or change (numbers, information and so on) in a skilful way or for a particular purpose'. If we add 'or to move in a particular direction' to this definition, it becomes clear that without moving customers, colleagues or suppliers in the direction of saying yes, no business would ever happen. The intention behind the manipulation is what's important.

Like any tools, persuasion and influence can be used for good as well as harm. Many of the principles and concepts in this chapter have been misused by many people and even been used for evil. They have been used for speed seduction, unethical selling, politics, warmongering and radicalisation, but that does not make the tools themselves evil. It is an unfortunate fact of life that there are clients who see these tools as ways to persuade people to make decisions that are not in the receiver's best interests.

You will find enough coaching clients who want to use persuasion and influence ethically. Better to turn a project down than engage in something that goes against your morals. Use this simple model to decide which projects to coach clients in and which to say no to. If the results are:

- ✔ **Win** (for the communicator) **win** (for the listener) say **yes.**
- ✔ **Win** (for the communicator) **lose** (for the listener) say **no.**
- ✔ **No** (for the communicator) **win** (for the listener) say **no.**

It Takes Two to Influence

Think of engaging, informing and influencing as an elegant interaction, like a dance between the communicator and the receiver. The communicator is the one leading the dance, manipulating and taking the receiver gently in a desired direction. The communicator pays attention to how the receiver reacts to his lead, and if the receiver starts to go off-track, the communicator gently guides him around by changing his communication so he follows. This process is known as pacing and leading.

The key to great influencing is to pay attention to the feedback from the listener or receiver of the communication and to test that you're getting the desired results or at least going in the right general direction. (For more on changing the direction, see the later section, 'If You Aren't Getting the Desired Results, Change Your Communication'.)

> *I know that you believe you understand what you think I said, but I'm not sure you realize that what you heard is not what I meant.*
>
> *–Accredited to both Alan Greenspan and Robert McCloskey*

The following tools all manipulate. When used in a win-win scenario, it would be irresponsible for clients not to use them to get people to say yes.

Paying attention

The following exercise on the power of paying attention can help improve your communication skills.

1. **Sit facing your client and ask him to talk to you about a hobby or activity that he loves and to keep going for three minutes.**

    This conversation should be one-way with only him speaking.

2. **For the first minute, pay undivided attention with your whole physiology. Add in lots of nodding, smiles and agreeable sounds without commenting.**

3. **After one minute, start to fidget and be distracted: yawn, pick dust off your trousers, clean under your fingernails or glance at a mobile phone.**

    At all times, while feigning distraction, pay attention to what he is saying so you can replay it back to him at the end of the exercise.

    One of two things will happen. He may talk to you more intently in an attempt to get your attention, but this happens rarely. The normal response is that he stops talking because you aren't paying attention.

4. **Instruct him to keep talking and remind him that you're listening.**

   He will reluctantly continue.

5. **Resume the distracted behaviour while listening intently.**

6. **After a minute, return your physiology back to paying full attention for the remainder of the time.**

7. **Then call a halt to the exercise.**

8. **Debrief him about his experience.**

   Common feedback is 'While you weren't listening, I felt uncomfortable', 'I was unable to talk' or 'I was annoyed'. Then relate to him all that was said while you were seemingly paying no attention; he will be shocked that you were listening.

This exercise teaches people two valuable influencing lessons. First, they find out about the power of paying full attention when someone is communicating – if people feel someone isn't listening, they tend to switch off. Secondly, they discover how easy it can be to misinterpret whether someone is paying attention.

Coach clients to

- ✔ Fully pay attention when someone is a communicating.
- ✔ Don't make assumptions about whether someone has heard the meaning of your communication; test his understanding.

  Test by asking questions and, if appropriate, get them to repeat back to you what's been said. This testing is invaluable during meetings when quite often people have been given instructions but haven't really heard what was said or have interpreted it differently to the way it was meant.

These two skills are essential, especially for negotiators, sales and customer service people, to master.

Listening actively

We call this exercise 'Parrot phrase not para-phrase':

1. **Imagine that you're a property agent, and have the client describe to you an ideal house.**

   Instruct him to describe the size, location, rooms and features of the property.

2. **While describing, listen for and make notes of these two things:**

   - The sequence and order he asks for the features in
   - The words he uses to describe how important and necessary they are. These words are called *modal operators* or MOs. The words to listen out for are:

     Wish

     Like

     Want

     Need

     Have/Has/Hasn't

     Must/Must not

     Can/Could/Couldn't

     Will

     Should/Shouldn't

3. **When he has described his ideal property, read back the list three times, and each time enquire into how the information is received. How does it sound and feel? Are you describing the ideal property?**

   For example, he says, 'I want a detached house; it must be in the country; it should have four bedrooms with two en-suite bathrooms. It has to be within a ten-minute drive of a train station, and I would like it to have an open-plan kitchen, and it must have a large garden, preferably with a patio for sitting out of an evening'.

4. **First, change the sequence around and test his reaction to the description.**

   'So it has to be within a ten-minute drive of a train station; it must be in the country; it should have four bedrooms; it must have a large garden, preferably with a patio for sitting out of an evening; you would like it to have an open-plan kitchen; and you want a detached house with two en-suite bathrooms. Is that correct?'

5. **Second, repeat the original sequence, change the modal operators and test his reaction to the description.**

   'So you would like a detached house; it could be in the country; it might have four bedrooms with two en-suite bathrooms; and you wish it was within a ten-minute drive of a train station; and it needs to have an open-plan kitchen; and you would like it to have a large garden, which might have a patio for sitting out of an evening. Is that correct?'

6. **Third, repeat the original sequence and use the modal operators as he presented them and test his reaction to the description.**

'So you want a detached house; it must be in the country; it should have four bedrooms with two en-suite bathrooms. It has to be within a ten-minute drive of a train station, and you would like it to have an open-plan kitchen, and it must have a large garden, preferably with a patio for sitting out of an evening'.

With the first two descriptions, he will struggle to recognise the ideal property and may even adamantly reject what you have said because simply put, it's not what he asked for. You weren't listening. By changing the sequence and the modal operators, you're giving a clear message that 'I have heard what you have said, but I'm not really listening and will now change it'. This description is the verbal equivalent of flicking dust off your trousers during a conversation. With the third description, you will see him visibly relax as he recognises your description to be the ideal property he described.

Giving the client what he asked for

In customer service and sales as well as negotiations, being able to listen purposefully and communicate exactly back to the listener so he feels you understand is an essential skill. It creates rapport between two individuals and demonstrates understanding.

Have your coffee just as you like it:

> **Customer:** 'I would like a large latte with soya milk, extra hot, with an extra shot of coffee, in a take-away cup, and two pumps of hazelnut syrup please. Oh, and a doughnut'.
>
> **Barista:** 'So you want a doughnut with a large latte with an extra shot to go, and two pumps of hazelnut syrup. You would like it made extra hot with soya milk. Is that correct?'
>
> **Customer:** 'I have no idea. I'll just have a glass of water!'

I'm not angry, I just want to be heard:

> **Customer:** 'I'm calling not to complain but because I'm disappointed that my fridge was delivered at 1 p.m. You had promised a morning delivery, and I thought you would appreciate the feedback'.
>
> **Customer service:** 'I'm sorry to hear you're upset. I will let our delivery team know that they wasted your morning'.
>
> **Customer:** 'Well, they didn't waste my morning. I had the day off. I just thought you would want to know that I didn't get the text message as promised. If the delivery was going to be delayed, I would have liked to have known so I could pop out if I wanted to'.
>
> **Customer service:** 'Yes, that shouldn't have happened, and I'm sorry you're angry. Sometimes the text messages are delayed. I will pass your complaint on to the delivery department. If it was important and you needed to go out, I understand why you're upset'.
>
> **Customer:** 'Listen to me. I wasn't angry, nor complaining, nor upset . . . but I am now'.

Building rapport

Communicating to engage, inform and influence is easier when a rapport is evident between the communicator and receiver. *Rapport* is when you have 'trust and harmony in a relationship'. Think of rapport as part of the dance – where the communicator who has the need to influence extends his hand as an invitation to dance. If the receiver feels comfortable, he extends his and gives the communicator permission to lead the dance. The communicator gains rapport in order to lead the receiver in a purposeful direction to the point of agreeing or saying yes.

Influencing is a four-step process, beginning with rapport:

1. **Rapport:** Gain rapport. Ways to do so are covered in the following sections.

2. **Understanding:** When rapport has been established, trust and harmony are present so the receiver feels understood.

3. **Permission:** Because the receiver feels understood, he (unconsciously) gives permission to be led. He is willing to engage in the communication.

4. **Influence:** He is now more willing to be influenced by the communication.

Creating rapport elegantly

Here are a number of ways whereby humans naturally experience and demonstrate rapport between individuals and groups, at the levels of:

- **Identity:** People who share the same perceived identity often have natural rapport, whether that's gender, race, religion or members of social groups, a team or organisation.

- **Beliefs and values:** Consider all the people you spend time with. At some level, you must have rapport in what you believe and value or you wouldn't associate with them. This concept is openly used by business when values statements are made public. An example is that of 'ethical' or 'fair trade', where companies proclaim ethical practice allowing customers with matching values the opportunity to decide to use their products and services.

- **Skills and capabilities:** People with qualifications or in the same professions demonstrate natural rapport by their credentials.

- **Environment:** Generally, people like places they're familiar with or that match their expectations and make them feel comfortable. In terms of rapport, consider a professional business coach who operates from a business centre, has training credentials on the wall, a nice clean tidy professional office and dresses professionally; compare this scenario to that of an equally skilled and qualified coach who works from his living room at home with family photographs on display and dresses casually. A client who visits the home office may value the more relaxed approach and have similar family values and find the family photographs create rapport, but generally it's best to create an environment that meets the environmental expectations of the majority.

You're well advised not to attempt to create rapport with identity, beliefs and values if none exists. Pretending to be what you're not is never a good strategy for creating trust. When no natural rapport exists, the easiest way to create rapport is with skills, capabilities and particularly behaviours.

Here are four ways to gain rapport at a behavioural level:

- ✔ Matching language patterns
- ✔ Matching body movements and gestures
- ✔ Matching voice tonality, volume and tempo
- ✔ With dress and attire

The purpose of creating rapport is to create a relationship so the receiver feels trust (even at an unconscious level) and understood so he gives permission to be influenced.

Understanding preferred representation systems

We all communicate using a combination of language that represents the five senses – visual, auditory, kinaesthetic, olfactory (smell) and gustatory (taste), or VAKOG. These are known as the *representation systems*. The sensory words that people use in communication to represent their experience are called *predicates*.

Most people have a preferred representation system, one they use more often and are comfortable with. If a person whose preferred representation system is visual and tends to communicate using predominantly visual predicates talks with someone whose preferred representation system is auditory, at times they may as well be talking different languages because they are out of rapport. For example:

> **Manager:** 'I keep telling you, but you keep saying you don't see what I mean.' (Preferred representation system is auditory)

> **Supervisor:** 'I hear what you're saying, but it still doesn't appear clear to me.' (Preferred representation system is visual)

Listen actively to the words people use in their language because they leave clues as to their preferred representation system by the predicates they commonly use. Table 15-1 lists some predicates that people commonly use in the business world.

Table 15-1	Commonly Used Sensory Words			
Visual	*Auditory*	*Kinaesthetic*	*Olfactory*	*Gustatory*
Analyse	Announce	Active	Aroma	Bitter
Appear	Articulate	Charge	Bouquet	Bland
Clarity	Converse	Concrete	Essence	Delicious
Examine	Discuss	Emotional	Fragrance	Flat
Focus	Enunciate	Feel	Musty	Salty
Foresee	Hear	Firm grasp	Odour	Sharp
Illustrate	Listen	Grip	Pungent	Sour
Look	Mention	Hold	Rotten	Sweet
Notice	Noise	Intuition	Smells	Tangy
Observe	Proclaim	Motion	Stench	Tasty
Perception	Pronounce	Pressure	Stinks	Zesty
Scope	Remark	Sensitive	Sweet	
Show	Say	Shift		
Survey	State	Stir		
View	Tell	Support		
Vision	Utter	Touch		
Watch	Voice			

Mastering rapport skills takes practice. The following sections offer four exercises for you and your clients to practise in the great laboratory of normal life.

These skills take practice but are powerful for creating rapport where there may be none. You will begin to see examples of people naturally in rapport whether linguistically or with their physiology all around you.

Identifying someone's preferred representation system

To identify preferred representation systems, try this exercise:

1. **Divide a piece of paper into five columns headed Visual, Auditory, Kinaesthetic, Olfactory and Gustatory (as in Table 15-1).**

2. **Work with a partner and ask him to talk to you for five minutes about a subject he loves.**

3. **Make a mark under the respective column when you hear, notice or get a sense that he has used a sensory predicate word.**

4. **After five minutes, simply count up the predicate scores for each sense.**

   The sense he has used most in his language is his preferred representation system.

If possible, have two or more people doing the tally so you can compare the totals. Generally, the two people will agree with perhaps a few discrepancies. To improve your ability to identify someone's preferred representation system so it becomes second nature, watch and listen to TV and keep a tally.

Matching someone's preferred representation system

To match someone's preferred representation systems, try this exercise:

1. **Work with someone who you have already identified has a predominant representation system.**

   If, for example, he was predominantly visual, talk to him for two minutes about a subject you like using predominantly visual predicates.

2. **After a few minutes, stop and repeat the conversation using other sensory predicates.**

3. **Debrief your partner about his experience.**

   Which of the two conversations did he prefer? Although the subject matter was the same, the partner almost certainly preferred the first version as you have been talking his language.

Matching body movements and gestures

Try this exercise to match body movements and gestures:

1. **Go to a quiet place like a library and choose an unsuspecting partner. Sit at a distance so you can observe him without being observed yourself.**

2. **Notice his rate of breathing.**

   This is best done by watching for the rise and fall of the shoulders.

3. **Match your breathing to his.**

4. **Do this breathing for a few minutes so breathing is synchronised and then slowly speed up or slow down your rate of breathing.**

   The unsuspecting partner will follow your lead. Although he will be unconscious of this phenomena, he is in rapport with you.

5. **Match breathing for a few more minutes, then make a gesture and wait for him to follow your gesture.**

   With practice, you can have people following your lead.

Creating rapport with a stranger

On persuasion and influence training in Florida, Steve was having breakfast in the hotel restaurant and decided to practise some of the skills that would be taught over the course. He sat back and, out of his peripheral vision six tables away, he saw a well-built man with a lumberjack shirt and large bushy beard having breakfast.

Steve matched his breathing and movements, lifting food to his mouth to match the man, drinking when he drank, turning his paper when the man turned his. Then Steve ran his fingers through his hair, and the man followed the gesture. Steve scratched his nose; the man followed again.

After a few minutes of this, the man closed his newspaper and stood up, looked across the room and headed towards Steve. Focusing intently on reading his newspaper, Steve cautiously looked up to see this giant of a man standing in front of him. 'Excuse me', he said, 'I don't mean to interrupt your breakfast, but I have really strong sense that I know you from somewhere. Have we met before?'

Matching voice tonality, volume and tempo

In this exercise, you match voice tonality, volume and tempo:

1. **Engage in a conversation with a colleague, paying careful attention first to his rate of breathing.**

2. **Then become aware of the speed and volume that he talks.**

3. **Match his breathing and talk to him at the same speed and volume that he talks.**

4. **Slowly reduce your volume and speed of conversation so he begins to also slow down.**

Choosing words that could, should, might make a difference

Have you ever met someone who said he would do something but didn't follow through with his actions? This sorry state of affairs is not uncommon in business, especially after meetings when instructions have been given or agreements made but people still don't do their part. In this section, we explore how modal operators give clues as to why this inactivity sets in and how you can coach your clients to listen carefully to others' communication and change their language in order to influence people to deliver on promises made.

Modal operators can be thought of as 'moody operators'. They juice up the motivational desire to take action by changing the submodalities of the mind pictures. Thoughts precede actions, and when people can literally see themselves taking the action in the movie in their mind and see the movie run to the end with a successful outcome, they will engage in the activity.

This exercise is called 'Juicing up the motivation to take action'. Use this exercise to personally experience how changing one word in a sentence has an influence on how you feel about taking action and how you are likely to behave.

1. **Play the sentences below, one at a time, inside your head using your own internal voice.**

   Say each sentence, stop and notice the feelings you get.

2. **As you go through the exercise, compare the feelings from one sentence to another.**

   On a motivational scale of 0 to 10 where 0 is no motivation to take action and 10 is totally motivated, note the motivation for each sentence.

   Start by making an assumption that, regardless of the reality and circumstances of your life, it is within your power to take Monday off work and say to yourself:

   • Say to yourself 'I *wish* I could take Monday off'. Notice the motivational feeling and rate it 0 to 10. Then test for:

   • 'I'd *like* to take Monday off'. Notice the motivational feeling and rate it 0 to 10. Then test for:

   • 'I *want* to take Monday off'. Notice the motivational feeling and rate it 0 to 10. Then test for:

   • 'I *need* to take Monday off'. Notice the motivational feeling and rate it 0 to 10. Then test for:

   • 'I *must* to take Monday off'. Notice the motivational feeling and rate it 0 to 10. Then test for:

   • 'I *can* to take Monday off'. Notice the motivational feeling and rate it 0 to 10. Then test for:

   • 'I *will* to take Monday off'. Notice the motivational feeling and rate it 0 to 10. Then test for:

   • 'I'm *going* to take Monday off'.

Notice that simply by changing one word in the sentence, you experience a different degree of motivation. Generally, for most people, as they progress down the list, they feel more motivated.

These language patterns and humans are all unique, so some people won't comply exactly with the usual patterns. Always work with whatever the unique individual human you're communicating with presents to you.

Now, do the same exercise again but this time pay attention to the mind pictures that you make as you say the sentences, becoming aware of which submodalities change.

Generally, the sentences at the top of the list are described as unclear or 'wishy-washy'; people experience low levels of motivation' and the activity is not likely to happen. As people progress down the list, the images become clearer and more active, and more motivation is present to take the desired action.

Try one further sentence and notice what happens. If we were to say to you, 'You *should* take Monday off', what happens to the picture? For most people, when someone else tells them what they should do, the mind picture disappears. Tell people what they *should* do and you're literally erasing the very thoughts from their mind. No thought = no action.

With this knowledge about how language changes the motivation and desire to take action, consider these sentences and whether the person saying them is likely to deliver or get others to deliver on their promise. Against each sentence is a reworked sentence using language designed to influence the listener and get the desired results.

- ✔ 'I would like the report to be concluded by Monday'. vs. 'The report must be concluded and delivered to my office on Monday'.

- ✔ 'We want to finish this project by the end of the month'. vs. 'Let's aim to finish this project and see it done by the end of the month'.

- ✔ 'The customers must be told they have to return the signed contracts before we can ship the product'. vs. 'Tell the customer to return the signed contracts and the product will be shipped to them by return'.

To improve your success rate in influencing people to take action, where possible completely remove the modal operators from the communication or use more motivating ones.

If You Aren't Getting the Desired Results, Change Your Communication

Native English speakers are renowned for their unwillingness to learn a second language. Do you know the joke about the Englishman who goes to Spain for a holiday? He goes into a restaurant and asks the waiter for 'a cup of tea and a full English breakfast'. The waiter doesn't understand what he means, so the Englishman helps him out with his extensive language skills by saying the same words only louder and slower.

Do you know the saying, 'The meaning of the communication is the response you get'? The more variety clients have in the way they communicate their ideas, the more success they have in achieving their desired results. Simply repeating the same message louder and slower just isn't enough.

Influencing clients by demonstrating what you can do for them

Steve was invited by an international TV and film company to review a series of TV adverts promoting a new series of documentaries. The brief was to appraise the adverts from a 'persuasion and influence perspective'. The client wanted to know two things: Firstly, could the adverts be improved to encourage viewers to stay on the channel during the adverts, rather than channel hop? Secondly, could anything be done to improve the viewers' recall about what the upcoming shows were and when they were being aired? The adverts had been failing to retain viewer attention in viewer research samples; not only were an unusually high number of viewers switching over when the adverts came on, but those who did watch the adverts were unable to recall what or when the documentaries were being aired.

After viewing the adverts, Steve asked the clients, 'Do you want the bad news first or the really bad news, which is really the good news?' The client was understandably confused and a little upset by this frank feedback but curious as to what Steve meant.

The client group was made up of senior executives as well as the team who had designed and filmed the adverts. Firstly, Steve explained to the group that from a persuasion and influence perspective, all communication is processed by the viewer whether consciously or not. In the first part of the advert, there was a sharp red arrow with a high-pitched musical accompaniment that flew through a beautiful series of landscapes and finished by aiming directly at the viewer. Although it looked artistic and the landscape was aesthetically pleasing, the human mind reacts negatively to fast-moving, sharp objects flying towards it, even if only on a screen. The red colour, which is unconsciously associated with threat and danger, and the sharp staccato sound only amplified this reaction.

Research has shown the impact on the neurology of sharp objects moving towards the body. By using tests with cutlery, it was discovered that sharp metal objects caused increased heart rates as well as rises in adrenaline. Steve was later able to demonstrate this effect by setting up tests using heart-rate monitors and software that showed that viewers experienced elevated stress levels while watching the first part of the advert. This was one reason for large numbers of viewers switching over or going for a cup of tea. The first part of the advert made them feel stressed, and what people perceive as stress, they tend to move away from and avoid.

In the second part of the advert, the main character in the new documentary appeared on screen looking to the top left of the monitor, while the show logo and scheduled viewing time appeared in the opposite top-right corner. The viewer would naturally follow the nonverbal communication of the character on screen and gaze where his eyes looked, totally missing the logo and time. This was one reason why viewers could not recall the name nor timing of the show. They hadn't looked at it; they had been misdirected.

In the advert, the show logo to the top right of the screen flashed on and off and then exploded into fragments and disappeared off over the horizon, all highly dramatic and visually pleasing. However, this animation had the same effect as giving the viewers virtual amnesia for the show and schedule. Steve demonstrated the effectiveness of this technique with Charles, the advert director, by having him think of a problem he had been worrying about unnecessarily and that he'd like to forget about. After doing the technique for five minutes, Charles found it difficult to recall what the problem was.

In summary, the first part of the advert made people feel stressed, which was bad. The really bad news was they would then feel bad by association about the upcoming show, but the good news was those who stayed on the channel, although were feeling bad, wouldn't remember what the show was anyway.

Although the group of executives were upset to hear the negative impact of their artistic creation, they now understood why their research figures for these adverts were so poor and why the adverts were failing to have the desired effects of engaging the audience, informing them of the upcoming show and influencing them to switch on at the aired time. The adverts were changed by making the accompanying music less physically uncomfortable, by blunting the end of the arrow and reducing the bright red colour down to a pastel shade. The main figure on the screen was reversed so he looked up towards the show name and time so the viewers' eyes naturally followed the nonverbal communication of his gaze. The show details were kept static for a few seconds, enabling the viewers to imprint these details into their memory. The research statistics for viewing retention during the commercial break and recall of the show afterwards both increased dramatically.

Social psychology experiments confirm that our decisions and behaviours are influenced by many things beyond our conscious awareness. In Robert Cialdini's book *Influence: The Psychology of Persuasion* (Harper Business), he identified six principles as influencing decisions unconsciously, all of which were tested and validated through social experiments.

Coaching clients to use these principles gives them a wide variety of ways to influence. Against each principle, we have given examples of how to use it effectively in business. The principles are:

- **Reciprocity:** People tend to return a favour. Businesses that offer free samples use this principle to influence a potential buyer to feel that they owe a favour.

    - Offer something first – allow someone to feel indebted to you.

    - Offer something exclusive – allow someone to feel special.

    - Personalise the offer – make sure they know the offer comes from you.

✔ **Commitment and consistency:** If people make a verbal commitment, they're more likely to follow through with an action because they want their actions to remain congruent and consistent with their word.

- Ask people to start from small actions – if they take the first action, they are more likely to take the next action.

- Encourage public commitments – people are less likely to back out of an agreement if they have made a public declaration.

✔ **Social proof:** People do things that they see others doing.

- Users – approval from current/past users, use ratings, reviews and testimonials

- Peers – approval from friends and people similar to the listener

✔ **Authority:** People tend to obey or comply with authority figures, perceived experts and celebrities:

- Experts – approval from credible experts in the relevant field

- Celebrities – approval or endorsements from people who are widely admired

✔ **Liking:** People are easily persuaded by people they like (see the 'Building rapport' section earlier in this chapter). This fact can be due to:

- Physical attractiveness – people are influenced by looks. This unfortunate fact of life is clearly demonstrated throughout the advertising world.

- Similarity – behave like a friend, not a brand. Show people that you can relate to, and understand them.

✔ **Scarcity:** If a perceived scarcity for a product or service exists, this scarcity generates a demand such as the following:

- Limited number – item is in short supply and won't be available when it runs out.

- Limited time – item is only available during a fixed time period.

- Utilising competitions – the inclination is to want things more because other people also want them. This tendency can be used in auctions, bids or countdowns that show a diminishing supply.

These principles are well-known and used in business, especially in online marketing and selling where the Internet and emails provide cost-effective platforms to offer incentives and multiple communications including all or some of the six principles.

The principles work because they unconsciously influence the decisions of the person receiving the communication. What we are unconscious of is difficult to disagree with because it bypasses any conscious resistance.

Part V
The Part of Tens

the **part of tens**

Check out the free article at www.dummies.com/extras/businesscoaching mentoring for ten ways to be a top-notch coach who your clients refer to others.

In this part . . .

- ✔ Find more than ten online resources that will spice up your coaching.

- ✔ Discover ten conversational ways to convince clients to change their opinions and behaviours.

- ✔ Find our top ten tips for leaders who coach or mentor people in business.

- ✔ Ask ten killer questions that will get clients to think about where they are, what they are doing and whether they are taking the business in the right direction.

Chapter 16

Ten or So Online Resources to Boost Coaching and Mentoring Effectiveness

*I*n this chapter, we share ten resources that can help you on your journey to becoming the most effective coach or mentor you can be. In fact, we provide more than ten resources because we give you groups of resources organised by type.

A multitude of resources are out there, and you'll have your favourites too. We're sharing a few we know and like, including our own. These resources can support you practically, add to your coaching skill set and stretch your thinking. We invite you to explore these and make this chapter your reference toolkit to support your development.

Resourcing You Online

We have identified a range of resources in this chapter and, as authors of this book, have shamelessly started with our own. We have some tips, blogs and products that will benefit you. Through these websites, you can also get in touch with us if you have questions about what we've written throughout this book.

Marie Taylor

Marie Taylor, one of the book's co-authors, has a range of written material and tips on her blog and Facebook page and free tips. She has also written three short books that are available on Amazon; you can link to those from her blogsite. She has videos on her blog on thinking and the enneagram (see Chapter 11). She also has a YouTube channel where she has a playlist of videos on a range of leadership and coaching topics listed by subject. You can follow her on Twitter or contact her on the blog with any questions.

- Blog site: `http://marietayloronline.com`
- Books: `http://marietayloronline.com/books/`
- Videos: `http://marietayloronline.com/videos/`
- Free tips on coaching, 21st-century leadership, well-being and change leadership: `http://marietayloronline.com/free-tips/`
- Taylored coaching Facebook page: `www.facebook.com/TayloredCoaching/timeline/`
- Twitter: `https://twitter.com/marietaylor`
- YouTube channel other speakers: `www.youtube.com/user/scarletdaisynancy`

Steve Crabb

Steve Crabb, the other co-author of this book, has three resource sites where you can find free rich online content in video, audio and written formats for coaching, business use and personal development. A plethora of coaching content exists to help you develop excellence in all areas with lots of demos showing you how to use various Neuro-Linguistic Programming (NLP) tools. You can also see videos of Steve using metaphor in his work.

- **Corporate and business coaching/training:** `www.empoweringbusinesssolutions.com`. This site contains video master classes demonstrating NLP, coaching and hypnotic techniques. These are designed to develop
  - The mind-set of the prosperous coach
  - The mind-set of the prosperous entrepreneur
  - The mind-set of the prosperous salesman
  - A stress-free mind-set

✔ **Personal and professional excellence:** `www.how2easily.com`. This site contains audio-coaching programmes for personal and professional well-being.

✔ **Steve's one-to-one coaching website for personal development and performance excellence:** `http://stevecrabbcoachingexcellence.com`. This site includes written articles, video and audio recordings of training and master class workshops demonstrating techniques in NLP, coaching and hypnosis.

Business Reading Lists

Increasing your business knowledge through reading is a great way to educate yourself and people in your business about business. If you're looking for inspiration, scroll around some reading lists. You can find lots of these around with some more readily accessible. We've picked just three and encourage you to keep exploring.

✔ Relephance: This is a great reading list resource. With lists for academic courses, you can see what business students are currently reading and keep up-to-date with key texts. If you search on 'business', you can scroll through the lists and see the comments and rating of books. Some lists are password protected, but most are open for anyone who registers: `www.relephance.com/mydashboard`

✔ Blackwell's university reading list where you can search by business courses: `https://bookshop.blackwell.co.uk/jsp/reading lists/selectlist.jsp`

✔ Good Reads lists of business books updated and commented on by readers: `www.goodreads.com/list/tag/business`

iTunes University

Take a look at what is available on the subject of running businesses, entrepreneurship and social entrepreneurship on iTunes University. Loads of public lectures are available on line on these topics. We particularly recommend the following:

✔ `https://itunes.apple.com/in/itunes-u/cambridge-judge-business-school/id536544066?mt=10`

✔ `http://itunes.stanford.edu`

✔ www.open.edu/itunes/subjects/business-and-management

✔ www.harvard.edu/itunes

✔ https://itunes.apple.com/gb/course/real-entrepreneur ship/id684932064

YouTube

A lot of irrelevant content on YouTube positions itself as business material, when it's really an advertorial sales machine. If you can cut through that, you get to some great educational and informative content.

The best videos are the relatively short ones with snippets of great advice or longer in-depth talks around a coaching subject. We've chosen a few here from coaches we like who are talking on aspects of coaching. The Kevin Roberts one is about creating brands and businesses people love and relates to Chapters 6 and 15.

✔ Richard Bandler on determination and adaptation (NLP): www.youtube.com/watch?v=-BheYPWb7ls

✔ Richard Bandler on becoming more motivated (NLP): www.youtube.com/watch?v=u1VZvytE5As

✔ Mandy Evans on choosing what you want and questioning beliefs (BREAK OUT): www.youtube.com/watch?v=Mx-y8pO7xQQ

✔ Byron Katie on questioning the belief that you need more money (The Work): www.youtube.com/watch?v=s78jm5PIUDI

✔ Steve Chandler audio book on overcoming procrastination and making effective use of time (Time Warrior): www.youtube.com/watch?v=QWfDCNGVOO8

✔ Robert Holden on being a coach and what is success?: www.youtube.com/watch?v=PD410AqTNUc

✔ Marshall Goldsmith on coaching for behavioural change: www.youtube.com/watch?v=Hwn_W-X2Rds

✔ Kevin Roberts on Lovemarks – being crazy and creative: www.youtube.com/watch?v=bOIbEKA7kzU

Podcasts

We've recommended two generic business podcasts here (by Peter Day and Jack and Suzy Welch) that both talk about everyday business issues. The entrepreneurs share their own take on their businesses and their views on business life more generally.

The Mike Lynch one is an honest and direct talk on his own experience of developing and leading an organisation.

Michael Hyatt's podcast, similarly, is about his current journey in business and the wider aspects of life and business using social media and online tools to self-organise and increase efficiency.

- Mike Lynch, founder of Autonomy on vision, product positioning and creating a culture of achievement: `www.cfel.jbs.cam.ac.uk/news/podcasts/index.html#2014_lynch_vision`
- BBC Peter Day's World of Business: `www.bbc.co.uk/programmes/p02nrwfk/episodes/downloads`
- Welchcast – Jack and Suzy Welch on aspects of business: `https://itunes.apple.com/gb/podcast/welchcast-weekly-conversation/id1007502096?_mt=2`
- Michael Hyatt on creating a business you love and life in general: `http://michaelhyatt.com/thisisyourlife`

Blogs

You can find myriad business blogs out there. We've chosen three generic business ones where you can find up-to-the-minute content on business and recent research summarised in article format.

The Linda Gratton blog takes a future look at how work is shaping up. Seth Godin writes about marketing, customers and creativity; if Chapters 7 and 8 catch your interest, he is worth a look. Ginger Lapid Bogda is an expert on the use of the enneagram, which we cover in one of the exercises in Chapter 11.

We've also included two sites that provide lots of NLP resources as we have used NLP as a framework in many chapters of the book.

✔ Linda Gratton London Business School on the future of work: `http://lyndagrattonfutureofwork.typepad.com`

✔ Huffington Post Business: `www.huffingtonpost.com/business/`

✔ Forbes: `www.forbes.com`

✔ Harvard Business Review: `https://hbr.org`

✔ The Enneagram in Business – Ginger Lapid-Bogda: `http://theenneagraminbusiness.com/blog/`

✔ Seth Godin on marketing, tribes and customers: `http://sethgodin.typepad.com`

✔ Robert Dilts's Encyclopaedia of NLP provides a free resource on NLP: `http://nlpuniversitypress.com`

✔ Dr Richard Bandler Society of NLP: `http://purenlp.com`

Ted Talks

We love Ted. All that free content with world-class speakers. The following are a mix of light-hearted and self-reflective talks to make you think. They're focused on stand-out leadership and on authenticity in yourself and your business. You could just plan to sit and watch one with no other distractions than a notebook. Turn all the gadgetry off as if you were in a conference audience. Afterwards ask yourself two simple questions: 'What did I learn?' and 'How can I use this?'

✔ 'On how we remain average and moving the average up' with Shawn Anchor: `www.ted.com/playlists/171/the_most_popular_talks_of_all`

✔ 'Smart failure in a fast-changing world' with Eddie Obeng: `www.ted.com/talks/eddie_obeng_smart_failure_for_a_fast_changing_world?language=en`

✔ 'What it takes to be a great leader in the 21st-century' with Roselinde Torres: `www.ted.com/talks/roselinde_torres_what_it_takes_to_be_a_great_leader`

✔ 'Dare to disagree' with Margaret Heffernan: `www.ted.com/talks/margaret_heffernan_dare_to_disagree`

✔ 'Why good leaders make you feel safe' with Simon Sinek: `www.ted.com/talks/simon_sinek_why_good_leaders_make_you_feel_safe`

Twitter

We could mention lots more feeds, but rather than giving you feeds on specific business concepts, we have suggested a few generic ones as they throw out content on a range of topics:

- ✔ It can be fun to follow a hot topic across a range of feeds and get different perspectives, and then play a little. Ask yourself these questions:
  - If I were running that business right now, what would I do?
  - If I were pitching an idea into *Dragon's Den*, what kind of pitch would I deliver?
  - If I were a dragon in the den, what would I want to hear in a pitch?
  - What kind of businesses would I like to hear from?
- ✔ Tweets on general business:
  - https://twitter.com/The_IoD
  - https://twitter.com/BizUSA
  - https://twitter.com/business
  - https://twitter.com/BBCBusiness
  - https://twitter.com/WileyBusiness
  - https://twitter.com/ForDummies
- ✔ *Dragons' Den* – pitching and business ideas:
  - https://twitter.com/cbcdragon
  - https://twitter.com/BBCDragonsDen

Facebook

Brands that have popular Facebook pages (more than 16 million likes) have a few things in common:

- ✔ Fresh content
- ✔ Clean look
- ✔ Fan-based content and fans encouraged to engage with each other
- ✔ Product launches and promotions

We know that large brands have a small army of social media specialists working with them and that some likes and fan commentary are 'manufactured', but nevertheless you can learn lessons here about communicating with existing and prospective customers.

Take a look at the Facebook pages of these four successful brands and ask yourself: How can I replicate some of these elements on a lesser scale within my business on our budget?

- ✔ www.facebook.com/BurtsBeesUK?brand_redir=51334529153
- ✔ www.facebook.com/Burberry?fref=ts
- ✔ www.facebook.com/cocacolaGB?brand_redir=40796308305
- ✔ www.facebook.com/converse

Chapter 17

Ten Ways to Overcome Objections and Change Opinions

. . . .

In This Chapter

▶ Agreeing to disagree and still be friends
▶ Getting your points across
▶ Changing other people's opinions

. . . .

*B*usiness coaching and mentoring is proven to be effective. It works when people follow instructions in a cooperative manner and fully engage in the coaching process. Engaging with clients so they're compliant is the first step towards improving your success as a coach and increasing the chances of successful outcomes for those you coach. Knowing how to get compliance and deal with client objections, disagreements or resistant opinions whenever they arise transforms your results.

In this chapter, we summarize ten simple conversational ways to encourage clients to reevaluate their opinions and to assist you to win agreements.

This subject is not about proving that your view of the world is right and theirs is wrong, but about creating the circumstances so clients are willing to hear and see another perspective from one that may be limiting them.

Preventing Objections

When is the right time to deal with an objection? Well, you can deal with an objection after it's been raised or before it's raised. Most coaches would rather wait for an objection to be raised rather than discuss something that's not yet happened. Intuitively this technique may seem to make sense but the strategy is flawed.

If you raise the objections before your client does and inoculate against them, they're less likely to occur and become an issue. A *linguistic inoculation* is similar to a medical inoculation in that you use it to ensure against ever getting the complaint. It's preventative rather than curative.

Consider the following: If a client raises an objection, even if it seems logical and valid, you're then in the position of having to change his mind. Getting people to change opinions once they've been expressed can be hard work. Whatever opinion a client expresses, he often defends in order to maintain his integrity and be seen to be congruent and right. If you wait for him to first raise the objection, you've missed an opportunity to get your client in the right mind-set for an effective coaching session and are unnecessarily creating hard work for yourself. The right mind-set is when clients are calm, relaxed with an open mind and willing to listen to learn rather than listen to see if they agree.

If you've been coaching for a while, you've probably heard many of the reasons and excuses clients construct that may prevent them from fully engaging in the coaching process at any stage of the programme. A few common examples are

- ✔ 'I'm too busy'.
- ✔ 'I don't get this'.
- ✔ 'I don't see how this will work'.
- ✔ 'I'm not seeing the results yet'.

Sample inoculations for the preceding excuses include

- ✔ 'Some people think they're too busy for coaching, so they don't fully engage in the process and miss out on so much. Don't be one of them'.
- ✔ 'Not everyone gets it first time, and that's part of the learning process'.
- ✔ 'It may be that you don't see how something will work for you. I invite you to be open-minded and to try it out before judging'.
- ✔ 'Not all coaching gives an immediate result. Some things take time to make a difference'.

Prevention is better than cure. Inoculate ahead of time and it transforms your and your client's results.

Butting Out the Buts and Adding in the Ands

The word 'but' is a powerful word when used with intention and damages many meaningful conversations when used indiscriminately. People randomly throw 'buts' around in their language, failing to realise just how they get in the way of getting people to change their opinions.

Imagine a client who says, 'I get the importance of coaching, BUT I have a busy week ahead of me'.

Are they likely to do any coaching assignments? The language they use tells you probably not.

What about a client who says, 'My manager said I did a great job, BUT they need it done quicker'.

Are they focusing on the praise received or the need to do the job quicker?

The mind processes all the information in the sentence. The part of the sentence before the 'buts' then gets ignored or even deleted, and focus and emphasis are only given to the second part of the sentence.

The person speaking is basically saying, 'I understand and have heard the first part of the sentence, BUT I am ignoring or deleting it and only focusing on the second part'.

If a client expresses an opinion and you reply with a 'but', what you're in effect saying to them is 'I hear what you say, BUT I am ignoring it and deleting it and replacing it with my opinion'.

When you reply with a 'but', the client won't feel like you've heard him or understood him, and you then encounter resistance from the client to any opinion or alternative point of view you offer.

Remember, the word 'however' is just a sneaky form of but!

To keep conversations going smoothly, replace the word 'but' with 'and', and notice how much more open they are listening to a different opinion.

Appreciating a Different Point of View

When two people have rapport, they're said to have 'trust and harmony in a relationship'. When a client expresses an opinion that may be limiting him and you want to challenge the opinion, you need to give a counter-argument without seeming to disagree. By doing so, you maintain your rapport with him.

Using these agreement phrases followed with the word 'and' (no 'buts' – see the preceding section) enables you to question and challenge a client's opinions without losing him:

- ✔ 'I appreciate what you have said, AND. . . (express your counterargument)'.

- ✔ 'I agree with you, AND. . . (express your counterargument)'.

- ✔ 'I respect that opinion, AND. . . (express your counterargument)'.

- ✔ 'I acknowledge that view, AND. . . (express your counterargument)'.

- ✔ 'I hear what you're saying, AND. . . (express your counterargument)'.

Softening the Questions

Part of overcoming any objection is being able to understand exactly what the other person means. The way to understand is for you to ask good questions to get more specific information that you can then question.

When asking questions to get clarity, use softener phrases to tease the information out of clients. If you come across as confrontational, challenging or doubting what they say, your attitude will lead to resistance.

Often when a client re-evaluates what he's just said, he naturally sees another perspective and changes his mind.

Use the following softener phrases:

- ✔ 'I'm curious. What do you mean by that?'

- ✔ 'I'm wondering, when you say that, what does it actually mean?'

- ✔ 'That's an interesting opinion. Why would you say that?'

- ✔ 'That's fascinating. What do you mean by that?'

Reframing the Conversation

Reframing means to literally put a new or different framework around an experience or idea, thereby transforming its meaning. If a client expresses an opinion or demonstrates a behaviour that is limiting him, you can reframe the opinion and behaviour in a way that the client is more likely to agree with you and won't feel he's being challenged, criticised or ignored.

Look for another way to describe the behaviour or opinion that may be limiting the client so he sees that there are other perspectives and ways to behave.

Reframes can be in the form of descriptive sentences where the sentence is given a different meaning or simple one-word reframes where the meaning of the word itself is changed by replacing it with another word.

Philosopher Bertrand Russell quoted these examples of reframes:

- 'I am firm, you are obstinate, he is a pig-headed fool'.
- 'I am righteously indignant, you are annoyed, he is making a fuss over nothing'.
- 'I have reconsidered the matter, you have changed your mind, he has gone back on his word'.

Here are some examples of how to reframe client objections:

> Client says, 'I get the importance of coaching, but I have a busy week ahead of me and can't see how I'll fit in doing the coaching assignment'.

You can reframe the objection this way:

> 'I acknowledge that you get the importance of coaching and you have a busy week ahead of you, AND that's why the organisation has invested in this coaching programme to assist you to be more effective and efficient at what you do'.

This reframe shows the client that his being busy is all the more reason to do the coaching assignment.

Reframing enables a client to see multiple ways of viewing a situation, making him more likely to agree with your perspective or one that doesn't limit him.

Understanding the Intention

Some say that 'every behaviour has a positive intention', and the same can be said for all beliefs and opinions. We all believe and do things for reasons, even if we may not be fully consciously aware of the reasons.

A particularly effective reframe is the *intention reframe* where a coach looks for the positive intention behind any behaviour or opinion if it's limiting the client in any way.

For example, if a client expresses the opinion, 'I don't see how this will work', you can use an intention reframe such as the following:

> 'I appreciate what you're saying, and I'm just curious why you might think that. Is it perhaps a way to stop you from engaging in the coaching process for fear of making mistakes and being judged? So perhaps you prejudge before giving it a try? Or is it something else?'

The assumed positive intention is to avoid making mistakes and being judged.

Using an intention reframe gets the client to question and re-evaluate what he's saying and why he's saying it. Re-evaluation often leads to a new way of seeing an opinion or behaviour which often makes it difficult for the client to defend or justify his original opinion.

Realising the Consequences

Every decision you make in the present has an effect on the future. This statement can cause people to radically rethink an opinion when they consider the consequences of their actions. The *consequence reframe* points out or gets a client to consider the possible future consequences of holding on to a belief, objection, opinion or behaviour.

Future consequences can be both positive and negative in nature. When using consequence reframes, consider pointing out the negative ones first and then direct the conversation towards the positive ones. This sequence acts as a motivational propulsion mechanism for the mind, directing thinking and behaviour away from the negative towards the positive and creating a compelling case for someone to change his opinion and take positive action.

For example, if a client is disengaged from the coaching programme and expresses the belief 'I'm not seeing the results yet', a possible consequence reframe is

'I appreciate you're not seeing results yet. The soft option would be to quit and remain stuck and see others improve around you because they hung in *(this highlights the negative consequences)*. The other option is to persevere and in time and with practice you will see results and be in a better position for promotion' *(highlighting the positive consequences).*

Making Objections Personal

A simple way to question an opinion is to offer a counterexample that contradicts it. If the counterexample is from the client's personal life, it may be difficult for him to disagree with its relevance.

For example, if a client says, 'I don't get this', you can counter with, 'I appreciate you don't get this yet, and I'm guessing that when you studied for your qualifications, you probably didn't get everything first time then either. Yet you saw the value of continuing your studying until you did get it, and it paid dividends in the end. This is the same'.

Remembering a Story

An elegant conversational way to overcome an objection or change an opinion is to wrap a new idea up in with a story or metaphor. Metaphors act like Trojan horses in that the meaning of the communication gets delivered into the listener's thinking with little resistance.

Useful metaphors are references to other clients whereby it can be demonstrated that others who thought the same changed their opinions or behaviours for the better.

For example, if a client expresses a limiting opinion such as, 'I'm too busy, and I don't have time for this', you can deliver multiple messages in one metaphor:

> 'I understand you are very busy. I've worked with many successful executives who felt the same thing. One in particular was so busy being busy, he never made time to do the important things. We were coaching and having a similar conversation to this when he suddenly had an insight when I said to him, "Busy is lazy, and it's often a way to distract from the really important things." He suddenly realised that to move on, he had to manage his time better and commit and schedule the time to do the coaching assignments'.

A metaphor enables you to be indirectly direct and offer counter-opinions without offending a client.

Provoking a Response

Fortune favours the brave, and sometimes you have nothing to lose and everything to gain by being brave with a client who insists on remaining stuck. Sometimes you have to draw out a new perspective from a client. The word *provocative* means 'to draw out', and a *provocative reframe* can often draw out new ways of thinking and new ways of behaving for a client.

A provocative reframe is where you deliberately and purposefully misunderstand the client. You can take your misunderstanding to a ridiculous extreme and seemingly offer no help or sensible solutions whatsoever. This kind of reframe is the coaching equivalent of using a sledgehammer to crack a nut.

A provocative reframe requires you to first have good rapport with a client and a good sense of humour. Always do provocative reframing with a twinkle in your eye and an open, caring heart. Remember, the limiting opinion or objection is what you're bringing into question, not the individual.

For example, if a client says, 'I don't get this', a provocative reply would go along the lines of

> 'I'm not surprised you don't get it. Some people are a bit slow on the uptake, and some quit before they start. Are we talking about a coin toss here, or do you know which you are? Or some people are slow quitters, and they hang on until they do get it. I'm guessing that's not you either, is it? Or is there another reason? You don't strike me as being particularly slow, but I'm happy to look at ways to dumb this down some more if that's what's needed. What do you think?'

Smile, sit back and *shut up*. Let him process what you've said and listen to the reply.

The provocative response 99 per cent of the time is wry laughter and a recognition that what they were expressing was ridiculous and that they can 'get it' if they try. For the 1 per cent of clients who may take the comments personally and react, you simply smile and explain, 'Look, I'm only teasing with all that. I get it you're a quitter'. Smile, sit back and *shut up*.

Provocative reframes require persistence as it may take a few taps of the hammer before the nut cracks.

Chapter 18

Ten Tips for Leaders Who Coach or Mentor People in Business

In This Chapter

▶ Leading people effectively using the skill set in your own organisation

▶ Developing leadership habits that create results

*G*ood business is created by the efforts of a multitude of people all delivering their part to create and deliver the whole. To motivate people, get the best from them, retain them and keep them engaged, leaders need to lead and manage people well. Leaders need to focus the people they're responsible for on delivering in the business while focusing themselves, their management team and board on both delivering and developing the business. This requires that leaders keep multiple stakeholders on track with the why, what, when and how of the business regularly. Keeping staff (or shareholding family members) aligned with business goals, values and culture is essential for ongoing success.

This chapter helps leaders reflect on their coaching and mentoring skills and provides tips for coaching people in specific circumstances. We invite you to try out some of the tips given in the chapter. Experiment. Create the conditions for those around you to recognise their talents. Work with them to identify the best ways to use those talents for the benefit of the business; then stand back and watch them shine.

The tips in this chapter are useful for

✔ Leaders coaching their own people (staff or family members in family-owned business)

✔ Leaders coaching or mentoring colleagues within their organisation

✔ Leaders who coach or mentor in organisations other than their own

You can find a few simple tips for leaders who coach on co-author Marie's blog under the resources section here: http://marietayloronline.com/free-tips/

Develop Talent in Those You Lead

Leaders are there to lead, and yet we see so many who want to focus on task delivery. They like the job title and the package, but for too many, the leadership role has been given to them as a promotion to extend their span of control in the business with little thought to the all-important part of leading and developing others.

We've worked with leaders who think their role is to handle every issue their people throw their way, to solve every problem and effectively become handling agents. They've become patriarchal problem solvers running around being too busy with the issues passed upwards by their team while their people find even more problems. It isn't surprising that their people get used to passing the problems on the minute the issue falls into the 'too hard' box.

If leaders keep taking these problems off their people, over a sustained period they too can end up in a hard box too early. They can burn out and end up lying in a graveyard near you with a headstone that says 'Busy unto death. Under him the multitudes learned how to pass a problem on'. You can almost see a group of staff sitting in cubicles emailing each other weeks later saying, 'I sent an email asking her what to say at her memorial but got no response'.

Equally, we've watched those who fail to delegate authority, responsibility and tasks properly. They get caught up in a web of confusion when things don't work out and results aren't delivered. The web is one they've created by their inaction and failure to delegate effectively. And we all know what happens to things that get caught up in a web, don't we?

Coaching leadership is the secret to staff engagement

NASA prides itself on the fact that, some years back, when a guy who sweeps the floors was asked what his role was, he replied, 'I help people discover planets and to walk on the moon'. It's no accident – NASA has had a coaching style of leadership that has encouraged staff to align themselves and their work to the ongoing space programme for many years. Coaching is used as a management tool to help people consider their individual contribution as part of the wider organisation. Coaching inside organisations helps facilitate that kind of engagement. To create that from the inside, leaders need to be able to use the coaching skill set and adopt coaching as an enabling tool.

Don't be one of these extremes – particularly not after you've read this book. That would just be embarrassing for us and downright careless of you. In our map of the world, developing talent is an integral part of what 21st-century leadership is. Invest in your own skills development and discover how to delegate appropriately and how to coach and mentor others well.

Sell More than Tell

Leadership is about creating effective followers who can contribute and stretch their range of capability. The desire to have all the answers in leading people is an indicator of autocratic leadership, not coaching leadership. Coaching leadership facilitates others to generate solutions to problems and to use their abilities to create solutions to problems that they don't even know they have yet.

People like to follow leaders who enable them to contribute. How are you challenging people to contribute and add value through your coaching? If you were observing yourself speaking to the people you coach, what would you hear yourself say? What language patterns are you using most of the time?

Notice the difference between

- ✔ 'You need to do A first, then B, then C. That should take around two hours and when those are completed, try F or G. You should have it completed by the end of next week'. (Autocratic style)
- ✔ 'We need to complete these project plan updates by the last Friday of the month from now on. How might you enable the team to deliver on that?' (Coaching style)

Mind your language when you lead and coach others. If you adopt an autocratic style, notice that you're doing all the work to generate the solution. When leaders do that, they keep the ownership of the problem. The person on the receiving end is delivering to task and rarely feels fully responsible for delivery of those tasks. This doesn't mean you shouldn't be directive as a leader from time to time; rather, in the coaching context, you want to motivate people to take appropriate responsibility and help them generate workable solutions for themselves, instead of being told what to do wherever possible.

Name the Elephant before Eating It

If you walk around any organisation, whether in the deep dark corridors of the traditional fusty dusty building or the brightest LED up-lit workspaces of cubedom, you can find these strange creatures who spend most of their working day rarely saying what the key problems are. They seem to find difficulty stating what they really want to say or what they really mean. So they dance around and say everything but what they mean. It's like the issue is in the room but written in invisible neon signage that everyone present is trying not to look at. The leader doesn't seem to be able to say the unpopular thing, so she dances the Hokey Cokey, sticking legs in and then out but never standing still long enough to say 'Actually, we need to talk about your dance moves. Your legwork is just awful. You need more practice to be in this chorus line'.

To coach effectively, you need to be prepared to find the elephant in the room and name it clearly. The elephant isn't going anywhere – it's bigger and stronger than all of us.

Take co-author Marie, for example. Marie was group coaching with a newly formed leadership team at Pens R Us (not their real name). The team were looking at their three-year vision and were made up of some existing directors and newly appointed directors. There was an 'atmosphere', and by coffee she knew, if left unchallenged, the work with the team would be okay but not great; they may have been able to develop a vision, but she doubted their ability to deliver that vision as a team.

After coffee, she started the segment with a single sentence:

'Why is there an atmosphere in this room, and how do we clear it?'

After an uncomfortable silence, people opened up. There was an unresolved trust issue between two people on the team that seemed to be affecting the whole team of eight. By discussing it, planning for the fears of what could go wrong and looking at how to build trust in the team going forward, it cleared the air. It made things clearer and easier for everyone.

Sometimes, as a leader who coaches, you need to help people clarify and name the problem so you can help them work out how they can resolve it or work around it. Becoming really good at proper naming of a concern and articulating it clearly can help leaders catch a concern before it becomes a baby elephant. Cute as they may be, baby elephants take up a lot of space.

Get Good at Asking Questions

The way you ask questions informs the kind of response you get. You need to use questions in coaching that are appropriate to the type of situation. Leaders in organisations working towards specific outcomes find it particularly useful to frame questions depending on whether they're generating a process, identifying potential problems or seeking a quick resolution to a problem.

Questions in coaching sit within a context. You have so many ways you can use questions to help others get to an outcome: ask similar questions in different ways to notice what works with the people whom you lead regularly; become aware of what kind of questions open up their thinking and help create a level of clarity that they need. This kind of questioning is about identifying what works and doing more of that.

Notice the difference between these three questions:

- ✔ 'Imagine you could create the perfect solution to a problem you're leading on. What would be the first step for you?'

- ✔ 'Imagine you could create the worst solution to a problem you're leading on. What would be the first step? . . . What will you do instead?'

- ✔ 'Imagine you could create a quick, workable solution to a problem you're leading on. What would be the first step for your team in the next two hours?'

Play around with your coaching questions a little. Help people move towards an outcome in different ways and pay attention to what works. The ability to ask good questions saves your time and empowers others to think and act.

Speak in Specifics and Minding Your Language

We've all done it. We speak in generalities and sometimes drop hints into the conversation in the hope that someone will get the message or understand what we're really trying to say without us having to say it clearly. When we coach within an organisation, we have this habit too. We can fall into the trap of buying into our coachee's generalisations. This mistake can happen because we have a shared experience or a shared set of assumptions, a kind of organisational shorthand. Sometimes this shorthand is just fine – but not if the collective assumptions need to be challenged.

Assumptions in business can result from a lack of clarity. When people don't speak up, those assumptions begin to sound like facts that everyone uses to justify behaviour. This situation can create organisational risk, myths and misunderstanding. When coaching as a leader, you are sometimes the one who needs to question assumptions and challenge generalisations.

In this area, it can be really helpful to challenge your own generalisations before speaking; get specific and challenge your coachee to do the same.

For example, there is a world of difference between

> *Option 1. Leader: 'The debt recovery team are useless at chasing customers up, and that delays our bonus payments. We need to rectify this. What ideas do you have?'*
>
> *Staff member: 'I know, they're useless. I can go and talk to Fred and see if he can get them to be more efficient on that in future. We can try and see if that shifts them. I can do that on Wednesday'.*

Notice how a generalised statement and call to action creates what sounds like a solution. Also, how the generalisation can invite collusion with the status quo.

> *Option 2. Leader who coaches: 'Some of our debts don't seem to be recovered as efficiently as others, and this seems to have created a knock on problem with the bonus payments for the sales team in February. It isn't the first time it has happened. We need to rectify that. What thoughts do you have?'*
>
> *Staff member: 'I know, they're useless. I can go and talk to Fred and see if he can get them to be more efficient on that in future. We can try and see if that shifts them. I can do that on Wednesday'.*
>
> *Leader who coaches: 'I didn't say they were useless, but that they contributed to the sales team not receiving their bonus. What I'm looking for are ideas on how you might help the situation improve'.*
>
> *Staff member: 'Oh. Well, I guess I can sit down with Fred to work back and see what happened in February. I can look at whether it's a problem with the chasing of debt or something else'.*
>
> *Leader who coaches: 'What could the "something else" be?'*
>
> *Staff member: 'Well, now that I think about it, I guess part of the problem may be timing. I can check what dates the sales team are passing on customer details to debt recovery for chasing'.*
>
> *Leader who coaches: 'Anything else?'*
>
> *Staff member: 'As it only happens some months, I wonder if anything is happening in those months or in the preceding month that causes the problem and whether the sales team are contributing to that . . .'*

You get the picture. By coaching and setting aside the assumptions and generalisations, you can help people generate specific thoughts and ideas that may actually address the problem.

Recognise the Value of Slowing Down or Shutting Up

Sometimes when people coach, they do too much talking. They may do so because they love the sound of their own voice, they have lots of ideas that they can't sit on or they simply feel uncomfortable with the silence in a conversation. When coaches are doing most of the talking, they're normally doing most of the work in the coaching conversation too. If this happens, they can start directing rather than leading or can end up generating solutions that the member of staff then doesn't recognise as her own. When the coachee hasn't generated the solution, it can be more difficult for her to implement it.

Noticing this situation happening is the first step to get the conversation back on track by either slowing down your pace of speech or using silence as ways to help others think.

 People tend to think more deeply when they slow down the pace a little. In coaching, you're looking to create the conditions to allow others to generate thoughtful, workable ideas and solutions rather than rapid-fire answers. Consider how you may make room for those you lead to generate their own solutions by simply slowing down the conversation. If you find doing so difficult, a simple technique is to practise speaking out loud by reading at a storytelling pace.

Being quiet and getting comfortable with silence can also help. The silence inevitably seems longer for the coach than the coachee. The person being coached is generating ideas and using the space the coach creates to solve the issue she is faced with. Get comfortable with the silence and, if it helps, tell the coachee that you're going to stop talking quite so much and leave a bit of silence from time to time in the conversation to allow room for her grey matter to get to work.

Try it and see what results you get.

Appreciate Differences to Be a Difference Maker

Globalisation and virtual workplaces are changing the role of leadership. Equally as we become more geographically mobile, managing people of different cultures in single location business is becoming increasingly important too. Cross-cultural coaching can be difficult for those who have limited experienced of cultural diversity.

We need to understand how cultural differences manifest themselves because they can present entirely different philosophies of life, of work and worldviews. With that comes a range of different values, assumptions and beliefs. To coach people effectively, you need to understand some of these differences and how you can respect those in the coaching process.

Ask people of a different culture what works for them in the coaching process and what they find useful, particularly if they've been coached previously within their own culture. Even basic manners and communication methods can be different from culture to culture. Being sensitive to these differences is important in terms of gaining and maintaining rapport with a coachee. You may need to switch out of your own cultural norms to serve your member of staff well. Knowing when to take the lead a little from the coachee is important. If you're male, shaking the hand of a Muslim woman may not be acceptable, for example. You need to become familiar with cultural norms and actively engage your staff in the conversation about what works for them.

Do you know what the cultural expectations are of work from the people you lead? What are the range of culturally specific celebrations and festivals in your team? How can you acknowledge those or take account of them in the coaching process? For example, if someone is fasting for a period of time, you may need to consider changing the timing of coaching conversations from afternoon to morning when the person may be less tired. Coaches need to be adaptive and flexible.

Create the Optimum Conditions to Coach at a Distance

When you coach people at different locations, you need to consider a few obvious things such as taking account of time differences and organising meeting times when both you and the coachee have the energy to coach and be coached. We both coach internationally and have had that experience of speaking to a client at midnight after a full day's work. Although we have techniques we can use to recharge our energy, in truth late-night calls are never a good idea. Reorganising your day to have a late start and learning the art of the ten-minute power nap are good habits to develop if working across different time zones.

When you have coaching conversations at a distance, it's a good idea to re-create the conditions of a face-to-face meeting as far as possible. The following checklist may help. The checklist is intended for use by the coach, and you can use it as preparation guidance for the coachee too.

✔ Use Skype or videoconferencing to see the person face to face. Check that the link works ten minutes before the call. If using the telephone, move away from the computer and any other distractions in the office.

✔ Have a clear desk and, if not using the computer, close it down and turn off any message alerts to avoid distraction. If you need something to take a note with, just have that available.

✔ Turn off any mobile phones or other phone lines that may distract you.

✔ If you're at risk of being disturbed, put a note on the door or by your desk asking not to be interrupted during the call.

✔ Before you dial in, get a picture in your mind of the person you're about to speak to. If you have a photo of her, have it in front of you with her name underneath.

✔ Review any previous meeting notes and recall what coaching models you have used with this person and what really helps her when you have coaching conversations. Get clear about any issues you would like to discuss with the coachee and what she's bringing to discuss with you.

✔ Have in mind how much time you would like to spend on each element that you're bringing to the discussion.

✔ Remind yourself to slow down the pace of your dialogue and actively listen even more than usual so you hear the nuance in the conversation.

✔ Clear your mind of anything other than having this focused conversation for the next X minutes.

If you're coaching by email or messenger service, keep your emails short and use a conversational rather than directive style. Use two different-coloured fonts – one each. That way you can see the dialogue at a glance. We would never recommend using email coaching as your only method. The richness of the coaching relationship is in the conversation. Email coaching can be useful between calls if your coachee gets stuck and needs additional support to check her thinking or if she wants to check that she is on the right track in delivering a specific outcome.

Support Your People during Change

When you're leading and coaching people through a change programme, remember that people can find change a challenge. If staff cannot recognise or articulate feelings of shock, anger and melancholy that can manifest during change, this challenge can be even greater for them.

Individual and team performance may suffer, and staff can feel deskilled and sometimes may find it difficult to transition to new ways of working.

The best thing leaders who coach can do during change is to:

- ✔ Encourage people to keep talking about the change and the process of change even if you feel you've heard their feedback ten times before.

- ✔ Acknowledge people regularly and be as specific as you can about what they are contributing, what you value about them and what you would like them to contribute in the next month, week or day!

- ✔ Be prepared to feel a bit stupid sometimes. You may not have the answers to their questions and may not have even thought of some of the questions that pop up. It's okay to say, 'I don't know, I will need to come back to you'.

- ✔ Be honest when you do know but are not able to share information. This can become an art form when coaching people during change. Most of the time, the best policy is to tell people that 'decisions are being taken that are not for sharing beyond the senior team at the moment' (if they are) rather than a blanket 'I don't know'.

- ✔ Help people to see their strengths and capabilities by giving lots of feedback and encouraging the coachee to review her own work and highlight her strengths. It can be a great idea to coach people to recognise and 'sell' her strengths during change, particularly if she may need to apply for a new role.

To help her, try working with these types of coaching questions:

- ✔ How are you experiencing the change process?

- ✔ On a scale of 1 to 10, how motivated are you to deliver what you need to get done this week? What would help to move you one or two points up the scale?

- ✔ If our team were to be just 10 per cent more effective in the next two to four weeks, what would you suggest we do? What would you have me do? What would you do?

✔ I can hear you're angry about the changes and the impact on your colleagues. What could I do more of to support you during this time?

✔ What do you absolutely need to deliver in the next week? What would you like to deliver if we can find another way of doing things by the end of this conversation?

✔ As a team, let's go around the room and on a scale of 1 to 10 indicate how informed you feel you are about the change impact on this team. Where are you on the scale in relation to your understanding of the organisational change as a whole?

✔ If I were to ask all of your internal and external customers what you have delivered and how you have delivered in the last three months, what positive things would I hear?

✔ What one thing would help to make the change process easier for you in the next four to eight weeks?

Educate Yourself about the Business

When leaders coach and mentor inside organisations, you need to know the business: to know more than they do about the vision for the business, the values it holds dear and what can help them succeed within it. Leaders need to be honest, but you can only say 'I don't know' so many times before your credibility as a leader is affected. The questions your people ask in coaching conversations and the issues they raise that you don't understand can provide some indicators of where your own knowledge gaps are.

We don't take the view that leaders need to know everything their people know, rather that you need an overview of the business and where the work your people are delivering fits longer term. You need to understand business terminology and the roles people play in making the business successful in order to be a great coach too. These can be divided into three areas:

✔ **People factors:** Being able to explain the role of the Board, the Executive Leadership, the different functions in the business and its customers. Being able to describe the relationships between key players in the organisation, any organisational politics and accepted ways of operating in the business.

✔ **Business process factors:** Knowing how to interpret the annual report, understanding key operational policy, knowing key milestone dates and deadlines. The rhythm of the business such as budget deadlines, Board paper deadlines, regular communications to read, any social calendar and the like.

  ✔ **Industry and market factors:** Understanding the business externally to help your people widen their perspective and knowledge base during their career. Sharing your knowledge of relevant professional networks and associations, or helping your coachee/mentee navigate her way through the key publications to read or understanding who the movers and shakers are in your industry.

This understanding is essential if you're helping your people develop their careers, and we believe that one role of leaders is to do that. Not that you would simply impart information to your staff like the career equivalent of a tourist information office. In a coaching or mentoring session, you want to encourage a degree of self-discovery and personal research. To do that, you need an informed internal and external view to help people know if they're heading in the right direction.

A good way for leaders who coach to consider this issue is for you to draw two mind maps and stakeholder maps. One shows your internal knowledge in the areas of people, policy, processes, vision and plans. The other shows your external relationships and knowledge in your industry, customer groups and professional expertise. These two maps can help you spot your own gaps and sometimes your own areas for development as a coach, a leader or professional. Possibly, you may identify areas where you may seek coaching or mentoring support yourself.

Chapter 19

Ten Questions to Keep a Business on Track

*K*eeping a business on track involves more than checking financial accounts, having regular progress meetings and measuring to see whether targets or objectives set have actually been achieved. Yet as a coach, these are always the first places to begin when coaching a business to keep on track.

We are always shocked by how many businesses fail to have these fundamental measures in place. They're the low-hanging fruit (the easy, early successes) for coaches to pick. Reviewing finances, assessing the way a business conducts meetings and evaluating how it measures its performance are always good places to review before doing any coaching. These areas often show if a business is on or off track and reveal the reasons why. Many businesses, especially small to medium enterprises, fail to have these measures in the first instance, so you must coach clients to have these in place if they don't already have them.

In this chapter, we offer ten powerful questions that go beyond financials, meetings and measuring. They're questions that can assist you to coach clients to see whether they're on the right track to begin with and to check whether they're still on track. The answers to the questions can also give clients insights into the adjustments they need to make to get back on track.

The questions can be asked of individuals, teams, in relation to projects and for organisations. In this chapter, when we refer to projects, you can read it to mean individuals, teams and organisations.

What Would We Create If Anything Was Possible?

The journey of a thousand miles begins with one step.

–Lao Tzu

On any journey, you want to make sure you head off in the right direction from the outset. You're a fool to head east looking for a sunset. Many businesses start off on the wrong track to begin with or head in a direction where if they knew the destination, they probably wouldn't have started the journey at all.

'What would we create if anything was possible?' is a great question to ask at the start of any project, throughout the project and at any time during the life cycle of a business to ensure that it stays on a worthy track.

While working on a project with his friend, best-selling author and self-help guru, Paul McKenna, it was Steve's responsibility to put together a business plan for an idea they had developed.

After months of working to check the Proof of Concept and to create a plan Fit for Purpose (see Chapter 9), they had a robust, well-researched plan that seemed worthy of investing their valuable time, money and effort into.

Late one evening, Steve received a telephone call from Paul, who was laughing hysterically. He had been discussing the plan with friends and advisors, all of whom are internationally recognised entrepreneurs. One advisor is a globally recognised branding and marketing expert. He owns, among other things, an airline and a football team. Paul was laughing because his friend couldn't understand why they were thinking so small with the project.

After getting his bruised ego out of the way, Steve sat with this feedback for a while and realised that his friend was correct. Neither Paul nor Steve think small – they had even referenced the plan 'Blue Sky Thinking' – but Paul's friend only thought on a global scale.

Steve revisited the plan and scaled it up from a national to an international project. The additional work involved in turning the plan into a global reality was small by comparison to that involved for a national project, and the potential return was also significantly of more value.

Ask this question of your clients to ensure that they're on the right track to begin with. Far too often, businesses think small and have the ladder of success propped up against a low wall. A lot of time, money and effort goes into projects that, even when successful, people often say, 'Is that it?' Coach the client to think bold and get on the right track to begin with.

Why Are We Doing This?

And it comes from saying no to one thousand things to make sure we don't get on the wrong track or try to do too much. We're always thinking about new markets we could enter, but it's only by saying no that you can concentrate on the things that are really important.

–Steve Jobs

When we ask clients this question, we are asking them to enquire into what's important to them. The 'Why?' question reveals their values.

If you think of values as unwritten, often unconscious rules that tell you what's right and what's wrong, then values can be used as a compass to let you know if you are on- or off-track with your actions.

Identifying the values for an individual, a team, project or organisation is a crucial enquiry and an exercise worthy of spending time on.

When you act in conflict with your own personal values, you get a sense of ill ease, it feels wrong and you are said to be incongruent. When you act in alignment with your values, it feels right and feels congruent. Right actions seem easy choices and obvious, and results often happen naturally and effortlessly.

Get clients to write their values down, keep them in plain view and encourage them to keep the 'Why?' in mind at all times. Doing so is a simple, elegant yet powerful way to use values as an inner compass to check that actions being taken are keeping the business on track.

What Would Richard Branson Do Now?

Don't think what's the cheapest way to do it or what's the fastest way; think what's the most amazing way to do it.

–Richard Branson

In Chapter 3, we explore the value of a different perspective. We all act through the perspectives of what we think are the right actions to take, and we see the world through the rose-tinted glasses of our own beliefs about what's possible and what's not.

By asking this question, you create the coaching space for a client to go beyond his own limited thinking. You can replace Richard Branson for any industry expert or person who would be a valuable advisor on a support team. Allow for out-of-the-box, blue sky and lateral thinking and explore all options and insights that the client has.

This question can often reveal quicker, better, easier or more amazing tracks to the one your client is currently following.

What Is a Better Way?

Many are stubborn in pursuit of the path they have chosen, few in pursuit of the goal.

–Friedrich Nietzsche

Projects and plans change over time, and what may have been a great plan at the start may no longer be the best plan. The phrase 'building the aircraft as we fly' is often used in a negative way, implying little or poor planning. Many businesses know the value of launching a project before it's perfect, gathering feedback from customers or staff and adjusting as they go.

If a business is rigid and inflexible and the leadership has its mind set on following a predetermined plan, that business is closing off other options. Use this question as a regular check to adjust plans and action steps as the project unfolds and evolves and as new information is gathered.

This question is a variation on the preceding one. It presupposes that a better way is possible. Allow for brainstorming and replace the word 'better' with 'quicker', 'easier', 'more elegant', 'more cost-effective' or 'smarter'.

Are We Still the Right People to Be Doing This?

Talent is the No. 1 priority for a CEO. You think it's about vision and strategy, but you have to get the right people first.

–Andrea Jung

As the golden glow of enthusiasm for a new project fades to the dull, tarnished glimmer of apathy, wavering enthusiasm can be a sign that the project or business is off-track.

Many projects stall or fail because of lack of enthusiasm and people failing to deliver. In such cases, they not only go off-track, but it often seems as if the track they were on begins to fade away before their very eyes.

If a business is in this state, always ask clients the first two questions in this chapter to check whether the project is a worthy and inspiring one and whether the project is in alignment with their values. If the answers to these questions are both 'yes', then wavering enthusiasm is often a sign that the business may not have the right people for the tasks.

It requires honest courage to ask and answer this question. Egos have to be set aside for the greater good of the project or business. A healthy business has the honesty to respectfully replace people with those better suited to the tasks.

Are We Busy Being Busy?

> *Being busy does not always mean real work. The object of all work is production or accomplishment and to either of these ends there must be forethought, system planning, intelligence and honest purpose, as well as perspiration. Seeming to do is not doing.*
>
> *–Thomas Edison*

Most people never have enough time in the day to do all the tasks that have to be done. The business world is full of people busy being busy without being productive.

Client time is often spent doing urgent rather than important tasks that would keep a project on track. Coaching a client to identify the 'busy-ness bug' is the first step in helping him to be more efficient and effective with his time.

Pareto's Principle states that roughly 20 per cent of actions produce 80 per cent of results, or 80 per cent of effects come from 20 per cent of causes. This principle is a simple and effective economic one that has been used for decades by business professionals to produce better results.

Coach clients by asking 'Are you busy being busy?' to focus their attention on the tasks that create results and they will be on track at least 20 per cent of the time – joke.

What Can We Do to Optimise or Streamline?

An organisation's ability to learn, and translate that learning into action rapidly, is the ultimate competitive advantage.

–Jack Welch

On an NLP Train the Trainers course, Steve heard Dr Richard Bandler (co-creator of NLP) explain to his audience that optimising a process or strategy involves taking out redundant steps. He went on to explain that he used to take clocks apart and put them back together again and have parts left over – and his clocks would always work quicker. The joke was missed by many, but the principle of optimising is a valuable one for keeping a business on 'the best track'.

Humans have a creative capacity for making things complicated. Asking clients this question on a regular basis ensures that they review their actions and find the simplest ways to achieve their goals. Think of optimisation as finding a new track, a shortcut to a destination. This approach can save a lot of meandering that takes time and effort and can result in missed opportunities and deadlines, which ultimately costs businesses money.

This approach can be summarised by the principle of Ockham's razor, first developed by the Franciscan friar and philosopher William of Ockham. Ockham's razor is more commonly described as 'the simplest answer is most often correct'.

Are We Going in the Right Direction?

Everybody who goes through the business will make mistakes. The big question is how big will the mistakes be? How fast will they learn from the mistakes, and how quickly will they get the business in the correct direction?

–Fred DeLuca

When an aircraft takes off from London Heathrow heading to New York, it never exactly follows the planned flight path. The pilot is always making course adjustments for wind speed, air pressure, turbulence, fuel and weather, and constantly changing altitude, air speed and direction. Yet the plane is always heading towards its destination, albeit not in a straight line.

Making small course corrections to a business is a lot easier than having to completely reorganise a plan if that plan has gone completely off course. This valuable question can often reveal whether a business is off course and that the original plan is now unworkable. Asking the question reveals when the time has arrived to change from Plan A to Plan B and to then think of Plan B as the new Plan A.

As long as an individual, team, project or business is heading in the right direction, they tend to eventually get there.

What Do We Need to Stop Doing?

Don't use a lot where a little will do.

–Buddhist proverb

This question is another way to help clients identify whether they're off-track by being busy or have made a project more complicated than it needs to be and what has to stop.

While answering this question, clients start to identify tasks or steps in a process that they can stop doing and still achieve their aims or outcomes. Doing so releases valuable resources such as time and effort that can be diverted into more useful tasks.

Are We All Still on the Same Page?

When you're surrounded by people who share a passionate commitment around a common purpose, anything is possible.

–Howard Schultz

Assuming that a company has regular meetings with updates on projects and milestones towards achieving its goals, it must still have regular reality checks to see whether all team members are still on the same page with the project. Decisions and commitments made at the start of a project may no longer be valid weeks or months later.

Remember that saying 'a chain is only as strong as its weakest link'? It's mission critical to know whether a team or team member has wavering commitment or is behind on a task, and to find out why. Adjustments can then be made sooner rather than later.

Many projects and businesses go off-track when assumptions are made that everyone is still committed to their decisions and a plan. Coach clients to engage regularly in this open, honest dialogue and to avoid making assumptions about commitment and engagement.

Index

• *F* •

• S •

About the Authors

Marie Taylor is an executive coach, speaker and facilitator of insight and learning. She established her own successful consulting and coaching practice in 2002 and has been coaching for more than 18 years. She works internationally, supporting leaders and their organizations to create success.

Marie has a post-graduate diploma in coaching and consultancy, and is a fellow of the CIPD, a master practitioner of NLP and a hypnotherapist. She also holds an honours degree and a master's in business from Cambridge University. An experienced facilitator and trainer, she has worked with leadership groups in areas as diverse as national government, technology and science-based start-ups, professional bodies, international corporations, TV, the arts and nonprofits. She runs a successful leader-as-coach program, training leaders how to integrate practical coaching skills into everyday management. Marie is a consummate learner and a pragmatist. She has written books on thinking, career development and the enneagram.

Her coaching philosophy can be summed up as follows: 'Possibility is the foundation of the human experience. Our true intention is what really matters most. Living life on purpose is the best way to create a purposeful life'.

Steve Crabb is an entrepreneur and business coach who has applied his professional coaching and business experience to working with individuals and organisations to bring about fast and lasting change in the name of business excellence. Steve has been the director of two multimillion-pound companies and has owned businesses in construction, IT, retail and training. During Steve's business career, he recognised the value of a stress-free attitude to life and the importance of being able to sell; this has led to his specializing in coaching and training clients in selling and stress management.

Steve is a master trainer of NLP (Neuro-Linguistic Programming) and was head trainer for Dr Richard Bandler (co-creator of NLP) and best-selling author and personal development guru Paul McKenna. Steve was responsible for selecting and training their UK NLP assisting teams. He is a certified master transformative coach and a qualified clinical hypnotherapist. He combines NLP, coaching and hypnosis in his work with individuals and groups to create deep and profound change for clients.

His coaching career spans 15 years, during which time he has worked one on one with thousands of clients. His clients have included famous sporting professionals, media celebrities, high-performing individuals, world-renowned entrepreneurs and businesses.

His coaching philosophy can be summed up by his motto, 'Using NLP, coaching and hypnosis to make the impossible seem possible, the possible seem easy and the easy so it becomes natural and effortless'.

Dedication

Marie: I come from several generations of people with the job title *hawker* (entrepreneurs without capital and plenty of enterprising ideas) on their marriage and death certificates. This book is for them, particularly my grandfather Thomas Taylor (1902—1973), who passed away when I was a child. His description of how to create a business always stuck with me: 'What do people want to buy, what will they pay for it and do you want to sell it?'

Steve: I dedicate this work to the people who matter most in my life. You know who you are.

Authors' Acknowledgements

Marie: My lovely clients who never cease to amaze me. My quirky, gorgeous family: Kathy, Keely, Claire, Nathan, Josh, Oscar, Scarlet, Daisy, Nancy, Colin, Andy and Marie, who are my greatest teachers on the subject of life. To my own coaches who have shone a light and walked with me in places where others fear to tread, in particular the lovely Mandy Evans in Palm Springs whose wisdom, intuition and skill know no bounds. To Cambridge University Business School for keeping me engaged with the school that taught me that I knew more about the realities of business than I thought back in 2001. Not least, my wonderful friends who have been eternally patient with me cancelling because of writing deadlines and for being supportive of me as a person who loves words. Not last, my friend and co-author Steve who has weathered the roller coaster with me despite his strained relationship with the apostrophe and mine with the comma.

Thank you to Wiley for commissioning this book. Flattery is underrated, and I secretly enjoyed being courted and cajoled to write it. Many thanks go to Mark Ryan, director of global talent at Wiley, for the original suggestion. Thank you to Steve Edwards for his support early on and to Annie Knight for getting us moving. Thank you in particular to Vicki Adang, who showed amazing patience with two busy people submitting chapters from planes, trains and tables in several locations around the world. I am grateful for your support in navigating the *For Dummies* template, for noticing the overuse of the split infinitive and the inappropriate use of the semicolon.

Steve: This book has been a personal journey of exploration and discovery into two subjects that bring me great joy in life: business and coaching. Without my co-author Marie Taylor, who phoned me up to ask if I was interested in co-writing with her, I would never have had the opportunity to indulge myself in spending so much time on these subjects. Thank you, Marie.

Without the Wiley team, there would have been many more sentences with my random punctuation, and some of my ideas would not have made as much sense as they do now. Special thanks to Vicki Adang; thank you for your infinite patience and gentle but firm guidance and willingness to keep asking me to rewrite and clarify.

There are two groups of people without whom I would never have been able to share what I have in these pages. Firstly, the amazingly talented and gifted people I have had the privilege to study and train with, notably Paul McKenna, Dr Richard Bandler, John and Katheleen LaValle and Michael Neill. They have all supported me and given me opportunities to work with them and continue to learn and grow, for which I am always grateful.

The second group that must be acknowledged are my clients and protégés. Without them I would never have had the opportunity to develop my coaching practice. Thank you for being willing to trust me as your coach and for being willing to try out some of the crazy things I ask people to do. There is madness to the methods.

Last but not least, thanks to my family and friends who have had to put up with me locking myself away for hours and asking not to be disturbed, especially Dani and Ben, who now get their dad's time back.

Publisher's Acknowledgements

Commissioning Editor: Annie Knight

Project Manager: Victoria M. Adang

Development Editor: Kelly Ewing

Copy Editor: Kim Vernon

Technical Editor: Sue Pullen

Production Editor: Kumar Chellappan

Cover Image: © Tuan_Azizi/Shutterstock

Take Dummies with you everywhere you go!

Whether you're excited about e-books, want more from the web, must have your mobile apps, or swept up in social media, Dummies makes everything easier.

FOR DUMMIES®

A Wiley Brand

BUSINESS

978-1-118-73077-5

978-1-118-44349-1

978-1-119-97527-4

MUSIC

978-1-119-94276-4

978-0-470-97799-6

978-0-470-49644-2

DIGITAL PHOTOGRAPHY

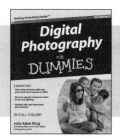
978-1-118-09203-3

978-0-470-76878-5

978-1-118-00472-2

Algebra I For Dummies
978-0-470-55964-2

Anatomy & Physiology For Dummies, 2nd Edition
978-0-470-92326-9

Asperger's Syndrome For Dummies
978-0-470-66087-4

Basic Maths For Dummies
978-1-119-97452-9

Body Language For Dummies, 2nd Edition
978-1-119-95351-7

Bookkeeping For Dummies, 3rd Edition
978-1-118-34689-1

British Sign Language For Dummies
978-0-470-69477-0

Cricket for Dummies, 2nd Edition
978-1-118-48032-8

Currency Trading For Dummies, 2nd Edition
978-1-118-01851-4

Cycling For Dummies
978-1-118-36435-2

Diabetes For Dummies, 3rd Edition
978-0-470-97711-8

eBay For Dummies, 3rd Edition
978-1-119-94122-4

Electronics For Dummies All-in-One For Dummies
978-1-118-58973-1

English Grammar For Dummies
978-0-470-05752-0

French For Dummies, 2nd Edition
978-1-118-00464-7

Guitar For Dummies, 3rd Edition
978-1-118-11554-1

IBS For Dummies
978-0-470-51737-6

Keeping Chickens For Dummies
978-1-119-99417-6

Knitting For Dummies, 3rd Edition
978-1-118-66151-2

FOR DUMMIES

A Wiley Brand

SELF-HELP

Cognitive Behavioural Therapy For Dummies
978-0-470-66541-1

Creative Visualization For Dummies
978-1-119-99264-6

Mindfulness For Dummies
978-0-470-66086-7

LANGUAGES

Spanish For Dummies
978-0-470-68815-1

Polish For Dummies
978-1-119-97959-3

British Sign Language For Dummies
978-0-470-69477-0

HISTORY

The Tudors For Dummies
978-0-470-68792-5

Medieval History For Dummies
978-0-470-74783-4

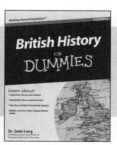

British History For Dummies
978-0-470-97819-1

Laptops For Dummies 5th Edition
978-1-118-11533-6

Management For Dummies,
2nd Edition
978-0-470-97769-9

Nutrition For Dummies, 2nd Edition
978-0-470-97276-2

Office 2013 For Dummies
978-1-118-49715-9

Organic Gardening For Dummies
978-1-119-97706-3

Origami Kit For Dummies
978-0-470-75857-1

Overcoming Depression For Dummies
978-0-470-69430-5

Physics I For Dummies
978-0-470-90324-7

Project Management For Dummies
978-0-470-71119-4

Psychology Statistics For Dummies
978-1-119-95287-9

Renting Out Your Property For Dummies,
3rd Edition
978-1-119-97640-0

Rugby Union For Dummies, 3rd Edition
978-1-119-99092-5

Stargazing For Dummies
978-1-118-41156-8

Teaching English as a Foreign Language
For Dummies
978-0-470-74576-2

Time Management For Dummies
978-0-470-77765-7

Training Your Brain For Dummies
978-0-470-97449-0

Voice and Speaking Skills For Dummies
978-1-119-94512-3

Wedding Planning For Dummies
978-1-118-69951-5

WordPress For Dummies, 5th Edition
978-1-118-38318-6

   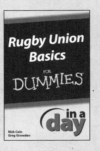